# Sermons On The Gospel Readings

## Series I

### Cycle C

# J. Ellsworth Kalas
# David J. Kalas
# Frank G. Honeycutt
# Stephen M. Crotts
# R. Robert Cueni

**CSS Publishing Company, Inc., Lima, Ohio**

Copyright © 2003 by
CSS Publishing Company, Inc.
Lima, Ohio

Scripture quotations are from the *New Revised Standard Version of the Bible*, copyright
1989 by the Division of Christian Education of the National Council of the Churches of
Christ in the USA. Used by permission.

Scripture quotations marked (RSV) are from the *Revised Standard Version of the Bible*,
copyrighted 1946, 1952 ©, 1971, 1973, by the Division of Christian Education of the
National Council of the Churches of Christ in the USA. Used by permission.

**Library of Congress Cataloging-in-Publication Data**

Sermons on the Gospel readings. Series I. Cycle C / J. Ellsworth Kalas ... [et al.].
    p. cm.
    Includes bibliographical references.
    ISBN 0-7880-1968-6 (pbk. : alk. paper)
    1. Bible. N.T. Gospels—Sermons. 2. Sermons, American—21st century. 3. Church
year sermons. I. Kalas, J. Ellsworth, 1923- II. Title.
    BS2555.54.S472  2003
    252'.6—dc21

                                                                    2003007603

For more information about CSS Publishing Company resources, visit our website at
www.csspub.com or e-mail us at custserv@csspub.com or call (800) 241-4056.

ISBN 0-7880-1968-6

# Table Of Contents

**Sermons For Sundays**
**After Pentecost (First Third)**
*When The Wind Begins To Sing*
**by Stephen M. Crotts**

## Sermons For Sundays
## After Pentecost (Middle Third)
### *The Transforming Power Of A Changed Perspective*
## by R. Robert Cueni

**Sermons For Sundays
After Pentecost (Last Third)
*Music From Another Room*
by Stephen M. Crotts**

# Sermons On The Gospel Readings

## For Sundays In
## Advent, Christmas,
## And Epiphany

### *Reading The Signs*

## J. Ellsworth Kalas
## and
## David J. Kalas

*To David —*
*son by birth,*
*by faith,*
*and by calling*

# The Signs Of Summer

The season of Advent is upon us, and with it is a spirit of heaviness. It is not the heaviness of Lent, when we are called to sacrifice and repentance, but there is a quality of darkness, nevertheless.

The music of the season shows it; much of it is cast in a minor key. It is the music of longing, hoping, and waiting: "Oh, come, oh, come, Emmanuel. And ransom captive Israel, that mourns in lonely exile here." The music and the mood are of an exile, far from a home never really known, but long and instinctively anticipated.

You and I may have some trouble with this mood — we already know the end of the story. We know that the "long-expected Jesus" has, indeed, come; and that we will soon be singing "Joy to the World!" Furthermore, we live in a culture where celebration is in the mood of the season and everyone seems to be occupied with shopping and party-going. It's difficult to take on the mood of mournful waiting — acting as if Jesus had not yet come when, of course, we know that he *has* come — when we are living on the right side of Calvary and Easter.

If that be so, we can take particular pleasure in our scripture lesson of the morning. It does not begin that way. To the contrary, the first impact of the passage is one that calls for mourning; it is a warning of coming judgment. A day is coming, Jesus said, when people will "faint with fear and foreboding of what is coming on the world" — a time of "distress among nations" as they struggle in perplexity with what is happening.

15

The normal reaction to such a scene is somewhere between despair and panic. We expect the populace to hide in terror, or at least to put in a frantic call to the psychiatrist. But Jesus has a better, happier word. "When these things begin to take place," our Lord said, "stand up and raise your heads, because your redemption is drawing near." The unbelieving and the unknowing may cringe with fear, but the people of God should be prepared to shout. The events of such a time are the sound of judgment to secular society; but for believers they are the sound of deliverance.

Then Jesus spoke a one-sentence parable. Look at the fig tree, or any other tree, he said. "As soon as they sprout leaves," you know that "*summer is already near.*"

So it is that the people of God read the signs of the times. We are not blind to what is happening in our world, and surely we dare not be insensitive to it. But neither do we see the storm clouds as a reason for terror. William Cowper, the eighteenth-century poet who was well-acquainted with inner anxiety, could, nevertheless, exult:

> *Ye fearful saints, fresh courage take;*
> *the clouds ye so much dread*
> *Are big with mercy, and shall break*
> *In blessings on your head.*

We are not looking for the winter of civilization. Through knowledge which is informed by faith, we see the signs of summer.

Mind you, there will be judgment. Judgment is necessary. A great preacher from the early twentieth century, Henry Sloane Coffin, once said there is no more comforting text in the entire Bible than this, "Our God is a consuming fire." That's our best promise that we will have a clean earth. It is also good evidence — even if painful — that God cares about our world. If God did not, at times, burn up the rubbish of our willful universe, we would become like a deserted neighborhood where no one bothers to clear away the debris. God loves our world, so he cleanses it. He loves it, and his love shows itself, at times and by necessity, in the consuming fires of judgment.

Judgment is not the end of the story. If our universe were run by blind fate, its judgments would be happenstance and without purpose. Faith tells us that God's judgment is to a worthy end. In 1755, a series of natural and political disasters swept over Europe. The Seven Years' War broke out in June of that year, then poor harvests, and the Lisbon earthquake. A severe cattle plague devastated western Europe. Even the very thoughtful felt that perhaps the end of the world was at hand.

England called a National Fast Day for February 6, 1756, and Charles Wesley — co-founder with his brother John of the Methodist movement, and the most prolific hymnwriter of Christian history — wrote seventeen hymns for the occasion. These hymns are vigorous in their descriptions of the disasters which were then occurring. They portrayed these events as the acts of a "righteous God" who was baring his arm in judgment. But Wesley could write, and the people could sing,

> *Whatever ills the world befall*
> *A pledge of endless good we call,*
> *A sign of Jesus near.*

There might indeed be disaster all around, but the Christian held to God's "pledge of endless good." Though plagues and war threatened, they were nothing more than "a sign of Jesus near."

This is no irrational whistling in the dark. It is not that Christians are naive about life, or that we proceed in a kind of Pollyanna happiness, oblivious to the hard facts of a cruel world. It is just that we possess some other facts, most of which have not occurred to the secular world.

We start with the primary fact of God, and what we believe his character to be. The secular world generally believes in God, but in a remote way. And what is worse, it is inclined to see God as indifferent, at best, and vengeful, at worst.

Christians see God, through the eyes of Jesus, as a benevolent Father, who wills good for his children. Like any truly loving father, God must work within the bounds of discipline and sometimes must reprove us. But his purpose for us and for this world is always good. So we can say, as Charles Wesley did in 1756,

> *The famine all thy fullness brings,*
> *The plague presents thy healing wings.*

We believe, too, that God works purposefully in all that happens in our world. I don't think everything which happens is the will of God; this is a rebellious planet which has given itself over to sin. I do believe that God is able to redeem even the worst of our rebellions and stupidities and to bring good out of them. Perhaps God's grandest and most demanding enterprise is to shape our confusions and our errors into patterns of symmetry and beauty. The secular mind looks at all the facts it can see and says, "Life is just one fool thing after another." The believer looks at the same facts, and adds one more: our belief in the character of God and his purposes. With that strategic additional fact in place, we say, "Life is sometimes a confusing combination of circumstances, but God is working with us for good, to bring order out of it all." God has a purpose for our world, and he works through creation and judgment to bring it to pass.

So Jesus looked at the signs of the times and promised that summer was on the way — signs in the heavens, distress of nations, people fainting with fear and foreboding. He said, "Stand up and raise your heads, because your redemption is drawing near." All these signs, Jesus said, are like leaves bursting forth on a fig tree; when you see them, you know that "summer is already near."

This is a good word for our times. It's clear enough that the hearts of many are failing them because of fear, and as we read and hear the daily news, their reaction seems logical. As some clever person recast Kipling's lines long ago, "If you can keep your head while others all around you are losing theirs / Brother, you just don't understand the circumstances." The times are, indeed, frightening. But, at such a time, we offer some additional facts: God, his character, his purposes. God, at work in history. And with it all we say, "Summer is near. Our Lord is at hand."

It is not a complacent word, calculated to make us settle back smugly while others fret and struggle. It is an empowering word, to encourage us to act. Free of paralyzing doubts and shapeless fears, we can stand firm even as we reach out to help others. We are able to contribute to the solution, rather than simply adding to the problem. After all, if anyone should be able to rise above the perils of the times and to help work on a solution, it ought to be the people of faith.

This is also a significant word for us as individuals. Most of our struggle is not with profound cosmic dread, but with the problems of our personal lives. These problems may be as wrenching as bereavement or major surgery, or as upsetting as a divorce or the loss of a job. More often they are those nameless, faceless feelings which seem to come upon us from the blind side, making us feel undone without our knowing why. An insensitive person might suggest that some of our upsets aren't big enough to matter; but, the fact is, when you hurt you hurt and no one from the outside is qualified to say it isn't so.

When we are in the midst of such personal turmoil, we need to remind ourselves that *we are a summer people.* We do not live with the clenched fists and gritted teeth of despair; we look for summer. We live in a world where God has chosen to manifest himself through his Son, Jesus Christ. It is a world great with promise. We believe that God's purpose for our lives is *good*; and, though surrounding circumstances may be negative, we expect the good to win. Even in those instances when we are ourselves responsible for our troubles, we still dare to ask God's help in finding our way out.

Usually God's deliverance comes in fairly predictable ways through the help and counsel of friends and a right use of our own ability. But sometimes we enjoy additional marks of God's gracious favor. John Donne, the great seventeenth-century poet-preacher, explained — in one of his poems — that God's heavenly seasons are not limited the way our earthly seasons are. "He can bring thy summer out of winter," Donne exclaimed, "though thou have no spring." We may limit God's grace by assuming he can work only through predictable progressions and developments.

19

Donne insists there are no such boundaries on God: "All occasions invite his mercies, and all times are his seasons."

It is because "all times are his seasons" that Jesus could point to signs which seemed to speak of winter and insist that summer was drawing near. Our Lord is not controlled by the seasons of life; he is Lord of the seasons. He is not victim of our winter of pain and discontent, for all times are his season. When the snow lies heavy on our lives, he can announce that summer is very near. And we, trusting him, can rise up to meet the challenge of the day.

"Stand up and raise your heads," Jesus said, "because your redemption is drawing near." Perhaps the music of Advent should have more of that quality — the raised head and the upward look. The child who is on tiptoe in anticipation of Christmas may not be stirred by the highest motives. Yet that child may be closer to the mood of the season than the person who mourns about the hopelessness of our world. Our redemption is near! How dare we sing sad songs at such a time?

A great Scottish preacher, Dr. George Morrison, often walked to a little village in valley not far from Glasgow. Running into that village were the remains of a wall which the Romans built in the first century. Dr. Morrison said that he liked going there on a Saturday, to ponder that the wall was a strong, new thing when John was writing the Revelation; and, at that time, the church was a little, hunted thing, apparently on its way to extinction.

Who would have guessed, Dr. Morrison said, that centuries later the wall could be only a heap of dust — a kind of historical curiosity — while the church bells would be ringing out clear and strong, in that tiny village?

Such is the faith to which we are committed, and such is the mood of this season. It is time to lift our heads and sing, for we are preparing again to celebrate the coming of our Lord. We have read the signs of the times and they tell us that summer is near. Whatever we pass through enroute, and whatever we may be called upon to do in order to save our world, we know the end of the story. We are believers in Jesus Christ, so we know that summer is near.

J. Ellsworth Kalas

# The Hinge Of History

Henry Ford said that history is bunk; but history has gotten its revenge on the pioneer auto maker. It has made Ford himself a benchmark of history, at least in its industrial and economic phases. Ford effectively disproved his own statement when he established Greenfield Village, which is probably one of the half-dozen favorite historical sites in our country.

Some of us love history, but even those who don't had better be ready to admit its significance. We want to know where we've come from and how things come to be as they are. When a driver slows his coach to point to some slabs in a field and tells the American tourists that they are looking at the oldest recorded writing on the British Isles, people quickly click their cameras. We want a record, fleeting and blurred though it may be, of our heritage.

By the same token, we like to feel that we are helping to make history. "I was one of the founders of the Student Council at that junior high school," a man told me as we drove through his town. It seemed a limited reason for pride in a grown man, but I understood it. All of us want to feel that we are making some mark on history, however small it may be. I dare to venture that this is some of the motivation in the youngster who etches his initials in fresh concrete. He might not verbalize it in such philosophical terms, but he's wanting to leave his mark behind. He hopes someday — maybe only a week from now, but we measure differently when we're young — to show somebody his *Kilroy* evidence.

We Christians are part of a faith which has respect for history. As the New Testament writer puts it, "We did not follow cleverly devised myths"; rather, first-century Christians were "eyewitnesses" of Jesus Christ and his ministry (2 Peter 1:16).

That first generation of Christians were very conscious of the historical integrity of their faith. They were surrounded by hundreds of gods and theologies — all based on fables and myths. But Christianity proudly pointed to its roots in actual historical events. Just as the Jewish faith looked back to its deliverance from Egypt, the first Christians spoke of one who had been born in a certain village during the reign of particular rulers; and who had been crucified in a given place after being tried before a specific Roman official.

The New Testament is so precise about this that its writers seem almost to be throwing down a challenge. "We offer you names, dates, and places," they seem to say. "Now, give us some hard facts regarding your gods and your beliefs."

Such is the style with which Luke's Gospel introduces us to the person and ministry of John the Baptizer. He identifies the opening of John's ministry by naming seven individuals who were filling government or ecclesiastical posts at the time.

Their identification is as all-encompassing as Tiberius Caesar, to such regional officials as Pontius Pilate or Lysanias, and to two religious figures — Annas and Caiaphas — whose role mattered only to the Jews.

All of this marshaling of history was to give us a setting for a Jewish prophet — John, the son of Zechariah and Elizabeth! John was unique, no doubt about it. He was a man so rare that he scorned the palace steps, from which some of his prophetic predecessors had delivered their messages, and proclaimed the Word of the Lord in the howling wilderness near the Dead Sea. He was a prophet who left behind no body of literature to compare with Isaiah, Jeremiah, Amos, Hosea, or even Obadiah. All the words recorded from his lips would hardly constitute three paragraphs in our daily paper, or the time of a long commercial on television. Yet his role is so significant that the Gospel writer lists seven historical figures to identify the time when his ministry began.

Today the situation is reversed. Only Tiberius Caesar has a place in history on his own; even his place is not dramatically significant. The six other personalities are remembered because their names are associated with Jesus or with John the Baptizer. If the tetrarchs of ancient Ituraea and Abilene matter today, it is because they touched human history at the same time as John, so that the Gospel writer recorded their names in association with the wilderness preacher.

For John was a hinge of history. When he declared, "Prepare the way of the Lord," he closed a door on the old and ushered in the new.

It sometimes seems that God shows his sense of humor with history. Halford Luccock once noted that Nero was sure that the most important happenings in Rome were the words he said, the laws he enacted, and the things he did. As a matter of fact, the biggest events in Rome at the time were some prayer meetings which were being held secretly in the catacombs. The Medici, he observes, must have seemed the key figures in Renaissance Europe, with their palaces, art galleries, and political power. Yet they are overshadowed by "a little boy playing about on the docks of Genoa," who would eventually open the seaway to the Americans.

So it was in John the Baptizer's time. One can easily imagine the pomp and circumstance with which Herod trampled about as tetrarch of Galilee. Wherever he went, people scraped and bowed. They waited for a disdaining nod and dreamed of some act of preferment from his hand. Herod was, indeed, a big man in Galilee in the first century. Today, all his pomp is simply pompous, and all his circumstance only circumstantial.

But John the Baptizer! — a great human being. He headed out into the wilderness, disregarding his safety in a land infected by natural perils. With his talent, he could probably have made a place for himself in the king's court where he could have been "dressed in soft robes" (Luke 7:25). Instead, he covered his body with camel's hair and a leather girdle and subsisted on a wilderness diet of locusts and wild honey. His message was as rugged as his garb and his diet: "a baptism of repentance for the forgiveness of sins" (v. 3b).

He became a hinge of history. I think the common people discovered him first, especially those whose hearts longed for a deeper

23

knowledge of God. Soon, people by the hundreds were beating a pathway to the wilderness to see and hear this man who seemed to fear no one. There, far from the conventional centers of power and influence, he declared the advent of a new age.

What made John a hinge of history? I could easily beg the question by saying that it was an act of God. But many people feel that usually God chooses his instruments with some logic. What is the logic in John?

Probably the biggest secret is this: John was pointing beyond himself. His goal was not personal advancement or position. He was "the voice of one crying out in the wilderness: Prepare the way of the Lord, make his paths straight" (v. 4). He was not a name to be reckoned with, but a voice to be heard. He was not building a kingdom for himself, but preparing the way for another.

And when the Other came, John had the ability to slip off center stage gracefully. Some of his friends pointed out, probably with devoted concern, that the crowds were now flocking to Jesus. John quickly reminded them that he had said all along he was not the Christ, but he had been sent before him. He described himself as "the friend of the bridegroom," who waits patiently until the bridegroom appears, then "rejoices greatly at the bridegroom's voice" (John 3:29).

A less-committed person could not have made such an exit. Praise and public recognition are intoxicating. They can make drunken fools of the most solid and reasoned human beings. John had been lionized for months, perhaps even years. He was accustomed to curious crowds and dedicated disciples. Now, almost overnight, all was lost.

Fortunately, John knew who he was, and he liked the role. He knew that his job was to prepare the way; not to be the Messiah who would travel on that way. He was not unhappy being the friend of the bridegroom. He was ready to play second fiddle.

If John had become carried away with his success and resisted the coming of Jesus, he would have been a pathetic footnote of history rather than its hinge. He would have been an absurdity. Not many of us can realize that when we see an opportunity to bask in the spotlight. A primary secret of John's greatness was his commitment to something and Someone beyond himself.

John's style does not fit well in our hype-and-publicity age. The late Andy Warhol said that we live in a time when everyone will be a celebrity for fifteen minutes. When we see how easily the media *makes* public figures and how Humpty-Dumpty-like they smash when they are ignored, Warhol's prediction seems rather true. The lifestyle of our times seems to justify self-promotion. "If you've got it, flaunt it," is the counsel of the cynical.

But don't be deceived. John's way is still the secret of greatness. The self-promoters come and go, but they make no lasting impression on human lives. How can they, when they are themselves all fluff and bluster? There was a toughness of spirit in John the Baptizer, demonstrated not so much by his wardrobe and diet as by a mind that could say, "I don't give a hang what happens to me, if only I do the job I was called to do."

Someone has said that no one can estimate how much good could be done in our world if no one cared who got the credit. Any local congregation can testify to the truth of that sentence, and so, too, can any community enterprise — from a scout troop to a peace caucus.

But it isn't easy to be so self-effacing. I have no trouble giving credit to others for what they have done; indeed, I find pleasure in honoring them. Yet something in me bristles when someone else takes credit for what I perceive to have been my accomplishment, without even a nod of the head in my direction. I'd like to say that it's just my sense of fairness which is offended, but I fear it's also my ego. It's pleasant to be recognized for what we have done, and it's hard not to seek such recognition.

John the Baptizer had a goal higher than himself. By nature he must have been a man of strong ego — he could hardly have preached such a demanding message otherwise nor have put himself in such a perilous ministry. But he had such a high commitment to the purposes of God that he could submerge his powerful temperament into his mission. In doing so, he became a hinge of history.

Now it is our turn. What will you and I do with that piece of history in which we live? Few if any of us expect to be a hinge for even a modest opening of history's door. Still, we shouldn't rule out the possibility. We may play a key role for some girl or boy who will develop some medical discovery which will bless the whole human race, or one who will write legislation which will make a strategic difference in the way human beings live. We never know, really, what greatness is residing very near us.

But we do know that God is constantly looking for people like John the Baptizer, who will gladly pave the way for God's grand purposes. And we know, too, that there is much work yet to be done and great causes still to be advanced.

There are great days to be alive. We are needed, my friends; you and I are needed. Our times need a new introduction to the Lord Jesus Christ, and you and I are favorably situated to be the introducers, the way-preparers. There could hardly be a more auspicious and challenging time.

We will not be dressed like John the Baptizer nor will we follow his diet — matters for which most of us are probably grateful. But we can commit ourselves to the same Lord, and with the same greatness of purpose. While we may not be the hinge on which the grand door of history will swing, we can serve at our own special, contributory place. If it be a place where God can use us, and where we can bless others, we can ask no greater place. Whatever that place may be, let us commit ourselves, like John, to prepare the way of the Lord. And we will leave history's hinge to the Lord of history.

J. Ellsworth Kalas

# The Divine Opportunity

Opportunity comes with so many different faces that we often don't recognize it. That's probably why we sometimes miss its call. A previous generation said that opportunity comes dressed in overalls. And they were largely right, for nothing succeeds like hard work. Our generation thinks that opportunity comes with a college diploma. It may, but there's no guarantee.

The divine opportunity comes in what is, to our human eyes, the most unlikely garb of all. It's no wonder we don't recognize it; or that, recognizing it, we resist it. This Advent season is an especially good time to experience the divine opportunity. Any time is God's season; but because you and I find certain settings and circumstances especially hospitable to religious experience, Advent and Lent are particularly attractive.

The first Advent preacher, John the Baptizer, offered opportunity in a compelling, almost ferocious way. When you read his words, you don't think he's offering opportunity; I expect that if we had heard him in person, we would have been even more doubtful. William Barclay said that John's message "was not good news; it was news of terror" (*The Gospel of Luke*, Westminster John Knox Press, p. 28). I understand what Professor Barclay was saying, but I see it differently. It seems to me that good news must sometimes come dressed in rough clothing.

That was surely the nature of John's approach. When we read the brief gospel summaries of his messages, we wonder why people went to so much trouble to hear him. Were they masochists courting abuse, or did they perhaps hope to hear him thunder against the sins of their neighbors? One way or another, the crowds flocked to him. And largely, I think, because they felt, in the integrity of his message, an opportunity which they had sought for a long time. His was a message of judgment; but in the judgment was opportunity. And opportunity was wrapped up in the word *repent*.

This was John's message, and it was a message of hope. "Repent," he cried, "for the kingdom of heaven is at hand." With the word *repent*, John was telling the people that they need not remain as they were. We are not held captive to our failures, our past, or our inadequacy. We can repent. We can get rid of the past. We can start over.

I'd hate to live in a world where there was no chance to repent. In a sense, you could divine hell as a place where there is no possibility of repentance. That's what makes it hell: there's no way out, no chance to get rid of the garbage of life, no chance to start again.

*Repent* is one of the loveliest words in our language. It pays us human beings a sublime compliment, for it says that we can do something about the course we have taken. If we were nothing more than poor animals, we'd have to go the way our instincts demanded. But you and I, humans as we are, can *repent*. If we are on the wrong track, we can turn around, or get on another train. We may not be able to change what we've already done, and we may not be able to fully escape the consequences of those past choices. But we need not continue in the same destructive path. We can repent, and start again.

Every life accumulates a certain amount of rubbish. No matter how earnestly and thoughtfully we live, we make mistakes — if not outright sins. In time, our sins, stupidities, and poor choices can become like a mountain around us, until we spend endless waking hours in the miserable enterprise of regret.

Thanks be to God, there is something better than haunting regard. Regret, you see, leads nowhere. It is a sea of misery in which we can wallow and fret until it destroys us. But repentance is a gift from God — a wholesome way to look the past in the eye, confess it for what it is, and leave it behind. On, then, to a new start.

Perhaps that's why people were drawn to John the Baptizer. They felt hope when they heard him preach. He spoke harsh, incisive words, but he led them to a door of hope. "You can repent," he said. "There is a way out of the dilemma you're in."

But the Baptizer made it difficult. When people began flocking his way, he sensed that, for some of them, it was easy religion. Even the most vital religious movements can become "popular" in a way that undercuts their integrity. "You brood of vipers!" he called. "Who warned you to flee from the wrath to come?" (v. 7). It was a figure of speech appropriate to the setting where John preached. The brushwood and stubble which covered the rugged area would sometimes set afire and the flames would leap quickly through the dry nettles. When this happened, vipers and snakes would scurry wildly from their hiding places to escape the flames. John's figure of speech wasn't very complimentary, but it was true to his sense of urgency.

For John presented his message in a take-it-or-leave-it fashion. I remember an automobile salesman who bargained faithfully for a time, then said, "This is my last offer," and, as he said it, walked away from me. Perhaps it was only a good sales ploy, but I was impressed. That was John's style. "I have something great to offer," he seemed to say, "and you'd better grasp the opportunity now that it has come to you."

Sometimes our hunger for repentance fails to achieve its goal. We need to do more than simply say, "I'm sorry." Repentance needs some means of action. I still remember an anonymous note which I found on a bulletin cover one Monday morning. "We all want to have a more victorious life," someone had scribbled, following what I had thought was a pretty good sermon. "But, Dr. Kalas, how do we get it?"

John the Baptizer got down to specifics. When the people asked, "What then shall we do," John answered with line-on-line counsel. If you have two coats, he said, give one to someone who has none. The same, he added, with your food. When tax collectors asked what course they should follow, John answered, "Collect no more than is appointed you." The secret of wealth for those first-century tax collectors was in cheating; and John quickly set them right. To the soldiers, John gave a two-pronged answer: "Do not extort money from anyone by threats or false accusation, and be satisfied with your wages" (v. 14b).

Perhaps the most notable thing about John's advice is that it was so practical. He didn't indulge in cliches, like "Pray about it," or "Seek the will of God," or "Work for a just social order." He spoke directly to the world in which his people lived, in terms they could put to work that very day.

I'm impressed, too, that he wanted them to live out their new faith in their present occupations and circumstances. Sometimes religion has encouraged people to show their faith by isolating themselves from the world they are part of. As a matter of fact, some of us might have counseled the tax collectors and soldiers to resign their positions and find some other kind of work. Both occupations had so many questionable factors that such advice would have made rather good sense. I can hear someone saying, "Tax collecting and army life aren't where godly people should make their living." John offered no such counsel. Perhaps he knew that these people couldn't possibly leave the work they were doing. At any rate, he told them to live out their faith where they were, by being honorable and godly in their current occupations. He didn't tell them it was going to be easy, but just that it was the right thing to do.

I'm interested, too, that John concentrated on the daily work of his hearers. "We are more than our jobs," we often protest. Some people don't like to be introduced by references to their employment. But our daily work plays a large part in defining who we are, whether we like it or not. Indeed, when we Protestants insist that every person's employment is his or her *vocation* — a call from God in which we live out our priesthood — our daily work has such significance that to minimize it is to minimize who we are.

How would we translate John's message in our day? What do we say to a world where people work with computers; sell insurance, securities, real estate; or teach, nurse, raise families, or practice law or medicine? What is the gospel for a truck driver or a farmer? There had better be a gospel for us in our workplace, or our gospel is too small. It is a good thing to write a letter to our senator; but it is a better thing to honor Christ in the day-by-day marketplace of our jobs. Here, especially, we are called to live out the gospel. Such was John's message to his generation; and would be his message to ours.

But John was able to offer more than one repentance. The people sensed that there must be more than what John was preaching. Was he, they asked, the Messiah? Was he the Christ of whom the prophets had spoken?

John's answer was in the best Advent tradition: Christ is coming, he said, and he brings with him glory and power such as my ministry cannot even suggest. "I baptize you with water; but one who is more powerful than I is coming; I am not worthy to untie the thong of his sandals. He will baptize you with the Holy Spirit and fire" (v. 16).

John was a man of powerful ego or he would never have cared to challenge the established power brokers of the day, and to speak with such directness. Yet, when he spoke of his relationship to Jesus, he was quick to bow in the most dramatic humility. "I can't even qualify to take care of his shoes." Perhaps it was the very strength of his ego which made it possible for him to submit so thoroughly to his supporting role with Jesus. He knew who he was and what he was called to do; and he was at peace with his role. Indeed, he gloried in it.

John gladly announced that his baptism could not even be compared with the baptism which Jesus would bring. His was a baptism with water, to symbolize a washing of life. But Jesus, he said, would baptize with the Holy Spirit and fire. Fire is itself a symbol of cleansing, but an interior cleansing quite beyond the reach of water; thus metals are put in fire to burn away their inner impurities. John seems to suggest that his baptismal cleansing is almost superficial compared with what Jesus would do.

Jesus was going to immerse us in the Holy Spirit. Water is a natural substance symbolizing a spiritual reality; Jesus deals not in symbols but in the realities themselves. He brings to the world, for all persons, a presence of God which formerly was experienced only by a select few on special occasions.

But again, John made clear, it is with a price. Our Lord is coming with a winnowing fan, to separate the wheat from the chaff; and he will burn the chaff "with unquenchable fire." We may be inclined to discount John's vigorous language on the ground that he was a dramatically emphatic man, so that he would speak of even Jesus in terrifying terms.

Perhaps we should remind ourselves that Jesus often spoke of himself in the language of judgment. We are so taken with the image of Jesus' compassion (which is a major element in his person and ministry) that we forget the anger he showed to hypocrites and to unworthy religious leaders, and the fearful language he used in describing the day of judgment.

We shouldn't hide from this quality in Jesus. Instead, we should seek to understand it and respond to him. If this One who has come as the ultimate expression of God's love is also an agent of judgment, then the judgment itself must be an act of mercy. Luke surely saw it as such, for he says that it was with such exhortations that John preached "good news to the people" (v. 18b).

This brings us back to our theme of the day. Repentance is the grandest expression of opportunity, because it is the door by which our Lord comes into our lives; and with him, all the favors of mercy and grace. As we repent, we sweep out the accumulated, burdensome rubbish of our lives and clear the way for God's love to fill us.

Sometimes I feel — as I look at neglected places in my own heart, and at the people of the church — that we Christians have forgotten how to repent. We act as if repentance were something only the ungodly should do; in truth, as the apostle said, repentance should begin at the house of God. Repentance is a particular gift to us believers; we know by experience what benefits it brings. We ought, therefore, to be all the more ready to put this good gift to use.

Right now we are in the best season for repenting. How better can we prepare for the celebration of Jesus' coming than by clearing away the trivia and troubles of past days, to make clear a highway for our God?

This is our season of opportunity. We can repent at any and every hour, but here we are at the best of all hours. Now is the time, here is the place, and opportunity knocks. Repent, the voice invites us, and begin afresh and anew. Thanks be to God for such an opportunity.

J. Ellsworth Kalas

Advent 4
Luke 1:39-55

# Songs Of The Season

No season of the year sings as well as Christmas. This seems to be true whether one is a saint or a sinner. The world about us has occasional songfests for patriotic days or school homecoming celebrations, but those songs are sung by selected groups in isolated places. Only at the Christmas season does the majority of the population choose to sing or to listen to the singing of others. Some of the songs which now mark the Christmas and Advent season are poor secularizations of the original Christmas theme. But even as derivations and deviations from the true theme, they carry some measure of the joy of the season.

This isn't surprising because Christmas was born in the midst of songs. The Gospel of Luke says it most specifically, but many of us feel it instinctively. It seems inevitable that the words spoken by Gabriel to Mary, by Mary and by Zechariah in their occasions of rejoicing, by the angels to the shepherds, and by Simeon in the temple were sung. They are too exultant to be spoken without benefit of tune and rhythm.

We turn our attention this day to songs given us by two remarkable women, Elizabeth and Mary. They were separated in age by probably thirty years; and, though blood relatives, were probably widely separated by social standing. Elizabeth was the wife of a priest and thus possessed some measure of position, while Mary was, no doubt, simply a peasant girl. But they had in common a deep faith in God, and a sublime willingness to be used by him. They were kindred spirits in the most profound sense of the word.

Elizabeth and her husband Zechariah had waited through all the years of their marriage for the common miracle of conception, but without fulfillment. Then, quite out of the blue, God promised that they would have a son, that his name would be called John, and that he would minister "with the spirit and power of Elijah" (Luke 1:17a).

Nearly six months later, Mary was visited by the angel Gabriel, with the message that she had found favor with God, and that she would bear a child who would be called "the Son of the Most High." When Mary asked how this could be, since she had no husband, the angel answered,

> *The Holy Spirit will come upon you,*
> *and the power of the Most High will overshadow you;*
> *therefore the child to be born will be holy;*
> *he will be called the Son of God.* — Luke 1:35

Then, as if anticipating the uncertainties and fears which lay ahead for Mary, the angel told her that her kinswoman Elizabeth had also conceived and that she was in the sixth month of her pregnancy. It was as if the angel were saying, "You'll find a sympathetic, understanding friend in Elizabeth."

So Mary wasted no time in finding her way to Elizabeth's village. She needed desperately to talk with someone who would understand her particular situation. It had to be a person who had herself experienced a miraculous visit from God; not just like Mary's, of course, but miraculous enough that she would not brush Mary's story aside, impatiently or with a sneer.

Mary did well in seeking out Elizabeth. The moment she greeted her cousin, an extraordinary thing happened. As Luke, the physician, reports it, "the babe leaped in Elizabeth's womb," and Elizabeth was filled with the Holy Spirit. It is as if John the Baptizer already recognized his calling; as if, in the womb, he hastened to declare his tie with the coming Messiah.

Then Elizabeth spoke. Most Bible translators do not set up her words in the structure of poetry, but they have the same rhythm and grandeur of expression as the words of Mary which follow.

Elizabeth's words are the simplest kind of testimony. They are marked by gratitude and excitement, and they are unashamedly personal. She makes no attempt at formal theology; all she wants is to tell Mary the joy she feels. She sees herself as a privileged woman, and she wonders why such favors should come to her.

Perhaps the best evidence of the quality of Elizabeth's testimony is to be found in Mary's reply. Mary's response is the glorious *Magnificat*. If one cannot write a great poem or compose some classical music, surely the next best thing is to inspire such creation from another. I wonder how many artists could credit a spouse or friend for the work of genius which came from their brush or pen? I've noticed that often a minister will note, in a preface to a book, that he or she feels indebted to the people of the parish for the help they have given. The ebbing coals of inspiration are often blown into a bright flame by someone's thoughtful word or attentive ear.

So it was, it seems, when Elizabeth and Mary. When the angel spoke to Mary, she answered only with questions; but when her cousin spoke to her, Mary cried, "My soul magnifies the Lord!" I hope I am not exaggerating the point when I suggest that God spoke to Mary as surely through Elizabeth as he had earlier through Gabriel.

I think Mary may have been tied in knots of fear and bewilderment when she came to the home of Zechariah and Elizabeth. Gabriel's message had, perhaps, become a dim and mystical thing to her. Doubts and double doubts may have begun whispering in her ear: Had this really happened; and if it had, was it a madness that could persuade only a peasant girl like herself? Having heard from God, Mary needed now to hear from some human being. Gabriel's majestic voice needed the support of Elizabeth's excited, loving response.

And so it could be with you and me. We might well speak the word which could set loose someone's Magnificat. We might well confirm an uncertain soul. I've known times when someone spoke just the right word to reassure me, often without knowing what he or she was doing. Gabriel may make the motion, but we need Elizabeth to second it.

I'm urging you, in the style of Elizabeth, to sing a song of encouragement. There could be no more appropriate song for the Advent and Christmas season.

Mary's song is one of such grandeur that I am tempted to say, "Read it," then pronounce the benediction. The great missionary-statesman, E. Stanley Jones, called it "The most revolutionary document in the world." Mary identifies herself as a "handmaiden" of "low estate," and from that point on, she makes a case for others like herself — with fair warning to those who walk with pride and arrogance.

Someone has said that this song contains "the first rough draft of Christianity." That may be an overstatement; but surely the mood of this song is reflected in the beatitudes, especially as those beatitudes appear in Luke's Gospel. Mary pictures God on the march against entrenched power and wealth. If, for a moment, we could hear these words as if we had never heard them before — indeed, as if they were coming from someone other than a biblical personality — I wonder how they would strike us? Listen:

> *He has shown strength with his arm; he has scattered the proud in the thoughts of their hearts. He has brought down the powerful from their thrones, and lifted up the lowly; he has filled the hungry with good things, and sent the rich away empty.* — vv. 51-53

At least two things must be said about this powerful statement.

1. Those who have wealth and power had better use these advantages with godly fear. Any form of power — whether talent, money, or position — is a divine trust and God will someday, somehow call it to account. Jesus warned that those who have been given much will be held to the most severe reporting.

This hazard, of course, is this: power of any sort inevitably breeds a certain kind of arrogance; and it blinds us, or at least dulls our sensitivities, to the pain of others. It is very hard to understand how someone on poverty row feels in a supermarket, if we can fill our own basket without undue worry. A person who is secure in their position can hardly imagine the pain of those who have been without work for months. "I'd make a job for myself," the self-confident answer; but they have not experienced the numbing pain of continued and humiliating defeat.

2. Mary's statement reminds us that the people who bear Jesus' name must always have a special heart for the poor. During the Decian persecution, the church was caring for a great number of the poor — windows, orphans, the physically handicapped, the hungry. One day a leader in the Roman community broke into the church and demanded that they hand over their treasures to the state. Laurentius the deacon pointed to the great circle of the poor, the maimed, and the disinherited and said, "These are the treasures of the Church."

It is true even today. If there is any substantial evidence that the church is rich, it is in the poor who are drawn to us or those whom we are able to serve. We must come to measure our wealth not in the size of our endowments nor in the beauty of our buildings, but in the poor of body, mind, purse, and spirit who find comfort in our precincts.

The very style of our churches makes it difficult for us to take Mary's song seriously. Clergy march down the aisle in impressive robes to bow at altars adorned by beautiful candles and ornate crosses. We seem to glory in conspicuous display. Would the peasant girl from Nazareth be comfortable in our pomp and pageantry? Or would she think of us as some of the "proud" who must be scattered, the rich who will be sent away empty? Somehow our denominational assemblies find it easier to apply the words of Mary to governments and corporations than to our own prides and prejudices.

But you and I will still miss the point of Mary's song if we pay attention primarily to the church as an institution. It is almost as easy to wax outrage for the church as for corporations and the distant rich. What shall you and I say about the wealth and power which is in our own individual hands? Have the proud imaginations of my own heart been humbled before God? Am I attentive to matters and people who are of low degree in the eyes of the world; or am I inclined to give special attention to those who have this world's goods? Am I impressed with life's real values, such as patience, humility, gentleness, compassion, and love?

Am I ready to share? Mary envisioned a day when God would exalt those of low degree. You and I could well be instruments of God in bringing such a beautiful thing to pass. Many people see themselves as persons of low degree because they don't receive enough attention to restore their egos. In some instances they need money, clothing, dental work, or education to restore some lost or never-possessed dignity. But in many instances they need nothing more than a caring human being. I don't want to over sentimentalize it, but I'm sure there are some people whose low estate could be substantially changed by little more than a word of sincere interest and appreciation.

And they're not necessarily people in poverty row. Most of us have no idea what loneliness and human hunger may exist in the heart of some person in our own circle of association. Even people living in physical comfort are sometimes, deep inside, convinced that they are of low degree.

It is a season for singing and for giving a song to others. Elizabeth sang, and set loose Mary's song. Mary sang in such a way that the challenge is upon us yet today. Now let us go out with a song, in Mary and Elizabeth's tradition. A word of kindness, a gift of money, an ear to listen, a heart to care; these make the music of the season. They are the songs of the Christ who has come, and who continues to come, through our acts and words of love.

J. Ellsworth Kalas

# God's Sneak Attack

I think I was eight years old the first time I got to be in a Christmas pageant. I played the part of a shepherd at our church during the Christmas Eve service that year. I didn't have any lines, but I remember that I had to kneel on one knee for a very long time.

The whole chancel area of our sanctuary had been transformed into a living nativity scene. There in the center was the manger, with Mary and Joseph on either side. Then we, the shepherds, came up along on one side. Next, the three gift-bearing wise men came up on the other side. And then, on a kind of balcony overlooking the whole scene, there were sopranos from the church choir appearing as singing angels in the skies overhead.

It was very exciting for me, as a child, to be part of that scene, for it was such a familiar and cherished scene to me. Among the many traditions that were part of the Christmas season in our home were certain decorations that my mother brought out in December of each year. And among those annual decorations was a little crèche that she would set up prominently on a table in the front hallway. It was a little wooden barn filled with ceramic figurines of shepherds and sheep, Wise Men and camels, parents and Child. My mother even had bits of straw that she placed on the floor of the little wooden stable for atmosphere.

That little crèche captured my imagination as a child. I moved the figurines around as a boy to reenact the story. I still vividly remember positioning my face right behind each of the Wise Men and each of the shepherds in order to imagine what they must have

39

seen that night. And so it was very exciting for me, as an eight year old, actually to be a part of that scene on that Christmas Eve.

In the many years since, of course, I have been in several more such Christmas pageants and plays, usually as a shepherd, and once as a wise man carrying myrrh. Each time, the scene has been basically the same: the manger in the middle, Joseph and Mary nearby, and the shepherds, Wise Men, angels, and animals flanking the scene.

That's the way the scene always looks, isn't it? We've all seen it, probably thousands of times. We've seen it depicted on Christmas cards, in churches, on front yards, in paintings, in pageants, and in plays. And every time, the scene is essentially the same: the manger in the middle, surrounded by the parents and all the familiar visitors.

In all of the depictions I have seen through the years, however, I have yet to see a pageant, a play, or a nativity scene that really depicts the whole Christmas story. For, you see, I have never yet seen a card, a painting, or a stage that is big enough to depict the whole Christmas story.

It would require a terribly large stage in order to make the nativity scene look small. And the truth of the matter is that if you really want to portray the whole Christmas story, then you have to make the nativity scene look small. Very small.

Luke tells the Christmas story for us, and he does a nice job of setting the stage — the whole stage — for the story. He begins with the headline of the day: "In those days a decree went out from Emperor Augustus that all the world should be registered." If there had been newspapers in the ancient Mediterranean world, this would have been the front page headline on every one of them. In Athens, Ephesus, Damascus, Alexandria, and Jerusalem alike, the big news was this decree from the Roman emperor. It would have been the lead story on every news broadcast and the hot topic of each roundtable discussion. It set people in motion all over the Empire, including a certain newly married couple from Nazareth.

See how Luke begins to set the stage for the Christmas story. Rome, not a manger, is at the center of the stage. The Roman Emperor, not a baby, is the star of the show — or at least the character with the top billing at the start. And the prospect of an Empire-wide tax, not some anonymous birth, is the headline.

Luke goes on to tell how the decree from Caesar Augustus prompted Joseph to travel from Nazareth, where he lived, to Bethlehem, which was his ancestral home. A traditional nativity scene puts the manger in Bethlehem in the middle. Luke's account reminds us, however, that Bethlehem was not only far from the center of the world's stage, it was not even at the center of Joseph's stage. His home was Nazareth, and going to Bethlehem was going out of his way.

Next, Joseph and Mary arrive in Bethlehem, only to find that there is no room for them in the inn. "I'm sorry, the motel is full ... but you're welcome to stay in the parking ramp!" This couple and this birth were not even a big fish in the small pond of Bethlehem. They were pushed off to the side of a town that was itself off to the side of a province that was off to the side of the Empire.

I've never seen the whole Christmas story depicted because I've only ever seen the manger at center stage. But the birth of Jesus was not center stage. Indeed, it practically happened offstage.

So let's reset the nativity scene in our minds. At the center of the stage is not a manger but a throne. It's Caesar's throne — the seat of the world's power — and it's in Rome. Off to the far right side of the stage, let's say, is a flat — a bit of background scenery — that represents the rather unimportant Roman province of Palestine. If it is portrayed to scale, then it will be little more than a link between Syria and Egypt. Painted on the edge of that flat, perhaps, is a dot barely visible to the audience. The dot represents Bethlehem, a little town that virtually no one outside of Palestine even knew existed. And somewhere out back, away from the main street in that speck of a town, is where we'll find the manger. It is not center stage at all. And that is where God came into the world.

The truth of the Christmas story is that God came into the world backstage. He came practically unnoticed by the world. He came to an unknown and unimportant place, and he came to unknown and unimportant people. He snuck in.

It is mind boggling to consider how God could have made his entrance onto this world's stage: the irresistible spectacle, the unmistakable glory, and the unfathomable power. That is likely how he will make his return (cf. Matthew 24:30, 1 Thessalonians 4:16) some day in the future. But that is not how he chose to make his entrance 2,000 years ago. The truth is that God came into the world backstage.

And yet, wouldn't you know it: God stole the show.

At that time in the Mediterranean world in which Jesus was born, dates were set according to the Roman Emperor — what year of his particular reign it was. Now, most of the nations of the world set dates according to this backstage Baby's birth — 2003 A.D., anno domini, the year of the Lord. At that time, Caesar Augustus, Quirinius, and Herod were big names, important men. Now they are just the supporting cast in the bigger story of Christ's birth. At that time, Rome was the most important city in the world, and Bethlehem was just a two-bit town in a conquered country. Now, Bethlehem is one of the most famous, most visited places on earth. And Rome's greatest claim to fame today and through much of Western history is, arguably, the role it plays in Christ's church.

I call Christmas "God's sneak attack" because he didn't come into the world marching through the front door. He didn't come with power or prominence, with influence or importance. He didn't come into the spotlight. God came into the world through the back door. He snuck in. And that continues to be his Christmas strategy. He continues to sneak into our world, into our lives, at Christmas time.

Stores, banks, and malls that wouldn't think twice about playing "Amazing Grace" or "The Old Rugged Cross" over their sound systems during the rest of the year will, at Christmas time, routinely play songs that say, "Let earth receive her King," "God and sinner reconciled," "Let every heart prepare him room," "In thy dark streets shineth the everlasting Light," and "O come, let us adore him." He sneaks into our world at Christmas.

I sometimes hear Christians lament the commercialization of Christmas. I wonder, though, if we have underestimated God and how he works. For I suspect that the effect may actually be flowing in the other direction: it is not Christmas that is being commercialized, but rather it is our commercial culture that is annually — unwittingly — infiltrated by the gospel.

A neighborhood that would never see a large illuminated cross on their yards will sport a half-dozen nativity scenes all lit up. Folks who pay little or no attention to church for eleven months of the year find themselves instinctively drawn back there during December. And families that practice no other devotional time together will light Advent wreaths and sing songs together as a family during this season of the year.

I suppose nearly every local church pastor knows the experience of looking out at an unusually large congregation each Christmas Eve. The preacher sees people in the pews on that night that he sees in church on no other occasion during the year. In my early days in the ministry, I found myself feeling annoyed by those once-a-year folks. In more recent years, however, my response has softened. I see a certain beauty now when I look out at that Christmas Eve crowd — not a beauty found in the limitations of some folks' commitment to the church, to be sure, but rather the beauty of God's gentle achievement each Christmas season.

Christmas was — and continues to be — God's sneak attack. He sneaks in through songs, through traditions, and through sentiment. He sneaks in through the generosity, the good will, and the festivity of the season. He sneaks in through the excitement that children feel as Christmas approaches, and he sneaks in through the longing that adults feel at that time of the year.

Philips Brooks, in his cherished Christmas carol, expressed the quiet, unassuming way that God worked in Bethlehem, and continues to work in human hearts today. "How silently, how silently, the wondrous gift is given; so God imparts to human hearts the blessings of his heaven. No ear may hear his coming, but in this world of sin, where meek souls will receive him, still the dear Christ enters in."

Christmas was God's sneak attack, and Christmas gives us a glimpse of what God is like and what he continues to do. God didn't come marching in through the front door, flexing his muscles, and demanding the spotlight. He could have, but he did not.

The movie star may arrive with his or her entourage. The sports team trots onto the court or field with fanfare, cheers, and applause.

The big-name performer receives a standing ovation. And the President, Prime Minister, and Queen are all welcomed by bands, red carpets, and protocol. But the King of the Universe arrived in swaddling cloths, mostly ignored by the world he had created.

And, still today, the Lord does not barge into our lives. Instead, he stands at the door and knocks (Revelation 3:20), and he waits for us to welcome him.

Take a good look at that familiar nativity scene and the elements there: Joseph and Mary, the little town of Bethlehem, a stable, and a manger. At Christmas, the Lord came into the lives of insignificant, common people. That's good news for you and me, for we are assured that he willingly comes into our lives, too. At Christmas, God came into a place that seemed small and unimportant. I'm glad to hear that, for my life and my home are small and unimportant. At Christmas, He came into a place that was dirty and unworthy of him. And that's good news for me, for my heart is dirty and unworthy, yet God comes to reside there.

Here is a God who is marvelously willing and able. He is willing to come in backstage, and then he is able to steal the show.

I have yet to see the whole Christmas story depicted on a stage, for it's hard to find a stage big enough for the job. But I have seen the Christmas story played out again and again in individual lives. It is the story of this God who could come bursting in, but does not. It is the story of this God who comes in gently and unassumingly, perhaps even unnoticed at first. And it is the story of this God who, bit by gracious bit, moves into the spotlight of our lives. He moves toward the center of our stage. And the God who comes into your life and mine backstage, by his mercy, becomes the star of our show.

I was eight years old when I first got to play a part in a Christmas pageant during a Christmas Eve service, and that was my privilege. But it is today my greater privilege — and yours, too — to be a year-round nativity scene: a life that depicts both how God comes and how God reigns.

David J. Kalas

# God Communicates In Humanly Understandable Terms

One Christmas morning, a young widow was doing her best to make Christmas happy for her two little boys. This was their first Christmas without their father. Unexpectedly, someone knocked at the door. "Who could that be?" she wondered. When she opened the door, she found her pastor standing with his arms full of toys and candy. This man, who was one of the most renowned preachers of his era, said quite simply: "I thought your boys might miss their father on Christmas morning." He spent the next two hours playing with the two boys and their new toys.[1]

That minister became a living parable of the meaning of Christmas! By his caring deed, he demonstrated the doctrine of the Incarnation fare more persuasively than he could have with his most eloquent sermon. Christmas means God humbled himself to come to the place where we live. The Incarnation of God in the flesh means God willingly shared in the joys and pains of *our* existence. The birth of Jesus means God took upon himself all the frailties and limitations of the flesh. Christmas means God *elected* to experience life on our terms.

This true story, which I have said is a parable, reminds me of a famous fictional story called *The Prince and the Pauper*. Only in recent years has the truth dawned on me that this tale is also a parable of the Incarnation. A young prince is depicted as having exchanged his rich garments and crown for the rags of a beggar. He gave up the comfort and protection of his palace for the rough-and-ready life of a street urchin. He moved upon the dirty, ragged, hungry, and looked-down-upon ordinary people. Only then did he begin to understand how the common people lived.

I also thought of a cross-country coach I know. He does not just teach by word. He runs alongside of his boys and girls. He demonstrates the art of running with his own body. He keeps in touch with the feelings of frustration and elation experienced by his runners. I thought of the contrast with my own college cross-country coach. He was a fine man and a successful coach. He used to drive alongside of us during a race or practice and yell encouraging words. With his 230-pound bulk, he could do little else!

The Incarnation is God choosing to share our common human lot. Much of the meaning of the Incarnation is encapsulated in the single event recorded from the growing-up days of Jesus. Our text is, therefore, an example of God communicating through Jesus in humanly understandable terms.

Our text shows God communicating to us by entering into the life of a boy who grew up like many other boys. The Gospel according to Luke emphasizes that fact by the way the account is begun and ended. In the prelude to this passage, we are told that "... the child grew and became strong ..." (Luke 2:40). The postlude summarizes by saying: "And Jesus increased in wisdom and in years, and in divine and human favor" (v. 52).

Romantic artists and writers have distorted the scene of twelve-year-old Jesus in the Temple with the elders. For example, the Apocryphal Gospel of Thomas gives extravagant but inaccurate, even repulsive, accounts of the young Jesus as an exhibitionist or some kind of "boy wonder." Christian art has sometimes depicted the incident under the misleading caption, "The Boy Jesus Teaching in the Temple." But scripture never portrays Jesus as a "boy wonder"! Luke never suggests the twelve-year-old was a precocious teacher of elders. Luke describes Jesus as "... sitting among the teachers, *listening* ..." (v. 46). Like any boy of that young age who has been raised in a devout home, he listened with *respect* to his elders.

So it was that his anxious mother and father, who had searched for him for three days, found him *listening*, respectfully. That scene must have become engraved indelibly in their minds. Years later, as she looked at her adult son and thought back to that incident,

Mary must have shaken her head in wonder. Do you remember that touching moment in *Fiddler on the Roof* when Tevye sings: "Is this the little girl I carried? Is this the little boy at play? I don't remember growing older. When did they?" ("Sunrise, Sunset" by Sheldon Harnick).

How often Mary must have thought something like that as she watched her special Son grow into manhood and become the magnificent preacher and healer! How often neighbors must have looked at the grown-up Jesus with such head-shaking wonderment and exclaimed: "I don't believe it! Is that the little boy at play? Is that really Mary's and Joseph's son? I don't remember growing older. Why did he?" Yes, Jesus must have been much like any other boy.

Perhaps Mary and Joseph had their first and only clue (other than the amazing events which surrounded the Nativity) that he was different in that moment in the Temple. Perhaps something deep and profound stirred within them as he answered their distressed question with the words: "Why were you searching for me? Did you not know that I must be in my Father's house?" (v. 49). These are the first recorded words from the lips of Jesus. In those words, we see the first emerging self-consciousness of his special identity. Here we see the earliest recognition of his unique Sonship to God! But, other than one moment, we have no reason to suspect Jesus had other than a normal boyhood. This is the greatness of God. He communicated to us by entering into the life of a boy who grew up like many other boys.

God also communicated in humanly understandable terms when he chose to have his special Son raised in a home like many others. He did not grow up in a wealthy home. We can tell Mary and Joseph were persons of small means by the humble thank-offering they brought to the Temple — i.e., "a pair of turtledoves or two young pigeons" (Luke 2:24). A well-to-do family might have offered a lamb. We can also tell that Jesus grew up in a good, law-abiding home. His parents showed respect for the *sacred* laws by bringing their son to the Temple on the proscribed eighth day for the required ritual of dedication called circumcision. Whoever has ever brought a young child to God's altar for Baptism can identify with that scene. So can any parent identify with the scene described by our text who has ever worried over and scolded a child who has lost track of time. Mary and Joseph were very normal. They worried when their son was missing. Then, when they found him, all their pent-up worry and anger poured out: "Child, why have you treated us so? Look, your father and I have been searching for you in great anxiety" (v. 48). Mary and Joseph could not have been more ordinary and human than when they revealed themselves in those words. This, too, is the greatness of God. He communicated to us in the humanly understandable terms of a very ordinary home — perhaps much like our own.

What is *most* precious about God coping with life on our human terms is that God did it his way! And, he did it successfully, victoriously, happily.

Jesus was attractive, admirable, strong, winsome, and blessed. Remember Luke's observation that, as Jesus grew, he "... increased ... in divine and human favor" (v. 52). Jesus blessed every life he touched. Too many people forget that! They think of him as a depressor or "wet-blanket" who ruins the joy of life. They react as if he were a curse instead of a blessing. So Walter Russell Bowie, writing in The Interpreter's Bible, says about our text:

> Many people since that time, both without and within the church, have made the mistake of the Pharisees. They have supposed that somehow there must be an incompatibility between religion and the bright enjoyment of this world. They have divorced it from poetry and turned it into dogmatic prose. They have divorced it even from beauty and made religion a thing of drab clothes and drab demeanor. They have turned it into a hard, inward discipline of spirit and have forgotten that all life ought to be baptized into a larger meaning if religion is to be true to the beauty of Christ. Worst of all, they have treated religion as though it had nothing necessarily to do with the everyday matter of keeping human contacts warm and lovely. Some persons of official standing in the church, both clerical and lay, have a kind of formal piety, but are poison to live with, like Mr. Murdstone in David Copperfield. It has been rightly

*said that not much credit can be given to any man's religion whose very dog and cat are not the better for it.*[2]

Let us so see Jesus. May you and I pray during this Christmastide season:

> *We would see Jesus,*
> *Mary's son most holy,*
> *Light of the village*
> *life from day to day;*
> *Shining revealed through*
> *every task most lowly,*
> *The Christ of God,*
> *the life, the truth, the way.*
>
> *We would see Jesus,*
> *on the mountain teaching,*
> *With all the listening*
> *people gathered round;*
> *While birds and flowers and*
> *sky above are preaching*
> *The blessedness*
> *which simple trust has found.*[3]

---

1. As told to Dr. Harrell Beck of the Boston University School of Theology speaking to a pastor's school in Bennington, Vermont, in 1975.

2. Walter Russell Bowie, *The Gospel According to St. Luke*, The Interpreter's Bible, Volume 8 (New York and Nashville: Abingdon, 1952), p. 69.

3. 1964 *United Methodist Hymnal*, No. 90, "We Would See Jesus; Lo! His Star Is Shining," Stanzas 2 and 3, by J. Edgar Park.

This sermon by Richard D. Campbell (originally published by CSS Publishing Company) has been included to correct an oversight in text assignments.)

# Christmas And The New Family

When Wilbur and Orville Wright completed their historic flight at Kitty Hawk, North Carolina, on December 17, 1903, they sent home a succinct telegram. In minimum words it reported that their venture had succeeded, and concluded, "Home for Christmas." Whether they knew it or not, their achievement had ushered in a new age. Along with that, their "coming home" announcement might seem very mundane. But any of us who have longed to go home for Christmas will understand that the two subjects of the telegram were of equal importance. Not to world history, of course, but to members of the Wright family.

Christmas is a family time, no doubt about it. Those who are without a family, or who cannot see their family fully joined together, almost hate to hear the word. Single people or those estranged from family sometimes say that Christmas is the loneliest time of the year. What could be worse, after all, than to be without family on the traditional family day and family season?

Let me hasten to say, therefore, that I am not going to talk about blood, marital, or adoptive ties. I am not even talking about the circle of friendship. The family about which I wish to speak is that new family which came to birth on Christmas Day. It is a family to which all of us can belong if only we desire to do so; and its potential for joy and fulfillment is almost unlimited.

You will find the story in our scripture — the opening verses of the Gospel according to Saint John. I don't know that there are any three or four paragraphs in all of literature with the sustained beauty, elegance, and power which can be found here. No actor is skilled enough to read them with proper power, and no preacher can hope to explain them adequately. Only through the Spirit of God can we begin to touch a fair measure of their grandeur.

"In the beginning," the inspired writer says, "was the Word." It doesn't seem a likely way to introduce the Christmas story; but John is anxious for us to understand that Christmas had its beginnings long before Joseph and Mary, and in a place utterly beyond Bethlehem. He wants us to realize that the One he is about to introduce was always with God, possesses the same divine nature, and that eternal part of God became one of us human beings in order to save us from our sins.

Thus John is still in the first paragraph of his story when he reveals the conflict which exists in our world. This Word is the light of our human race, he says, but the light has to shine in the darkness. After all, what is light for, except to overcome darkness? But the very existence of darkness tells us there is a battle to be won.

How much of a battle? This: though "the world came into being through him; yet the world did not know him" (v. 10). He is the Grand Playwright who appears in the middle of his own production; and the amateur actors don't recognize him, don't sense that the words they speak are of his giving, the costumes they wear of his designing and making.

John says, "He came to what was his own, and his own people did not accept him" (v. 11). There are few verses in the Bible more extraordinary and more wrought with tragedy than that one. He is rejected by those to whom he belongs, and who in turn belong to him.

As the Gospel of John tells the Christmas story, Jesus was not only shut out of the inn to which Joseph and Mary came, he was shut out of his home. It is shocking that Christmas, the great season for homecoming, began with our Lord shut out of his home!

But the story doesn't end there. Jesus came to his own home, and accepted rejection there, in order that he might establish a new home for our human race — that he might begin a new family. I shall dare to call it the true Holy Family.

The details are given to us in the twelfth and thirteenth verses of this first chapter of John's Gospel. "But to all who received him, who believed in his name, he gave power to become children of God, who were born, not of blood or of the will of the flesh or of the will of man, but of God." A new family is about to come into existence — a family born of God.

We need some background to appreciate and understand what is happening. The Old Testament scriptures tell us that God gave our human race an utterly beautiful start by setting us in a garden of perfect delight. But we human beings rebelled against God, and chose to listen to the voice of the intruder — sin. As a result, we became a wayward race. By creation we were the children of God, but by our own choice we became the children of this earth; in the classic language of the scriptures, we became the children of the devil. The Bible doesn't really give us any middle ground. If we do not choose to follow God, we have only one alternative. We may call that alternative by a number of less offensive names; but in the final measure, if we reject God, we become the children of destruction.

When you stop to think of the condition of our world, that isn't too hard to believe. The daily headlines demonstrate how given we are to destruction. War, hate, prejudice, pornography, hunger, poverty: these words are the language of destruction, and they seem to dominate our human scene. It's a far cry from Eden. Something has gone violently wrong.

The major part of the Old Testament tells us of God's continuing efforts to bring this wayward planet back to himself. It is a story that concentrates on a chosen people — the Jews — who are meant to be the special channel for God's working; and on God's efforts to help that people fulfill their calling.

And at last, in what the apostle calls "the fullness of time," God sends forth his Son. Christmas is God's ultimate effort to bring our world back to himself. He seeks to restore Eden by way of Bethlehem.

It is also by the way of the family. God wants a relationship with us human beings which is beyond king and subject; he is our Father, and it is that relationship which he wants restored. When we receive Christmas we become *children of God*, brought back to our rightful place in the Holy Family.

Someone once said that this verse — "all who received him ... he gave power to become children of God" — could well have been placed at the very beginning of the New Testament. It would be the key to all that follows in the Gospels, the Epistles, and even in Revelation; because the climax of the whole biblical story is a kind of family reunion in eternity. And it is the explicit summary of what Jesus was sent to do. He came not simply to teach or to be an example, but to do what he alone could do: prepare the way for you and me to become children of God.

The Bible wants us to realize that this is God's achieving. We must be born, the writer says, "not of blood or of the will of the flesh or of the will of man, but of God." I'm not sure that we can distinguish particular meanings for each of these phrases; perhaps it's primarily that the writer wants us to understand that there is no other factor involved than the purpose and power of God. If we are to come into a renewed relationship with our Heavenly Father, it will not be by our human efforts, our struggling for acceptance, or our admirable deserving. It will be God's doing. God alone can bring about this marvelous reunion.

And it *is* a reunion. It is not that we are strangers to God. Rather we are prodigals who have left home and now need to be restored to the family. We all have that divine breath which came to the human race at creation, when God breathed into the creature of clay the stuff of divine life. Now it is a matter of our coming back into the family which is rightly our home.

There are many times when you and I need to remember that our rightful human place is in the family of God. I must tell myself this, for other people, in those instances when I despair for someone's in humanity and degradation. Whatever that human being may seem at this moment to be, no matter how debased or unlovable he may have become, he is still someone whose original family ties are with God. I dare not give up on any human being; because he or she has the potential, by God's action in Jesus Christ, to rejoin the heavenly family.

Nor dare I give up on myself. On those days when I look at myself more harshly than I would ever look on any other human being — and when I can see no measure of worth in me because I am obsessed with hell's estimate of unworth — I must remember that my eternal roots are in the family of God, and that God wants so much for his family to be whole that he sent Jesus Christ to give us the power to become children of God. This is a word to throw in the teeth of despair, self-loathing, and unreasoning fear. It is a word to speak to hell itself.

The key to this transformation, John tells us, is in our believing; specifically, the promise is to those who believe on his — Christ's — name. It is in accepting Jesus Christ for who he is that you and I can become what we were meant to be. This is not as mystical a thing as it first seems to be. Whoever is Lord of my life has power over it. If I choose to believe in despair or materialism above all else, they will rule me. But if I believe in Jesus the Christ, he gives me the power to become a child of God. We belong to that which we believe. That's why our believing is such a powerful thing.

It is by this believing that we receive the power — or the right, as other translations put it — to become the children of God. Believing releases us to take advantage of what is already possible. When the prodigal son was in the far country, languishing in the pigpen, he was in fact a son of his father, but it was doing him no good. It was not until he believed that there was an opportunity in his father's house — an opportunity he underestimated — that he rose up to go home. He would have died in the pigpen if he hadn't believed enough to leave it. In his rising up and leaving, he received the power to become, effectively, his father's son.

So the Christmas story is a family story. Not because some of us remember happy family celebrations, and not because some of us have had such celebrations this season, but because Christmas makes possible the renewed family of God. Because of Christmas, the power is available for us to become the children of God, and for the family of God to be restored.

G. K. Chesterton probably said it as well as anyone since the writer of John's Gospel. Chesterton is known to many as author of the Father Brown mystery novels, and to others as a passionate defender of the Christian faith. In his poem, "The House of Christmas," Chesterton first describes the state of our human souls.

> *For men are homesick in their homes,*
> *And strangers under the sun,*
> *And they lay their heads in a foreign land*
> *Whenever the day is done.*

We are all "strangers" on this planet, as long as we are estranged from God. Even when we are in the midst of family and friends — surrounded by the familiar appointments of home — we feel some unexplainable homesickness. Why? Because, as Chesterton says, "We have hands that fashion and heads that know, but our hearts we lost — how long ago!" How long ago? Back at the earliest part of the human story, when we began wandering from the Father's house.

But God has made it possible for us to return. Chesterton recalls both the language of the Gospel of John and the rejection which Joseph and Mary experienced at the Bethlehem inn. So he rejoices:

> *To an open house in the evening*
> *Home shall men come,*
> *To an older place than Eden*
> *And a taller town than Rome ...*
>
> *To the place where God was homeless*
> *And all men are at home.*

God, in Jesus Christ, became homeless at Bethlehem so that you and I and all the human race might have a home. In sublime love, our Lord accepted rejection in order to bring the family together again. This is the Holy Family of Christmas: the family which you and I make with the Heavenly Father. Welcome home, this Christmas season!

J. Ellsworth Kalas

# Epiphany: Glory
# Beyond Our Expecting

In 1986 a relatively unknown basketball team from the University of Arkansas at Little Rock defeated the highly-favored Notre Dame team in the NCAA basketball tournament. Reporters who crowded around Coach Mike Newell following the game wanted his analysis of the victory. He answered, simply and significantly, "Your only limitation is your imagination."

Our lives are often fenced in by our low expectations. This is true not only of what we expect of ourselves, but also of what we expect to happen in our world, and what we think might be the purpose of God in our times.

It was so with a generation of Jews over 21 centuries ago. Their nation had not had a powerful prophetic witness in perhaps four centuries. Their knowledge of the glory of God was almost entirely historic. They could read in their Jewish scriptures of the wonders of the Lord as experienced by their ancestors of times long past; but they had never seen such glory, nor had they ever talked with anyone who had.

Thus, when John the Baptizer appeared on the scene, people had no standard by which to judge him. Obviously he was a man sent from God, but jut how far-reaching was his ministry? Was he only a passing prophetic figure; or was he one of those persons whose role had been predicted by earlier prophets? Was he, perhaps, the one the people wanted most to see — the Messiah?

John quickly advised the people that their expectations were too low. We read his words with a reverence which limits their sting. He all but ridiculed their confusing *him* with the Christ. My baptism, John said, uses water; his will be with the Holy Spirit and with fire. Could there be a greater contrast?

What a shock that must have been to the crowds. Although John used water for his baptismal rites, his style was anything but water-like; if any word could aptly describe John, it would have been fire. And it was fire, John said, that would characterize the baptism of the Christ who was coming. "You think I'm important enough to be considered a prospect for the Christ?" John continued. "He's so much above and beyond me that I can't even qualify to be his valet; I'm not worthy to untie the thongs of his sandals." John was trying to tell the people that their expectations were far too low. The Jewish people had been without a prophetic voice for so long that they were elevating the forerunner to the position of Christ.

What qualities made the ministry of Jesus superior to that of John the Baptizer? How can Jesus be referred to as a source of fire, when John himself seems much more fiery a personality? A scholar in another day says that John's style had "the quiescence of a negative and prudential morality," while Jesus offered the living, vital energy of a true moral and spiritual enthusiasm.

John's call to repentance was necessary and noble; and we must begin there. But that kind of negative morality is not enough. It's sad that we Christians seem to get bogged down at that level of moral power. We often measure our goodness by the number of things we refrain from doing, rather than moving on to the positive righteousness of holy enthusiasm. "Don't tell me what you *don't* do," a backwoods preacher in another generation once said to his negatively-inclined people. "The nearest picket fence doesn't do those things, either. Tell me what you *do*! Tell me something positive that's happened to you, for Jesus' sake!"

Jesus calls us to such positive goodness. Entrenched evil will never be overcome by *reacting*; there must be something alive, compelling, and persuasive in our goodness.

That ought to be clear to us simply in the three key words of the Christian life — faith, love, and hope. These are not reactive words. They are positive, aggressive, and challenging. Hope is not a word to characterize retreat, but advance. So, too, with faith. Faith is a power which reaches out; it is a marching, advancing term.

And love! What a positive word that is! Hate is a reacting good, dependent on the face, manner, or conduct of the other person. But love doesn't wait to react. Christian love sets the pace in a relationship, rather than simply reacting or responding to that which others have done. It doesn't wait to see what the other person's manner or conduct may be: it is resolved to love, whatever. And in those cases where the conduct of the other party is negative and destructive, love has the power to overcome.

It is ironic that we Christians are often thought of as a negative people, when everything about our heritage in Jesus Christ is positive. True, we say *no* to many things: hate, war, poverty, sin, meanness, and fear. But we say *no* to those qualities simply because they are negotiations; and it is by saying *no* to them that we can say *yes* to life. We follow one who came into the world that we might have *life*, and have it abundantly. Our Lord's purpose in the world was not to restrict and limit our lives; but to set us free, so that we might take more of life's conquest.

One of the ancient documents of Christianity records Jesus as saying, "He that is near me is near the fire." I think it is almost impossible for us to grasp such a picture of our Lord. We have lived all our lives in a world — particularly in the western world — which has benefitted from the fire he brought to the earth. We cannot easily imagine a society without many of those benefits and glories. Let us discover how many ways Jesus Christ came as fire.

The modern Russian novelist, Boris Pasternak, put it powerfully in his novel, *Dr. Zhivago*. First-century Rome, he said, was "a flea market of borrowed gods and conquered peoples, a bargain basement on two floors ... And then, into this tasteless heap of gold and marble, He came, light and clothed in an aura, emphatically human, deliberately provincial, Galilean, and at that moment gods and nations ceased to be and man came into being ..." (p. 43). Jesus sent the value of the human creature into a whole new level. A society which looked upon children as of limited value — to be pushed to the background — watched in amazement as the Great

Teacher interrupted himself to take children on his knee for blessing. A world which was surfeited with the halt and the blind, and which told such persons to stay out of the way, was baffled by the One who stopped his procession to heal a blind beggar.

This was *fire*. It was a burning of the old values and prejudices, clearing the way for the birth of compassion.

It showed itself, also, in the world of human prejudices. The best people of Jesus' day knew only one way to deal with people they judged to be sinners, and that was to shun them. To their amazement, Jesus — who was himself clearly a good human being — chose to associate with such persons. It was not that he condoned their sins; to the contrary, he gave people a passion to be done with such a life, so that — like Zacchaeus — they became transformed and productive citizens. That was no tame "water" approach, but fire.

It cut another way, too. The super citizens, who paraded their religion, were condemned by Jesus. He called them hypocrites and playactors — people who made a performance of religion without offering any reality. Those who the people had been taught to revere were suddenly cut to size. That was fire, for sure!

So, too, with the world of human fears. Violent insanity terrified the first-century world, and it still unnerves ours. They called it demon possession; and whatever that term may lack in scientific precision, it is wonderfully accurate in the picture it provides. Jesus walked boldly into such cases, offering a declaration of freedom for those who had been bound by hell. Leprosy was the most dreaded disease of the time — not only because in some instances it was contagious, but because in its worst forms it was dreadfully destructive. The leper was required to warn others to avoid him, and people quickly responded, in terror, to such a warning. Jesus chose not to flee, but to walk into the world of the leper. He touched the untouchable, and made them whole. That, surely, is fire. John's water is tame by comparison.

At times, Jesus invaded even the domain of death. "She is not dead, just sleeping," he told a group gathered to mourn the passing of a girl. It was an absurd word to those bowed by grief, a word so far removed from the realm of possibility that they would hardly give it a hearing. But Jesus made the absurdity into a fact. When someone walks into the domain of death and emerges with life, that is *fire*.

We find it hard to read these stories with fresh and open minds. As a result, we probably fall into the same error as did the people in John the Baptizer's time. They were looking for a messiah who was cut to John's specifications. He seemed to them to be just about "the right size." You and I are likely to do the same thing today. We continue to domesticate Jesus, to make him manageable. We make him a Lord of water rather than of fire.

Our expectations are almost always too small. We shut God out of too many areas of our lives. Sometimes it is because we fear that if we let him in, he will make demands on us which we aren't ready to fulfill. Sometimes we deprive ourselves of beauty and blessings because we simply do not seem to understand that God wants our lives to be victorious and fulfilling. Jesus Christ has come to bring fire into the world.

Perhaps our problem is even greater than that encountered by the people in John's day. They had limited expectations because they had never seen anyone like Jesus. Thus they thought the Messiah would be nothing more than a slightly enlarged version of a prophet; and John fit that description very well. But we've read about Jesus and we've heard about him since we sere children, so we think we know what to expect. And, in most cases, we aren't expecting fire or glory. That's a pity, because we're likely to get what we expect.

John the Baptizer knew that the Christ was to be someone far beyond his dimensions, and beyond the expectations of the crowds that had come to see him. As a result, he was all the more surprised and nonplussed when Jesus came to him for baptism. As Matthew reports it, John hesitated to baptize Jesus: "I should be baptized by you," he said, "not you by me."

But Jesus insisted on receiving John's baptism. People often ask why. After all, John's baptism was for repentance from sin, and we understand that Jesus was free from sin. Why, then, was it necessary for him to be baptized?

Jesus' own answer was, "Let it be so for now. For in this way we shall do all that God requires" (Matthew 3:15). That is, Jesus was ready to fulfill the routine requirements of his calling.

His answer and his attitude are instructive. Many of us are inclined to become restless with the requirements of life. We seek shortcuts. Some of the prerequisites of education, profession, family life, and citizenship seem petty and unnecessary. Perhaps sometimes they are. But it is important for us to bring ourselves under the disciplines of life. They usually have a purpose.

Perhaps Jesus especially wanted by this act to identify himself with us human beings. For him, baptism was not necessary for cleansing from sin, but it was an opportunity to declare himself part of our human race; in our needs, as well as in our potential glory.

I welcome the prospect of a baptism as I enter into this new year; and so, I hope, do you. I need a renewed sense of my baptism in water. I want to feel again the sense of cleansing; a freshness and a lovely purity.

But I want, also, a baptism of fire. I want to feel the grand expectation that God has invested glory in this year; not only in some general sense, but in a specific way, for you and for me. I don't want to limit God's purposes and possibilities in my life by a low expectation. Why should we settle for water when God's promise for you and for me is fire? Thanks be to God for high expectations, and for a Lord who waits graciously to fulfill them.

J. Ellsworth Kalas

Epiphany 2
Ordinary Time 2
John 2:1-11

# Epiphany: A Faith
# To Work Miracles

I consider it divine good fortune that we have a scripture lesson so early in the year which encourages us to ponder a miracle. You and I need to become more sensitive to the possibility of miracles. Such a sensitivity will help us recognize present miracles, which we either do not see or which we take for granted; and it will prepare us to receive still more miracles.

Walt Whitman felt that "each part and tag" of his own person was a miracle, and that "a mouse is miracle enough to confound sextillions of infidels." He reminded us that we are surrounded by the glorious and the miraculous and do not know it. Science ought to have increased our sense of awe, as it has unfolded the marvels of the heavens above and mysteries of our bodies within; but we take the attitude that if we know how far it is to a given planet, we have, therefore, encompassed all its significance.

We need to know that God is at work in our world. The affairs of this world, and of our individual lives, often seem to be out of control. At such times we can be reassured by the knowledge that God has worked wonderfully in days past, and that he is still at work.

So I direct our attention today to a story from the Gospel of John, generally referred to as Jesus' first miracle. I am impressed that this miracle came to pass, not in the confines of a place of worship, nor even in a uniquely religions occasion; but where people were celebrating one of the happy social events of our common life — a wedding.

In the course of the wedding feast, the family ran out of wine. That was a more serious matter in first-century Palestine than it would be in our culture, because a wedding was a unique social occasion. For a family to be inadequately prepared was almost unthinkable. Jesus' mother turned to him expectantly, as if she felt he could solve the problems; and Jesus answered that his hour had not yet come. Several times in this Gospel, Jesus expressed such a sense of divine timing.

But Jesus' mother was not to be put off so easily. She instructed the servants to do whatever Jesus told them. Jesus gave in to his mother's request. He instructed the servants to fill some nearby purification jars with water; then told them to draw some of the water out of one of the jars and take it to the steward of the feast. When the steward tasted the wine, he praised it as the best of the occasion, marveling that they had saved this special wine until the last.

In many ways, this is a troublesome story. I can find logic for most of Jesus' miracles — especially those where he heals the sick and relieves human misery. But this miracle seems so much like a performance, a mere demonstration of power. In a way, it hardly seems worthy of our Lord. What is the meaning of it?

Some scholars feel that it was purely a symbolic act. They question whether it actually happened, and think of it rather as a kind of dramatic parable, to show the power of Christ to bring excitement and renewal into human life.

Others say this is a beautiful way of showing God's care for the common business of life. In a way, it is a living-out of Jesus' statement that the hairs of our head are all numbered — God is concerned about the most routine details of our lives, even though they have no eternal significance.

Still others say this miracle is God's way of saying that heaven is ready to celebrate with us in the happiness of life. God is not a killjoy who waits to make life miserable. Rather, he is a benevolent Father who rejoices in our happiness and brings exuberance to our best celebrations.

I find a bit of satisfaction in each of these interpretations; you may take your choice. I'm more anxious to rejoice in the miracle and to learn what circumstances brought it to pass.

To be specific: How many participants are needed in order to make a miracle? The devout might say that one is enough; miracles are God's business, so only God is needed. The very secular, on the other hand, might reply that it's a moot question; there is no such thing as a miracle, thus any questions about the number of participants are meaningless.

The truth lies somewhere between these extremes. I will not concede the miracles do not exist; the essence of this sermon rests on the conviction that miracles are a fact of our lives and we ought to rejoice in them and enlarge their scope. Secularists and I might differ widely on the definition of a miracle; but I think I would show them, in time, that they, too, leave a place for miracles and mystery in their lives, even though they are troubled by the terms. They might resist using the word *miracle*, since they may find the word offensive. That won't bother me, since a rose by any other name still smells as sweet.

As for those who argue that the miracle is God's province alone, I expect that their definition is too small on the other end of the discussion. We would soon discover, as we looked at specific miracles in the life of that devout person, that God used several human instruments in bringing the miracle to pass.

The miracle at the wedding feast in Cana began with Mary. It began where many a less-remembered miracle has begun — with an unabashed, indomitable, undiscouraged mother.

The scriptures do not give us many insights into the thinking of Mary. We're told that after the shepherds' visit, "Mary treasured all these words and pondered them in her heart" (Luke 2:19). And again, a dozen years later, following the remarkable experience in the temple at Jerusalem, "His mother treasured all these things in her heart" (Luke 2:51b). In truth, I imagine that Mary's mind and heart were a beehive of wonderings, glories, and apprehensions. Many things about this son of hers must have confused her.

But one thing was sure — she knew he was different and special. So when the word slipped out at the wedding feast that refreshments had run out, Mary knew exactly what to do. The Gospel record is succinct. "When the wine gave out, the mother of Jesus said to him, 'They have no wine'" (v. 3). Probably any of us who have memories of our mothers will hear the inferences which are waiting to be drawn from those four words. From anyone else, "They have no wine" might be simply a statement of fact. From the mother (also, sometimes, from our children), the tone of voice says, "What are you going to do about it?"

Very clearly, Jesus got the message. He responded, not to a statement of fact, but to the implied request for help. "Why are you asking me?" Jesus countered. "It's not my time."

Mary proceeded as if she hadn't heard Jesus' objection. From the human point of view, hers was the style of many a mother: while you complained that you were not going to school, Mother continued to pack your lunch. From a faith point of view, Mary was doing what we need to do more often: she was riding over the objection without giving it undue credence. She simply instructed the servants to do whatever Jesus told them. And in the process, she was telling Jesus what to do!

The second major contributors to the miracle were the servants. I'm not sure to what degree they were impressed by the innate authority which people were beginning to see in Jesus, or were intimidated by Mary's insistence. One way or another, they did exactly as they were told.

What they did was very remarkable. The pots which Jesus ordered filled were not containers of drinking water; rather, they were wash water — the jars for purification. When Jesus instructed the servants to take some water from those jars and deliver it to the steward of the feast, he was asking a reckless venture. Water in place of wine was bad enough, but *wash water*? The servants are the unsung heroes of this story. I marvel that they would hazard their jobs in such an absurd risk.

When the steward sipped from the cup and pronounced it something very special, the miracle was complete. The power belonged to Jesus; but the miracle belonged to Jesus, Mary, and a small team of unnamed servants. The occasion of the miracle would never have been established if it hadn't been for Mary's insistence in the face of Jesus' apparent reluctance. And the delivering of the miracle wouldn't have happened if it hadn't been for the servants. In that structured first-century society, Jesus couldn't have delivered the wine for himself. He was dependent on the cooperation of the servants — and their *daring*, almost foolhardy cooperation.

And that's the stuff of which miracles are made. God hardly ever does a miracle unaided. Just as God works with us in the routine business of this world, so he works with us in the extraordinary and the miracles.

Sometimes our human involvement is so much in the normal course of things that we hardly know a miracle has occurred. The first asylum for the blind was founded by a Christian monk, Thalasius. The first hospital of record was founded by a Christian woman, Fabiola, in love for God. Apollonius, a Christian merchant, opened the first free dispensary. Are these the stuff of miracles? Indeed! In a world where compassion was essentially an unknown quality, and where the sick and handicapped were a burden to be ignored, it was altogether a miracle for someone to be captured by a spirit of unselfish love. Their concern was completely against the tide of the times. It grew out of soil which was hostile to such caring. It was, spiritually speaking, a case of health bursting forth from a plague-ridden atmosphere. Miracle, indeed!

But God didn't do it alone. Thalasius, Fabiola, and Apollonius were the servants who bore the water which Christ could then change into wine.

Sometimes you and I are privileged to participate in very small, yet very real miracles. Have you, with sudden unexplainable impulse, sent a card or note to someone, then had them tell you that your greeting card came at just the right time? "How did you know," the person asked, "that I needed something like that at that very time? How could your timing be so perfect?" Yes, how? Is it only a coincidence that you felt the urge at such a special time? Do you suppose such "coincidences" would happen more often if we were more ready to bear water for our Lord?

You and I live in a time and place where miracles are badly needed, and in short supply. We are so trained to be skeptical, not only of God, but even of our own generous impulses, that the miraculous must struggle for any kind of hearing.

That's why it's so important that those of us who believe in God, and who believe deeply in love, compassion, and service to others should be sensitive to our potential agents of the miraculous. Many prayers are left unsaid, or are spoken tremulously, because we have been conditioned to expect nothing; and expecting nothing, ask for nothing. Many ventures, some grand and some ordinary, are never begun because we don't have the faith to dare. Larry Sachau says that most Christians have "an almost terminal case of practicality." I fear he's right. God seems to find a stronger voice for hope and daring venture among secular leaders than among some of the people who claim to be his disciples. We Christians ought to be an expectant people, because we follow One who has the power to set the world right.

Much of the living of our time has taken on the quality of a wedding feast in which the celebration has faded into silence. A miracle is needed, which will bring a true and worthy intoxication to life. Jesus Christ waits in the wings, ready to introduce such gladness. He waits to perform that great and necessary miracle: the enlivening of life.

But it is a miracle which calls for helpers: a "mother" who will insist on giving Jesus a place at the feast, and servants who will dare to deliver the water-made-wine. Our Lord Jesus Christ will do the rest. But he counts, as always, on our doing what only we can do.

J. Ellsworth Kalas

# Epiphany: The
# Joy Of Fulfillment

I've read some books where it seemed the author had no purpose in writing. When that's the case, I'm glad if I can discover it early, so I don't invest too much time in a meaningless search. In some instances, however, I've been slow to recognize the problem, perhaps because I've been looking so earnestly for the author's point that I didn't realize he was without one.

No such charge can be made against Luke, the Greek physician who gave us the Gospel which bears his name. He knew why he was writing, and he was obviously excited about his assignment.

In a sense, you and I can feel that we are eavesdropping when we read this Gospel. Luke addresses himself, in the opening paragraph, to someone named Theophilus. We don't know who this was. Some say he was a friendly Roman official who had only a disorganized knowledge of the faith, to whom Luke wanted to give more basic instruction. Others say that this is only a general term to refer to all who "love God" or "are loved by God" — the two ways the name "Theophilus" is translated. However that may be, we are sure that Luke's Gospel speaks to us and that the purposes which he meant for the unknown Theophilus are being fulfilled in us as well.

Luke explains that others have "done their best" to write reports of the things they knew, from eyewitnesses, about the lif~ of Jesus. We don't know how many such books or tracts were ɛ able in the first century. With the kind of impact the gospe making on so many lives, it was natural that anyone whc anything about Jesus either first- or secondhand — would

69

tell others their version of the story. The best and most significant of these accounts survived, perhaps simply because God meant it to be so. But from the human side we can see a reason, too: no doubt the most beloved books were copied and recopied for sharing. We know as much by the fragments which remain to this day in such relative abundance.

But Luke has his own reason for telling the story. It is partly, as he says, because he had "carefully studied all these matters from their beginning," and now he felt qualified to "write an orderly account" (Luke 1:3). Luke may have felt uniquely qualified, as a Gentile and a physician, to offer insights which others might overlook. Certainly it's true that his Gospel has some special factors.

More than anything, though, Luke wanted his readers to "know the truth" about the whole story. In the language of the King James Version, he wanted Theophilus to "know the certainty of those things wherein thou hast been instructed."

That first generation of Christians felt a magnificent certainty about the way of life they had chosen. If they hadn't, they wouldn't have put their lives on the line so freely for their beliefs. It is sometimes pointed out that, though the four Gospels and the several epistles are so different in style, and though they clearly come from a wide variety of authors, they have one characteristic in common: the quality of certainty. There is no querulous tone, no hesitancy, not even a reasonable caution — just this grand, "I *know* whom I have believed...." They may differ regarding the time and order of events. That's typical of eyewitnesses even in something as simple as a traffic accident. But they are unanimous in their certainties about the nature, person, and power of Jesus the Christ.

Their profound assurance is all the more remarkable when we consider the circumstances under which they believed. They took their stands with Jesus at the peril of their lives. It was not like joining a luncheon club! Some of them had seen Jesus discredited in the series of trials, and reduced to an apparently helpless, dying form, hanging from a cross. You and I sometimes envy the generation that saw Jesus in the flesh. Perhaps their faith was more tested than ours, for they saw Jesus with all the marks of humanness that we usually blot out.

Yet, with it all, they *believed* with such certainty that they could turn the world upside down. What was their secret?

Part of the secret is made clear in the latter portion of our lesson for the day. As Jesus explained scripture for the first time to the people in his hometown of Nazareth, he spoke from one of the most cherished portions of the prophet Isaiah:

> *The Spirit of the Lord is upon me, because he has anointed me to bring good news to the poor. He has sent me to proclaim release to the captives and recovery of sight to the blind, to let the oppressed go free, to proclaim the year of the Lord's favor.* — vv. 18, 19

Then, sitting down in the manner of a rabbinical leader, he declared, "Today this scripture has been fulfilled in your hearing" (v. 21).

At first the people responded warmly to "the gracious words." But they soon began to be troubled by the fact that he was one of them. They knew Joseph and Mary, had seen the boy grow up, and stopped often to visit with him in the carpenter shop. And when Jesus pressed the issue with them, nothing that a prophet is not honored by his own people, their questions grew into resentment and, at last, into open violence.

But Jesus' ministry went on, and grew, and continued to grow after his death and resurrection, even to the present time. As we view what is happening in much of Africa, Korea, and Indonesia, this twenty-first century might well prove to be the greatest century yet for the Christian faith. But how has it happened? How has the cross of Christ, as the poet put it, continued too "tower o'er the wrecks of time"?

It is because Christ is surely the *fulfillment*. The first Christians and the Gospel writers saw him especially as the fulfillment of prophecy. They had studied the prophets, heard the scriptures expounded by their rabbis, and waited for One who would fulfill these grand expectations. Now they could spread out the prophecies of the scriptures alongside their experiences with Jesus and conclude that they matched. Jesus was the fulfillment.

But he was far more than the fulfillment of prophecy. If that were all we could say about our Lord, he might become to us no more than a kind of mystical novelty, something to be speculated on in a cheap newspaper or an offbeat book. The glory of Christ is this — he is the fulfillment of our human longing and need. He fits the empty space in our human galaxy. His voice and his power turn our discordant sounds into music. He is the fulfillment of life.

I think that's what a scholar meant, in the mid-twentieth century, when he heard that the Christian faith does not stand or fall with the trustworthiness of the Gospels. The gospel, he said, was preached to the world before a single Gospel was written — for nearly a full generation — and it would continue to be preached if all the written Gospels were discredited or destroyed. The Christian faith has been conveyed to us in the scriptures, and we cherish and honor the Book. We are grateful that we have it as a written record of the faith we firmly believe. But great as the scriptures are, they would not convince us if it were not for the fulfillment we have seen during these passing centuries, in literally millions of human lives. And more than that — far more! — if it were not for the fulfillment you and I have experienced in our own lives. The people of Samaria came to look Jesus over after hearing wonderful reports from the woman who had met him at the well. But afterward they said, "It is no longer because of what you said that we believe, for we have heard for ourselves, and we know that this is truly the Savior of the world" (John 4:42). By God's grace, we ought to be able to speak in the same way.

Jesus Christ is the fulfillment of our human longing and our human need; we rejoice this Epiphany season in that grand fact. It is as if his role were written not only into the scriptures, but even into our very natures. Saint Augustine said that we human beings have a God-shaped void which only God himself can fulfill. Jesus Christ came to our planet as the visible expression of God. He "fits" the void which is inherent in us human creatures.

I continue to marvel that this need is basically the same regardess of all outward differences in us, and that the same Jesus Christ fulfills the need. About forty years ago I visited, outside Addis Araba, with a missionary nurse who was ministering to a hidden Ethiopian tribe which had no written language (thus not one literate person) and where primitive rites still included drinking fresh animal blood. As she spoke of the people with whom she worked, I thought of the upwardly-mobile young executives in the congregation to which I would return, and asked myself what her people and mine had in common. I realized that they both longed to know God, and their longing could be fulfilled in Jesus Christ. The tribesman might muffle his longing cry in worship of trees or stars, and the suburban family in pursuit of material satisfaction, but the longing refuses, ultimately, to be extinguished.

And the marvel is this: Jesus somehow fits the void in all the farflung instances of human longing. When medieval European artists painted the Holy Family, they usually painted them with typical German, Italian, or Flemish features. It was not imagination or prejudice which made them do so, but the instinctive feeling that Jesus belonged to them; he was one of their people. In our time, Christian artists in Africa and the Orient paint the Holy Family with features and coloring appropriate to their world. Again, it is because they feel that Jesus belongs to them.

The mountain church, where a duet twangs out country-western music on a guitar, may seem to have little in common with a Bach rendition from a four-manual organ; but each is seeking to show its adoration of Jesus in its own best way. Here is the common bond between a ghetto storefront church and the massive Gothic structure some miles away: they both bear the name of Jesus Christ; and they each seek, in their own way and setting, to fulfill the human longing.

What about you and me? What is the longing in our lives which Christ has filled? "Today," Jesus said, "this scripture has been fulfilled in your hearing." For you, for me?

To what degree are we in the business of fulfilling the scripture in the lives of others? Those of us who have seen the glory of Jesus Christ want to extend the benefit to others. When we read that he came to preach good news to the poor and recovery of sight to the blind, and to proclaim release to the captives, something in us w' to make this happen.

It is easy in these post-Christmas days to lose the spirit of Christmas. The Christmas decorations have now been packed away for another year (well, for most of us!), Christmas mail has been answered, and all that seems left of Christmas is reckoning with the charge account balances we've accumulated. It's hard to concentrate on the joy of giving, which seemed so important a few weeks ago. Even though this is the season in the church when we recall the visit of the Wise Men and their giving to the Christ Child, our own disposition is more in the mood of "Let's go on with normal life."

If we're to get on with normal life, let us not do so by leaving Christmas behind. Let us remind ourselves that our Lord came, not to institute a season of cards, celebrations, and Christmas trees, but to bring good news to the poor and release to the captives. You and I can be agents of the good news. Some of it we do through our part in the work of the church, which, even at its weakest, is still in the forefront of relieving human pain. And some of it we can do personally, one to one, as we extend kindness, love, and deeds of thoughtfulness to people in need. Those people in need may be closer than we sometimes think, because only a few of life's needs are measured in dollars and cents.

Luke knew why he was writing his book. He had been a secondhand witness to the blessed fact of Jesus Christ. Now he wanted others to know the fulfillment which had come to the world, in wondrous certainty, through him. Let us, you and me, go out into this week with the same gladness and the same grand certainty.

J. Ellsworth Kalas

Epiphany 4
Ordinary Time 4
Luke 4:21-30

# Epiphany: The
# Tragedy Of Rejection

In the church, most of us think of Epiphany simply as a season on the church calendar, and sometimes as a season we don't understand too well. We may recall that we are celebrating particularly the revealing of Christ to the Gentile world, via the Wise Men, but not much more.

The dictionary, however, adds further dimension to the word, listen: "a sudden, intuitive perception ... into the reality or essential meaning of something, usually initiated by some simple, homely, or commonplace occurrence or experience."

That definition applies in a profound and unique way to our Lord Jesus Christ. We have good reason to write his Epiphany with a capital "E" because it is not only a special day on the calendar, but a revealing which sets the pattern for all other revealings.

True to the literary definition of the term, Jesus brought perception "into the reality or essential meaning." He stripped the superficial away from life and the artificial from religion. What we need, he told Nicodemus is a new birth: not just a reformation or higher resolves, but an utterly new start. To the woman of Samaria he prescribed water which would satisfy the deep, eternal thirst. For the rich young ruler, he commanded a whole new set of values, a change which the man, unfortunately, was unwilling to make.

But in every case, Jesus went below the surface — down to reality. Even the physical changes said as much: the blind could now see, the deaf hear, the leper feel new flesh. To Zacchaeus he revealed, without saying a word, that his grasping publican values were meaningless; so Zacchaeus gave exuberantly to the poor and righted his economic wrongs. But when he pointed out their hypocrisies to the scribes and Pharisees, they began seeking ways to destroy him. An epiphany may be exciting, but it may also be upsetting.

Such is the story in our scripture lesson of the day. It is the account which we began last week — Jesus' visit to his home community of Nazareth, after his ministry had begun to make him a topic of conversation elsewhere. After reading the magnificent prophecy of Isaiah about One who would proclaim liberty to the captives and recovery of sight to the blind, and who would set at liberty those who were oppressed, Jesus announced that the scripture was being fulfilled that day.

The first reaction of the synagogue gathering, as Luke reports the story, was one of approval and amazement. They "spoke very well of him," because the words were *gracious*. They sensed, in spite of themselves, the wondrous hope which he embodied. At that moment they had an *epiphany*. They saw the possibilities of God in their lives, the prospect of being set free, and of sharing in the freeing of others.

True to the dictionary definition of epiphany, the experience had come through a "simple, homely, or commonplace occurrence." What could have been more commonplace to the people of Nazareth than a visit by their native son, the boy who had grown up in the carpenter shop? Commonplace, indeed! The sabbath service in the synagogue was an every-week affair; and while it is true that Jesus had gotten some notoriety by his teaching and miracles in other places, he was no stranger to the people of Nazareth. Now grace was coming to them through his lips.

But the initial response of wonder was quickly put aside. The "commonplace" channel by which God's graciousness was being revealed was simply too commonplace. A murmur began to slip through the synagogue gathering: "Is not this Joseph's son?"

You and I understand that. Most of us appreciate the wisdom of our parents better after they are dead. We quote them avidly then, because they've gained the authority which comes from distance. But it's hard to appreciate their wisdom when we dwell in their house; and sometimes also when we are a bit older and they come to visit in ours. Very few prophets get a good hearing in their own country. We may feel great affection for the person next door, but it's hard to see him or her as an authority; however, people in another, farther place might.

Jesus sensed their attitude, and threw down the gauntlet. "Doubtless," he said, "you will quote to me this proverb, 'Doctor, cure yourself!' And you will say, 'Do here also in your hometown the things that we have heard you did at Capernaum' " (v. 23). Then Jesus reminded them that a prophet is never welcome in his hometown.

Perhaps if he had stopped there, the people would have admitted, grudgingly, that it was difficult for them to look at him as outsiders might. But he pressed the issue in way that offended them. Jesus reminded them there were many widows in Israel in Elijah's day, but, for some reason, God chose to use a widow in Sidon to care for Elijah. That stung their national pride and their sense of chosenness. Then Jesus underlined the point by recalling that in the days of Elisha there were many who suffered from leprosy, but that the one who was healed was Naaman, a Syrian.

I can easily imagine what they said, and so can you. How dare this carpenter's son tell us that God chooses Gentiles? Who gave him the authority to instruct and even to insult us? They knew the examples he used were true, but that didn't make them any less offensive. A preacher must be careful, you know, in his choice of texts!

They became so angry that they dragged him outside the city, to the precipice bordering their town, intending to throw him over the cliff. It was a strange, horrendous development — after, at first, being impressed with the graciousness of his words. Somehow these words bout the Sidonian widow and the Syrian leper were not gracious! But when the people were about to cast Jesus over the cliff, "he passed through the midst of them and went on his way" (v. 30). Bruce Barton contended, in a popular biography of Jesus, that this was a demonstration of the unique power of the Master's personality. The mob spirit which was set on violence was somehow cowed by Jesus' sublime inner strength.

Our lesson of the day does not stop with the incident in Nazareth, but goes on to introduce us to some of the happenings in the Galilean town of Capernaum. There, as in Nazareth, he taught the people on the Sabbath. This time we're not told what Jesus said. But Luke reports that the people "were astounded at his teaching, because he spoke with authority" (Luke 4:32).

To the good fortune of the people of Capernaum, they were not handicapped by hometown images of Jesus. They did not lay the insight and power of his words alongside the discrediting measuring stick, "Is not this Joseph's son?" They accepted Jesus' words and person in their own right, and they saw authority. And as a result, they were privileged to see miracles.

An epiphany — a wondrous revealing — is only as good as our ability to receive it. A dour soul can look out into a morning of inexpressible beauty and say, "Bah! Humbug!" An indifferent person can sit through a superb rendition of Bach or Beethoven and be bored. The people of Capernaum listened to Jesus with open, unprejudiced minds, and were filled with awe; while the people of Nazareth found it necessary to discredit him, and then, in bitterness, to seek to destroy him.

The Nazareth tragedy is compounded by the fact that the people were at first inclined to hear Jesus appreciatively. But then something in them made them want to cut Jesus down to size. Specifically, their size. They wanted to be able to "manage" him, by remembering that he was the boy they had seen through the years in the carpenter shop.

Our culture still tries to make Jesus manageable. Flannery O'Connor, that perceptive modern novelist, observed one very painful thing about writing as a Christian — that which is the ultimate reality for the Christian, the Incarnation, is something which nobody in her reading audience believed. Her readers, she said, were largely people who thought God was dead. To speak of a God who has come to earth in Jesus Christ, who is not only alive but profoundly involved in human affairs, is offensive in the extreme.

So, too, with Jesus of Nazareth. The secular world is happy to recognize Jesus as a fine teacher and an admirable moral example. That is the modern equivalent of seeing him as Joseph's son. Jesus is manageable, if we can keep him in the categories of logic and human morality. But when the secularist is asked to see him as the singular revelation of God, Jesus becomes an intellectual embarrassment.

We church members have our problem with him, also. We, too, like a manageable Jesus: one to whom we can come in times of trouble, who comforts us and sympathizes with our human need. This *is* a true picture, as far as it goes. But he is also King of kings and Lord of lords; and, as such, he insists on being Lord of all of life. At that point Jesus becomes difficult. We are tempted, in our own fashion to follow the people of Nazareth in pushing him over some cliff.

Our hymnals contain a variety of hymns which plead for an epiphany — a moment of revelation. "Be thou my vision, O Lord of my heart," we sing. Or, "Open my eyes, that I may see / Glimpses of truth thou hast for me." And again, "Talk with us, Lord, thyself reveal, / While here o'er earth we rove."

But I'm not sure how ready we are for such a revealing. Often the revelation begins with new insight into ourselves; and that "revealing" is usually a painful process. The people of Nazareth managed pretty well with Jesus' revealing of himself; they found his words gracious. It was when he began to reveal their own persons to them that they became upset. His suggestion that they were like their ancestors in Elijah and Elisha's day — who were bypassed for blessing while "outsiders" were favored — was utterly unacceptable.

No significant glory is going to burst into our lives, however, unless we deal honesty and earnestly with ourselves. We cannot be healed until we acknowledge that we are ill, we cannot learn until we confess our ignorance, and we cannot find fullness of life until we admit that we are not presently complete. If the people of Nazareth had bowed humbly before Jesus' analysis and had sought deliverance from the blindness and pride which consumed them, they might have been the setting for far greater manifestations of the glory of God. Instead, there were virtually no miracles there, because of their unbelief. And their unbelief stemmed not from some inherent spiritual lack, but from their unwillingness to confess their sins.

A good word must be spoken for those people who come to the house of worship week after week. The church is the only institution in our world which challenges us, again and again, to be better than we are. We come to a service on Sunday morning, or to one of the small group or class sessions, knowing that someone will speak on a theme which will lead ultimately to the conclusion: "We aren't all that we ought to be. God meant us to be more than this, and we must commit ourselves to that higher goal." Whatever the failings of the church and of church people, we are virtually unique in our willingness to put ourselves in a setting where we will be challenged and corrected.

If we accept that challenge, the potential is almost unlimited. The people of Nazareth, unfortunately, rejected it. When the gracious revealing of Jesus became a painful revealing of themselves, they wanted to be done with the upstart carpenter. We're always in danger of following their example.

But the past 21 centuries have been highlighted by these beautiful human beings — some well-known, but most of them virtually unknown — who have seen the revealing of Jesus and of themselves, and have accepted the challenge. For them, it has been a path from faith to faith from glory to glory. Like the people of Capernaum, they have seen the authority of Jesus Christ, and life has been made anew. Let us, this day, join their company.

J. Ellsworth Kalas

# From Empty Nets
# To Full Lives

It's funny what experiences and phrases will stay with you from childhood. I still remember a line from a song which apparently was popular, for at least a short period of time, in my early childhood. It was a half-funny, half-pathetic little lament from someone who felt rejected and unsuccessful. As I recall, each verse ended with the phrase, "I guess I'll go eat worms."

Most of us can understand the mood of the song, if not the dietary remedy. Every one of us feels like a failure at one time or another. Some people — Father, have mercy on them! — feel that way most of the time. On some occasions we don't know why we feel so defeated and unlovable; but at times, nevertheless, we do feel that way.

Jesus came, one day, upon a trio of defeated men. He had met them before, when they were associated with John the Baptizer. Now they were about their customary work — fishing. But this was a very bad day. They had fished all night and had caught nothing. If you fish for recreation, such a period is simply frustrating; but when it's your life's occupation and the source of your daily bread, a night of empty nets is thoroughly demoralizing. We say that misery loves company, so perhaps the pain was at least partly relieved by the fact that all three men were in the same boat. Nevertheless, the misery was running very deep.

Now it was morning, after a night of failure, and the men were washing their nets so they'd be ready for the next night's work. Suddenly Jesus of Nazareth, the rising young teacher, stepped into

Simon's boat. "Put me out a bit from the land," he said to Simon; and from that position, Jesus began to teach the people.

There's no record of what Jesus said, nor even of how long he talked. Nor is there any indication of how much attention Simon and his partners, James and John, paid to Jesus' teaching. We only know that when Jesus had finished teaching he said to Simon, "Put out into the deep water and let down your nets for a catch" (v. 4).

It was really quite audacious for Jesus, a landsman, to tell three professional fishermen how to do their business. Perhaps he sensed they were so defeated that they were ready for any kind of counsel, from anyone. Or perhaps he was counting on the fact that they had confidence in him from their earlier experiences with him.

Simon refused at first. "Master, we toiled all night and took nothing!" It is the language of someone who already feels so defeated that he doesn't want to submit himself to the possibility of still another failure. However, he quickly added, "Yet if you say so, I will let down the nets" (v. 5).

Again, it's hard to know why Simon responded as he did. It would have been easy to put Jesus off with a polite refusal. Maybe Simon answered out of the spirit that says, "I've tried everything else without success, so why shouldn't I try this?" Or perhaps it is just another dramatic evidence of the fact that Jesus "spoke with authority." Something about the Master's utterance must have made it difficultly to refuse him.

So they threw out the nets from Simon's boat and engulfed a great shoal of fish. So great, in fact, that the load strained their nets to the limit, and they had to enlist help from the other boat. Now both boats were loaded with fish. It was probably more than a night's catch, and they had harvested it within a matter of minutes.

So it was that their dark night of failure was turned suddenly into glittering success — greater success than they had ever known in all of their fishing career. It wasn't just the catch that was so satisfying, but the complete sense of turn around. Victory is always exhilarating, but especially such an unexpected victory.

If this is where the story ended, it would be an increasing but rather inconsequential little miracle. It might feed our desire for a gospel of success in business and good grades in school, but it would hardly be worthy of our Lord Jesus Christ.

Fortunately, Simon Peter saw more than just the miracle. He was captured by the Lord behind the miracle. Thus, instead of responding with the bravado of a winner, he pleaded for forgiveness. Falling at Jesus' knees, he begged, "Go away from me, Lord, for I am a sinful man!" (v. 8).

At first glance, that may seem an unlikely reaction to a moment of success. Sometimes, however, it is the experience of achievement which forces us to see how superficial our victories are. Andre Thornton, a home-run hitter with the Cleveland Indians in the 1980s and an exemplary Christian, predicted that there might be a very real religious awakening among athletes as a result of the exorbitant salaries so many are receiving. He felt that when they found themselves suddenly so financially secure they would realize how little their wealth really means, and would thus be driven to look for deeper values.

The truth is, a person can have full nets but still have an empty life. After you've sold the fish in the market and have put a share of the money in the bank, you may still feel an emptiness deeper than empty nets and a yearning more poignant than the desire for economic security. You and I know some people like that; and there are many others in this category.

It is sometimes said that the miracles of Jesus are parables in action; they teach a lesson. Jesus surely used this miracle in that fashion. "Do not be afraid," he told the frightened Simon Peter; "From now on you will be catching people" (v. 10).

It was both the contrast and the reassurance Simon needed. At the contrast level, what could be more dramatic than the difference between fish and human beings? No doubt there had been a time in Simon's life when he dreamed of being the best fisherman on the Sea of Galilee. A person of Peter's personality must have had big dreams for himself. But all of our dreams are limited. Because Peter's experience had been confined almost entirely to the area of Galilee and to the vocation of the fishing villages, he probably had no expectations beyond what might be envisioned within those borders.

He could hardly have imagined that people would still talk about him 21 centuries later. And surely he couldn't have dreamed that someday the term "the Big Fisherman" would be a synonym for Simon Peter! How paltry "best fisherman on the Sea of Galilee" sounds compared with that. As paltry, in fact, as fish in a net seem when compared with human souls.

Simon needed such reassurance. As a matter of fact, as mercurial as he was, he would need it again and again. He would have to be told often that he was more than he had ever imagined himself to be. But just now, when he felt so unworthy, it was electrifying to hear that the Master had work for him to do. Far from being rejected for his sins, as he felt he ought to be, he was being called to a grand assignment. Jesus wanted him to become a fisher of human souls.

How often do you and I settle for an achievement or a dream with boundaries no larger than the Sea of Galilee? I am thinking particularly of our capacity for goodness and Christian quality. We think little of Jesus's command that we should be perfect as our Father in heaven is perfect (Matthew 5:48). We discount the words as a kind of ancient hyperbole, or we push it aside with self-deprecating laughter: "Perfect? Who, me?"

As one of your very imperfect brothers, I understand such feeling. But I don't want us to rule out so easily what God's grand purposes might be. I'm not calling for compulsive self-examination; I'm only saying that our Lord had something serious and possible in mind when he called us to such a goal. Robert Browning, in "Andrea del Sarto," said that a person's "reach should exceed his grasp, / Or what's a heaven for?" I'm willing to leave some of the ultimate achievements to heaven, but I think the promise of heaven ought to inspire us to a greater reach in the here and now.

Nor do we take seriously enough our potential for the fruit of the Spirit. Love, joy, peace, patience, and kindness are such beautiful qualities — and ones we are so glad to find in others; so why don't we pursue them more hopefully and expectantly for ourselves? It is partly because we have boundaries as confining as the Sea of Galilee. Jesus wanted Peter to fish for human souls. Until the moment of that revelation, Simon Peter apparently would have been content to spend his nights on Galilee. That's not to disparage the fishermen of Galilee. It's only to say that a person should not too quickly place too small boundaries around his or her soul.

The focal point of the story is Jesus' call to Simon Peter, James, and John to become fishers of human souls. Many of us would be glad to skip this part of the story because we are uneasy with the whole concept of soul-winning. We can't imagine ourselves buttonholing people, offending them, or intruding upon their privacy. We have all kinds of negative images in mind; those images prevent our giving serious attention to our calling to be witnesses of our faith.

Perhaps our greatest problem is that we try to make such witnessing an isolated part of life; the occasions ought, rather, to be part of the natural flow of living. That's the impressive thing about Jesus' own pattern of faith-sharing. His encounters with Nicodemus, the Samaritan woman, and the rich young ruler don't seem to be structured and set up. They "just happened," so to speak. And it's especially significant that each individual was treated in a specific way. They were *persons* to Jesus, not people to be met with a formula.

Most of our witnessing is likely to happen in passing moments of conversation — those occasions when we show, in relatively minor ways, who we are and to whom we belong. I think of a suburban woman who was playing tennis with her good-but-quite-secular friends. In a conversation break between sets she began referring to something she had read that morning. It would have been easy to say, "I read something this morning...." Instead, with my attempt at piosity, she simply introduced one word: "In my *devotional* reading this morning." It is not a major soul-winning engagement. It was, however, a true sowing of seed. By a word, she had opened the door for some further conversation.

Perhaps our greatest problem in becoming Christ's fishermen is that we are not enough in earnest to grasp the opportunities that come to us; or we are so possessed of the idea that we must say something dramatic and far-reaching that we fail to say the small, immediate, and potentially significant thing.

To put it in the language of our lesson for the day, most of us really don't act as if we even have a call to "fish." We're out in the waters of human need every day, but we don't seem to know it.

The issue is not that we should become more aggressive about sharing our faith. It is that we should be more sensitive to the needs of the world around us, and more sensitive to the subtle prodding of the Holy Spirit. The two sensitivities are wonderfully intertwined. To be sensitive to the Holy Spirit must mean that we will be more sensitive to people and their pain; to be more sensitive to people ought to make us more open to God and his purposes.

Put another way: every human soul is a collection of fears, joys, strengths, weaknesses, sins, and goodness. God is able to meet the human soul at any of these points of reality, and ready to do so. If we are willing to be a channel by which God can touch the life of another person, even in the most routine way, God is finding a place in that person's life. And that small place, like leaven in the lump, can eventually influence the whole life. We don't have to be theologians to do this — or blazing witnesses. All we need is to care enough about others to want to help, and to believe deeply enough in God that we will tell them that he can help.

Who knows what a catch we will make? Who can say what an eternal achievement an be ours? The opportunity came to Simon Peter in the wake of a night of defeat. The same opportunity awaits us each day in all our passing relationships. You and I have allied ourselves with the One who will lead us into a life of full nets. Such is his purpose for each of us.

J. Ellsworth Kalas

**Epiphany 6**
**Ordinary Time 6**
**Luke 6:17-26**

# At The Corner
# Of Church And Main

Once there was a great intersection in the ancient city of Bethlehem.

We know a little something about great intersections. When we travel by car, we discover that the intersection of interstate highways becomes the epicenter of all kinds of activity: lots of traffic, and with the traffic come motels, restaurants, gas stations, fast food places, and more. Furthermore, within certain cities, some particular intersections have gained worldwide fame. The corner of Hollywood and Vine in Hollywood, Piccadilly Circus in London, Times Square in New York City — these intersections have all gained renown beyond their towns.

And we have other kinds of busy and important intersections — ones that are not just the juncture of roads. Train tracks and commuter traffic made Grand Central Station synonymous with hubbub and activity. Busy airports in cities like Chicago and Atlanta mark the modern intersections of flight connections. (I heard a preacher say years ago that, whether you go to heaven or hell, you'll probably have to make connections through Atlanta.) And recent years have introduced us to a whole new kind of intersection: the worldwide web. Without leaving our chairs, we are able to cross paths with people, institutions, and information from around the globe.

The ancient world, too, had its great intersections. Trade routes, favorable harbors, and convenient terrain turned certain ancient towns into important intersections, and with that into great cosmopolitan cities.

Well, there was once also a great intersection in the ancient city of Bethlehem. Unlike some others, however, it was not the junction of two major highways, for Bethlehem was just a bit off the beaten path. Nor was it the corner where two or three great avenues in the town crossed, for this intersection was probably nearer to something like an alley or a driveway.

No, this was not merely the corner where thoroughfares met. This was no less than an intersection of Heaven and Earth.

We see it time and again in the Christmas story. When the angels above bring good tidings to the shepherds below, it is an intersection of Heaven and Earth in the fields outside Bethlehem. When a star guides the Magi, it is an intersection of Heaven and Earth. And, most and best of all, when Mary conceives a child by the Holy Spirit — the Incarnation is the grandest, most profound intersection of Heaven and Earth.

Not since the Creator first breathed into that formed dust called Adam had there been such an intimate intersection of the Divine with the human. And this intersection in Bethlehem was even greater than that one in Eden: for originally God had only breathed into Adam's flesh; now God climbed into Adam's flesh.

In our world, you know, some roads are not allowed to intersect. An interstate highway does not entertain junctures with ordinary residential streets or country roads. These must go above or below. And if the highway is a turnpike, then still fewer roads are given intersections with it. In our world, highways are not interrupted with stop signs, runways do not cross driveways, and turnpikes do not intersect with parking lots. Such planning would be foolish and unreasonable.

Likewise, by all rights, the intersection that took place in Bethlehem was an utterly unreasonable one. That the immortal God should put on mortal flesh, or that the Throne should be exchanged for a feeding trough, or that celestial glory should be replaced by stable odors, or that the Almighty should confine himself to such fragility: these are all too foolish even to suggest. What took place in Bethlehem that night was an astonishing intersection of Heaven and Earth.

And it turns out that Christmas was only the beginning. For what begins in the Christmas story continues throughout the Gospel accounts of Jesus' life and ministry.

Luke reports that crowds from as far as Tyre and Sidon came to hear and to see Jesus. It is the incarnate Son of God, however, who had actually made the longer trip in order to be met by them there. For while they had made the trip to Galilee all the way from the Phoenician coast, Jesus had made the trip from heaven. Every encounter between Jesus and the crowds, therefore, was a profound intersection of Heaven and Earth.

And a gracious intersection, too. The scene becomes especially poignant when Luke says that people were coming to Jesus to be touched by him, to be healed by him. These are not just the intellectually curious who have come to hear a provocative speaker. They are not merely spectators who have come to gawk at the latest magician. No, these are a needy lot. And when the Divine touch heals their frail bodies, when the eternal Son of God restores their corruptible flesh, it is a lovely and gracious intersection of Heaven and Earth.

In the subway systems of some great cities, the trains and their tracks do not all run at the same depth. Some lines are deeper underground than others. At some junctures, therefore, one line runs below another, and making connections means going up or down flights of stairs.

So, too, with the intersection of Heaven and Earth: the intersection occurs at several levels. At the one level, there is the Incarnation itself — Heaven and Earth intersect in Jesus Christ. At another level, we see the angels and the shepherds, the star and the Magi, the crowds around Jesus — Heaven and Earth intersect by contact with one another, though always at Heaven's initiative. And, at another level still, we find the teachings of Jesus — Heaven and Earth intersect in ethics and lifestyle.

We have before us Luke's version of the teachings we call the Beatitudes (so named because of Jesus' recurring use of the word "blessed"). The underlying Greek word, *makarios*, can mean "blessed," "fortunate," and "happy." The Amplified Bible also includes "to be envied" in the connotation of the word. It is a supremely cheerful word.

If your experience was like mine, then perhaps you grew up seeing these Beatitudes on a poster in a Sunday school room or on an embroidery in the church parlor. We cherish these familiar teachings. I wonder, though, what the reaction was of Jesus' original audience. I wonder if they resisted these Beatitudes. They are, after all, quite surprising. Even counter-intuitive.

Blessed are the poor? Fortunate are the hungry? To be envied are those who weep? That makes little or no sense to us. Happy are you when you are hated? Excluded? Reviled and defamed? These kinds of blessings I think I can do without.

We Christians say that we love the teachings of Jesus. In fact, I have found in my years of parish ministry that most church folks typically prefer Jesus' teachings above almost every other part of scripture — certainly over everything in the Old Testament, apart from the Psalms. And yet, I fear that our love for his teachings is more sentimental than practical. After all, do we strive to be poor or hated? Of course not. Do we actually rejoice when we are excluded or defamed? No. On the contrary, we fuss about it and feel sorry for ourselves. Perhaps we complain to God about it — or even blame him for it.

And when Jesus goes on to say "woe" to those who are rich, those who are full, those who laugh, and those who are spoken well of, do we hear him speaking to us? Here I suspect we are not so eager for a contemporary application of the scripture. Here, perhaps, we are content to leave the teaching in its historical context, pointing at the Pharisees and other first-century hypocrites.

But the truth for most of us is that we are rich and we are full. We don't think of ourselves as rich, for we see the income and lifestyles of others in our culture — professional athletes, entertainers, corporate CEOs, among others — who have so very much more than we do. When we compare ourselves to the income and lifestyles of most of the world's population, however, then we are forced to confess that we are, in fact, rich. And we are certainly full. Our tummies are full. Our closets are full. Our drawers are full. Our basements and attics and garages are all full.

Is Jesus saying "woe" to me? Is that possible? After all, I'm just an average, middle-class guy. I haven't stolen from anyone. I don't cheat anyone. I don't oppress the widows and the orphans. I'm just an ordinary guy who is trying to make a living and provide for my family, just like the next guy.

Of course, it may be that I am not meant to be just like the next guy. Perhaps I am called to be different from him. Even an example to him.

The Greek word *ouai* is what we translate "woe," or sometimes "alas." As you might guess from trying to pronounce the unusual all-vowel word, it is not a harsh kind of exclamation. It doesn't have the kind of bite to it that makes for a curse word. Rather, it might better be understood as an articulate sigh, an expression of grief.

When Jesus says "woe" to those "who are rich," "who are full," "who laugh," and such, therefore, he is not shouting out a condemnation. Rather, I would say that he is crying out his sorrow. "How sad for you," he says. "How terribly sad."

As a parent, I know the difference between things my children do that make me angry and things they do that make me sad. Because I love them, I naturally want what is best for them. And so I am sad when they make choices that miss the best.

To paraphrase another teaching of Jesus: "If we, being evil, know how to feel sad for our children, how much more will our heavenly Father feel sad for us when we miss out on what's best?"

And so our Lord says, "Woe," to us. He is sad when he sees us make decisions that preclude us from what is best, from what he has in store for us. And, like children, those decisions we make are typically short-sighted. An impatient child might say he'd rather have a treat now than enjoy a feast later. And that may be essentially our choice, too.

Jesus says, "Woe to you who are full now." Perhaps the key word for us is neither "woe" nor "full." The operative word may be "now."

Our human instinct is to live for "now." And even the "laters" — college, marriage, vacation, retirement, and so on — that the most prudent of us might save and prepare for is still "now" in spiritual terms. Whether we are by nature impulsive or deliberate, whether impetuous or foresighted, for as long as we are preoccupied with this life and this world, we are living for "now." And the kingdom teachings of Jesus invite us to live for "later" — to see this world's sorry little treats for what they are compared to the great banquet in the kingdom.

Here, then, is the final intersection of Heaven and Earth. It is not the far-off experiences of the shepherds and the Magi. It is not the one-time event of the Incarnation. Rather, it is the intersection you and I experience daily. Indeed, it is the intersection that is our very address, for we live at the juncture of this world and the kingdom of God.

I live my life in this world, but not for this world. Your residency is in Heaven, even while your residence is on Earth. If I live for this world only, then I shall avoid poverty, hunger, sorrow, and ridicule at all costs. If I live for the Lord and his kingdom, however, then I shall follow him at all costs — even including poverty, sorrow, and such.

*The Poseidon Adventure*, the award-winning 1972 disaster movie, tells the story of a cruise ship capsized by a tidal wave, and follows the struggle to be rescued by a small handful of the passengers. The massive ship is turned over in the water, and so this small band of eventual survivors reasons that, in order to reach the "top," they must work their way toward the ship's bottom. It is an upside-down pursuit, and some of the other passengers on the ship disagree with the approach. In one eerie scene, the small band whom we as viewers follow crosses paths with another desperate group looking for the way out. They, too, are wet and scared. And they, too, are equally confident that they are heading the right direction. In the end, however, they perish.

The teachings of Jesus invite us to our own kind of upside-down pursuit of salvation. Seeking the top, we make an unlikely journey toward the bottom. It is an approach to living in this world that runs contrary to what seems natural and reasonable. Once we recognize, however, that this world has been capsized by sin — that this world is, in spiritual terms, upside down — then it will make more sense to us to follow Jesus' directions to the bottom of this ship.

So it is that the Lord grieves — cries out "woe" — for those doomed souls who are headed the wrong way. Naturally disoriented by the Fall, they push headlong toward all that is perceived as the "top" in this world. Meanwhile, Jesus urges them — urges us — to turn around: to live contrary to our self-serving instincts. Not to be afraid of this world's "bottom" since, in the end, it leads to the kingdom's "top." To have the wisdom and foresight to live for the glorious "later" in the 'now.'

This is our address — yours and mine. This is the great intersection at which we live. It is the natural place, isn't it, for the servants of that God who became Incarnate? It is the embassy for those citizens of Heaven who are called to be ambassadors to Earth. It is the witness of Christ on Main Street: sometimes ignored, sometimes ridiculed, and sometimes saving. But no matter the response, how happy, how fortunate, and how blessed we are to live at the intersection of Heaven and Earth.

David J. Kalas

# Saints In Shorts

Seven years ago, our family moved from southern Virginia to northeast Wisconsin. As you might expect, spring comes later here. Fall comes earlier. And winter is a much different experience in northeast Wisconsin than it was in southern Virginia. The same temperatures that seemed bone-chilling in Virginia are good reason to leave the mufflers and mittens at home in Wisconsin. Of course, many of the retired folks in my congregation here take their cue from the geese and fly south for the winter each year. Florida and Arizona are the desired destinations as they leave behind the piles of snow, the sub-zero temperatures, and the bitter cold wind.

Set aside for a moment, if you will, the comfortable, climate-controlled setting in which you are probably sitting just now, and picture yourself living in some of the fiercest winter weather you can imagine. A local television or radio station in that cold community publicizes a special promotion: an all-expenses-paid two-week trip to some warm and sunny spot. The trip can be to Florida, the Caribbean, Cancun, Hawaii — you name it. And all you have to do to be eligible to win this very desirable prize is to show up at a particular place at a particular time.

The date comes for the prize to be awarded, and so you and hundreds of other folks head out to the spot where the winners will be selected. The setting is a strange one — a gimmick, you think, to make the trip seem all the more desirable. The contestants are asked to gather in the middle of the night in an open field outside of town.

You arrive at the field and discover that the snow is up to your knees, except in the spots where it has drifted even higher. The night air is frigid. And the wide open space of the field encourages a strong, cold wind. It is a bitterly cold time and place.

Everyone there is dressed for the occasion. You could be standing next to your best friend and not even know it, for every inch of every person is covered. Heavy coats and long underwear, mittens, mufflers, boots, and snowsuits are everywhere on everyone. All the people there are layered and insulated. Everyone, that is, except for one nut — there's one in every crowd, right? — who is standing there with shorts on. He's wearing no shirt and no shoes, no coat, no gloves, no scarf.

It's obvious that he is shivering and miserable. And his misery is soon compounded by some folks' pointing and taunting. A few thoughtful persons in the crowd, meanwhile, express concern for his health and well-being, and they offer him some of their winter wear. "Would you like my gloves?" asks one man. "I could just keep my hands in my coat pockets." "I've got an extra scarf," offers another. But the half-dressed man turns down all the offers, though his teeth are chattering and his body is shivering violently.

If we can imagine someone so uncomfortably out of place — and so seemingly out of touch with the reality around him — then we are prepared. We are prepared to read the New Testament. We are prepared to think about the kingdom of God. We are prepared to hear the teachings of Jesus. And we are prepared to understand the kind of people he calls us to be.

We are dealing here in Luke 6 with some of the very familiar teachings of Jesus. Conventional wisdom says that "familiarity breeds contempt." I expect in some circumstances of life that is true. Perhaps when it comes to familiar scripture passages, however, familiarity may breed something even worse: a kind of deafness to God's word. After all, once I think that I already know what a passage says, I may stop listening carefully to it. And if it happens that a familiar passage of scripture says something more or something other than what I thought, I stand very little chance of hearing that, for I have stopped listening carefully to it.

New translations of old, familiar texts can help to break the logjam in our understandings. Eugene Peterson, a retired Presbyterian pastor and professor of theology, offers us such a fresh translation of these teachings of Jesus. Peterson's version, called *The Message*, includes this insightful and startling translation: "To you who are ready for the truth, I say this: Love your enemies. Let them bring out the best in you, not the worst. When someone gives you a hard time, respond with the energies of prayer for that person. If someone slaps you in the face, stand there and take it. If someone grabs your shirt, giftwrap your best coat and make a present of it. If someone takes unfair advantage of you, use the occasion to practice the servant life. No more tit-for-tat stuff. Live generously" (Luke 6:27-31).[1]

Jesus' instruction to "turn the other cheek" is one of those very familiar passages of scripture. It is so familiar to us, in fact, that it has become something of a cliché. We may need to take a closer look at that cliché, however, in order for it to have real meaning and application in our lives.

For myself, I don't suppose that I have been struck by anyone since a playground spat in the fifth grade. And I don't live in a setting where I am likely to be struck by anyone. Still, I have a hunch that this instruction has daily meaning for me.

It is worth noting that Jesus does not say, "If anyone attacks you with a knife ..." or "If anyone stabs you with a sword...." First-century Palestine certainly had its share of violence, but Jesus chooses a different kind of offense. The example he chooses — being struck on the cheek — is not a life-threatening kind of attack. If I am struck on the cheek, what is it that is really at stake? A slap on the face is perhaps more of a blow to my ego than my body. It is not so much that my life needs to be defended as it is my pride that wants to be avenged.

You and I may not live in settings where we are likely to be physically struck, but we are almost certainly in settings where our egos get slapped around a bit. That can happen even without any deliberate malevolence on the part of a spouse, a co-worker, a friend. And when someone has dealt my ego a blow, whether accidentally or quite intentionally, what shall be my response?

Egos, by their fallen nature, tend to be quite big and very sensitive. They beg, therefore, to be defended and avenged. And so my instinct when I am struck, in whatever form, is to strike back in kind. It seems that the reasonable ethic for Jesus to teach, then, might be that I should just walk away. Swallow my pride, bridle my tongue, sheathe my desire for vindication, and just walk away.

I was in a small fellowship group recently where folks were sharing a bit about their daily struggles to live lives that are pleasing to God. They came to the subject of stressful family relationships, and two people in the group reported that they were learning just to walk away from the harsh and berating speech they sometimes hear. The most Christ-like alternative to retaliatory words or action that they had found was to beat a hasty exit. The only choice they saw was fight or flight.

That is the kind of advice a caring mother would give, I suppose, if her son found himself in some antagonistic setting at school, on the playground, or in the neighborhood. "Just walk away" is the policy most likely to keep him out of fights and away from harm.

On the other hand, our "just walk away" ethic — which seems very reasonable — leads to all sorts of broken relationships and abandoned commitments. If being hurt in a situation — or the likelihood of being hurt again — is best resolved by my walking away, I will find ample cause to walk away from a whole lot of people and situations in my life. I will walk away from my family, from my friends, and from my church. I may try to find ways to walk away from myself, as well.

Quite the opposite from walking away, however, Jesus tells his followers to hang in there: to stay in that situation, that relationship, where we have just been hurt or offended or bruised. He not only denies us the seeming pleasure and satisfaction of retaliating, it appears that he wants us to leave ourselves deliberately vulnerable to being hurt again. After all, if I am going to stay there with the person who has just struck me on one cheek, I should at least brace myself: protect myself lest that hurtful person lash out at me again. But, no, I am to leave my other cheek available, leave myself exposed.

Jesus' words seem, at first blush, to be nonsense. What possible good could come from such a strategy of vulnerability? Could it be that Jesus wants us to be hurt?

No, not at all. Jesus wants something far better, lovelier, and more profound than that. Jesus wants us to be like God. "You will be children of the Most High; for he is kind to the ungrateful and the wicked. Be merciful, just as your Father is merciful" (vv. 35b-36).

If turning the other cheek sounds like nonsense to us, we might look more broadly at the teachings of Jesus to see if that one is just a fluke — a misunderstanding, something lost in translation.

But, no, we discover that the nonsense is everywhere. Love your enemies. Do good to those who hate you. Bless those who curse you. Pray for those who abuse you. If anyone takes away your goods, do not ask for them again.

Who can take seriously this sort of advice? Are these teachings excerpted from a sermon titled "How to Be a Doormat"?

No, these are teachings about how to be like God. This is, after all, the God who sent his Son into enemy territory "in order that the world might be saved through him" (John 3:17b). This is the Father who welcomes back with open arms and new clothes the irresponsible prodigal. This is the One who reconciles his enemies to himself at his own expense (Colossians 1:21-22). And this is the One who prayed on the cross for his taunting executioners to be forgiven.

Several years ago, I saw someone wearing a t-shirt featuring the traditional symbol of the fish that Christians have used to identify themselves since the days of persecution in the Roman Empire. The fish on the t-shirt was not alone, however. There were a great many other fish — including some rather menacing looking ones — all swimming in one direction, while this lone Christian fish was swimming in the other direction.

That's a pretty good depiction of life in this world for the person who would follow Jesus. Perhaps we do not always have to swim alone, but we are surely called to swim upstream.

This Christian ethic of going against the flow is not just for the sake of being contrary. No, we swim in the opposite direction from much of the rest of the world simply because we are swimming toward a particular destination. And you can't reach that destination — the kingdom of God — by living in the same direction as the fallen, sinful world.

Or perhaps the truth of how we are called to live goes still one step deeper. More than just living toward our destination, we Christians are called to live like our destination.

The old traditional traveler's wisdom said, "When in Rome, do as the Romans do." And that's fine, if you want to fit in in Rome. But the Christian lives with a different ethic, for the Christian has a different ultimate goal. We may live in the world, but we do not aspire to fitting in here. Instead, since our citizenship is in heaven, as the Apostle Paul says, we speak the language and live the customs of the place to which we belong. Simply put, we live like heaven on earth.

That should not come as a surprise to us. In the most familiar of all prayers — a prayer many of us speak once a week or more — we pray for God's will to be done "on earth as it is in heaven." If that is what we pray, then surely that should also be how we live: on earth as in heaven.

Return with me now to that frigid field in our imaginary vacation contest.

I imagine the contest judges climbing up on the platform and surveying the crowd. Hundreds of people are there, eager to be chosen for the all-expenses-paid trip to Florida, the Caribbean, or the like. The judges consult with one another only for a moment, though, and then they point to the shivering fool in shorts. He is selected from the crowd. He is helped onto the makeshift platform to join the contest officials, and there they award him the much-desired trip.

A murmur of surprise and confusion flows through the shivering crowd. Then the contest officials explain their decision to the bundled bystanders: this man won the trip to the Caribbean because, simply, he was the only person who was dressed for the Caribbean.

And so it is with you and me.

We are invited to enjoy an all-expenses-paid eternity in the Kingdom of Heaven. The expectation of the Judge, however, is that we will "dress" for our destination, even while we are here. Even though we live in the bitter cold of a fallen, sinful world, we are to live like the warmth of love, humility, and holiness that characterize our destination. The apparel — the lifestyle — that is fashionable in heaven may leave us shivering and vulnerable here. Kingdom-bound folks are bound to being teased and misunderstood, for we look and live so out-of-place. But that temporary discomfort is a small price to pay in the end. For the Lord has graciously promised his shivering saints in shorts, "Your reward will be great" (v. 35).

David J. Kalas

---

1. Eugene H. Peterson, *The Message* (Colorado Springs: NavPress, 1993), pp. 131-132.

# Whether You'll
# Weather The Weather

Every so often, toward the end of a hot, still, muggy day here in the Midwest, we'll have a television show interrupted by an alarming beep and a printed message scrolling across the bottom of the screen. It's tornado season, and so the message usually features one of two words from the National Weather Service. It's either a "watch" or it's a "warning."

A tornado *watch* means that the atmospheric conditions are ripe for the development of a funnel cloud. A tornado *warning*, on the other hand, means that a funnel cloud has actually been sighted somewhere in the area. If the National Weather Service issues a watch, you are encouraged to be alert. If the National Weather Service issues a warning, however, you are instructed to take cover.

Jesus has issued a warning.

Jesus tells the story of two men, each of whom builds a house. The two men make different choices, and their stories have different endings. Please note, though, that the two men are more alike than they are different. We might miss that fact, for our natural instinct is to focus on their differences. Before we can appreciate their differences, though, we ought first to take a measure of their similarities.

The first great similarity is in the weather. The one man, you remember, builds his house on a foundation of rock, and so his house survives the storm. The other man, however, builds his house without a foundation (or on the sand, according to the more familiar version of the story in Matthew 7). The second man's house is devastated by the storm.

103

Perhaps we ought to have an alarming beep sound each time we read this teaching of Jesus. Perhaps it should be printed periodically as a crawl across our television screens, for in this teaching Jesus has issued a warning. It's a severe storm warning. And it is not just a watch.

We might say that the first man is wise and the second man foolish. We might conclude that the first man is obedient to God and the second man is not. And those would be fair characterizations. But see that it makes no difference to the weather in Jesus' story. We would like very much to believe that the wise, the righteous, and the faithful would be exempted from life's storms. Not so here, though.

Our sense of fairness — and perhaps also our theology — expects that where the wise man chooses to build (or how the faithful person chooses to live) is a place less susceptible to storms. And there is surely a scriptural basis for that presumption. In the Old Testament Law, as well as much of the wisdom tradition of ancient Israel, there is a straightforward cause-and-effect paradigm: obedience brings blessing, while disobedience yields disaster.

At the same time, however, the Old Testament people of God were not naïve on this point. They cherished the stories of Joseph, David, Job, and others whose sufferings were unfair and undeserved. Many of the Psalmist's prayers are cries for justice in the midst of unjust persecution and troubles. And the faithfulness of people like Jeremiah, Daniel, and Nehemiah seemed only to create trouble for them.

The path of the righteous, we discover, has mixed results. On the one hand, it steers one clear of all the self-inflicted troubles that come with sin and wickedness. On the other hand, in this fallen world, it may also lead a person directly into the troubles of persecution and unjust suffering.

Both the wise and the foolish builder live with the same weather. That is the first great commonality they share. Saints and sinners alike experience life's storms. And so it is that Jesus' story does not offer a storm watch, but rather a storm warning. No matter who you are, no matter where you build or how, storms are coming. Other elements of the story are variable, but the storm is a given.

The question, therefore, is not whether the bad weather will come. It will. The question is whether you'll weather the weather.

And so it is that, right on the heels of the great similarity between the two builders, comes the great difference between them. Their weather is the same. How they weather it is not.

Last summer, as we were preparing dinner one evening, we heard the telltale beeping on the television. We turned to read the crawl. It was the real thing: not just a watch, but a tornado warning. And so the announcement was accompanied by a series of urgent instructions about where to go and what to do.

Typically, the instruction during such severe weather is to go to your basement. That's the most secure place to be during a tornado. Basements are usually concrete and underground: a foundation of rock, if you will. And so that's where you want to be — where you *need* to be — during a storm.

As it turned out for us, no tornado touched down in our immediate area, and so our shelter was not sorely tested. Both men in Jesus' story, however, do have their shelters tested. Both experience the same potentially devastating kind of storm, but they are not equally devastated in the end. The house with a rock foundation survives, while the house without such an enviable base is utterly destroyed.

I am reminded of Jesus' parable each time I go to the beach with my two young daughters. Only half of their beach fun, you see, is playing in the water; the other half is playing in the sand. And a standard part of playing in the sand at the beach is building sandcastles with Daddy.

My older daughter and I have endeavored some pretty elaborate structures together. At first I set down my reading to embark on the sandy assignment as just a favor to my girls, but soon I find myself thoroughly engaged in the project. I work on tunnels, bridges, and towers, while my daughter adorns our proud structure with stones, sticks, and seashells.

In the end, of course, our sandcastle's fate is always the same. The tide begins to come in, and the little constant laps of water prove devastating to our project. Gradually we watch our work being undermined, crumbled, and washed away. It comes with the territory, for that is the nature of sand.

Such vulnerability is harmless enough in a sandcastle. In fact, it's rather fascinating to watch. When it happens on a larger scale, on the other hand, it is truly disturbing to watch. You have no doubt seen, as I have, news footage of people's homes being battered and twisted by hurricanes, or leveled by tornados, or suddenly disappearing down the side of a hill in some California mudslide. It's a frightening scene.

And it's worse still when the wreckage is not a structure but a life. That's what Jesus is finally talking about, of course, in his storm-warning parable. The risks that come with a fragile foundation in a human life are even more poignant, more tragic than the sight of a building being devastated by some natural disaster.

I expect that we've all seen it. We've seen lives buckle and crumble. We've seen the human wreckage left in the wake of some storm.

Of course, unless we are very close to the situation, we may not see it coming. It's difficult to perceive from a distance that a person's foundation is being gradually eroded away. The final "crash," therefore — the suicide, the divorce, the crisis, the breakdown, the addiction, or whatever other form the crash may take — often catches us by surprise when it comes. "I had no idea," we exclaim when we hear the news. "I had no idea he was going through that." "I had no idea that was going on in her life."

As a parish pastor, I do a fair amount of counseling with folks. That counseling is not initiated by me. Rather, it is typically precipitated by some storm in a parishioner's life, and they come looking for help. I have thought sometimes, while trying to help some soul cope with the present storm, that perhaps a variation of Jesus' parable would be appropriate. Perhaps there is a third category of people — those who did not build on the rock at first, but who frantically run to find a firm foundation once the storm hits.

The real estate agent will readily tell you the axiomatic truth of his trade: "Location, location, and location!" As a pastor and preacher, meanwhile, I would bear witness to my work's version of that truth: Foundation, foundation, and foundation!

In my roles as a preacher and a teacher, I endeavor to help people build on the rock while the sun is shining. In my role as a counselor, however, I reckon myself out there in the rain and the wind with them, trying to help them find the rock to build upon, even in the midst of their crisis. It's a desperate effort. And it's a poignant sight.

I remember some years ago a woman in the church asking for an appointment to meet with me. I had no idea what she wanted to talk about, and when she arrived and began to tell me, I was caught completely by surprise. She told me about the situation in her home and her marriage — about the affair her husband had been having with another woman for years, about how she finally discovered it, about how he had been treating their daughter, and about the state of their marriage. It was shocking stuff. He was a respected leader and Sunday school teacher in the church. No one had any idea what had been going on.

Now here was this woman in my office, suddenly hit by one of life's potentially devastating storms, and she was looking for help. As we talked, it became painfully apparent that she had no real foundation of faith. She was foundering, and had no sense at all of the God to whom she belonged. She had been in church her whole life, and yet still there was no solid foundation in place when the storm came.

That brings us to the second great similarity between the two house builders. The first, you remember, is their weather. The second, it turns out, is their opportunity.

"I will show you what someone is like who comes to me, hears my words, and acts on them," Jesus says, and he goes on to describe the person we think of as the wise house builder. "But the one who hears and does not act," Jesus continues, "is like a man who built a house on the ground without a foundation."

The second great similarity between the two house builders is that both persons heard the Word. Both had the opportunity to build on the rock.

I suppose that's why we are right to think of the two builders as "wise" and "foolish." If the difference between them was that one had heard the life-changing, life-saving Word and the other had not, then we might label them "lucky" and "unlucky," "fortunate" and "unfortunate." But they had the same opportunity. They heard the same Word. But in the end, one responded wisely to the Word, and the other did not.

In so many of the parables Jesus tells, you and I are presented with a choice of characters. Am I more like the priest and the Levite or the Samaritan? Do I more closely resemble the wise virgins or the foolish ones? Do I live like the first two stewards or the third who buried his talent in the ground?

And here, too, in this parable: Both characters experienced storms, and both characters heard the Word, but each one responded differently to what he heard. Which of the two builders am I like? Which of the two characters are you like?

Have we acted on what we have heard from the Lord? Have we responded to his Word with our lives?

Every so often you hear the story of a scam artist who manages to bilk some poor, trusting souls out of their life savings. He makes promises, he offers guarantees, and they invest most or all of what they have in his proposal. But then both he and their money suddenly disappear, leaving them devastated.

The original scam artist, of course, was known as the most subtle and crafty of all the creatures in the Garden. He, too, made promises and guarantees. Eve believed him, and in the process she and Adam lost virtually everything they had.

And still today the Deceiver tries to sell folks a bill of goods. Or, in the parlance of our parable, he tries to sell us a piece of property. "Come build your life here," he urges. "Here you'll have everything you need!"

Not everything. Not a firm foundation.

We human beings keep buying property and building structures on flood plains, fault lines, and along hurricane-vulnerable coasts. It's a calculated risk, and many thousands of folks seem willing to take it.

There is no risk calculation to be made, however, when it comes to the life-storms represented in Jesus' parable. We do not need to assess the probability of being hit by one (or several) of these storms.

They are a given. And yet, still, people go merrily on, building vulnerability into the structure of their lives.

Perhaps we have been advised too early and too often not to "put all our eggs in one basket." After all, the prudent key to sound investing in our world is to diversify.

That's fine when only money is at stake. When it comes to the weightier matter of our life's foundation, however, diversification is not so wise. "All other ground is sinking sand,"[1] declared nineteenth-century hymn writer Edward Mote. The wise ones have discovered, when it comes to investing your life, your hopes, and your faith, that you need to *un*-diversify. Retract the far-flung hopes and reliance, entrusting instead the whole weight of your life onto the one sure foundation.

"Which of all the airy castles can the hurricane endure?" asked Joachim Neander over 300 years ago, concluding that "built on sand, naught can stand by our earthly wisdom planned." And so he resolved, "All my hope is firmly grounded in the great and living Lord; who, whenever I most need him, never fails to keep his word. God I must wholly trust, God the ever good and just."[2]

Modern meteorology is a highly sophisticated science, and many of us depend on it daily in the routine matters of predicting temperatures and precipitation. And, from time to time, we also depend upon it to alert us to danger, to warn us of storms.

We don't have such a sophisticated and reliable means of predicting life's storms. But Jesus has done us two great favors. First, he has issued a warning: the storms are a given; you can count on them. And, better still, he has offered us a firm foundation: his rock-solid and reliable Word; you can count on him.

David J. Kalas

---

1. Edward Mote, "My Hope Is Built," *The United Methodist Hymnal* (Nashville, Tennessee: The United Methodist Publishing House, 1989), p. 368.

2. Joachim Neander, translated by Fred Pratt Green, "All My Hope Is Firmly Grounded," *The United Methodist Hymnal* (Nashville, Tennessee: The United Methodist Publishing House, 1989), p. 132.

**Transfiguration Of The Lord
(Last Sunday After Epiphany)
Luke 9:28-36 (37-43)**

# Awake To Glory

Today we celebrate one of the most neglected passages in the Bible. It's possible that more sermons have been preached from some of the obscure places in First and Second Chronicles than from this tremendously significant scripture which describes the transfiguration of our Lord. At the time of the transfiguration, Peter finally broke the awed silence, but the Gospel writer says that he knew not what to say. I expect we preachers and teachers still feel a bit that way when we approach this story; probably some of us fear that, when we finally have our say, our words will be as inept or inadequate as were Peter's.

Let's review the story to see why it awes us. It was one of those occasions Jesus took Peter, James, and John — his three closest associates — to be alone with him. We see this as a signal that something special was about to happen. I wonder if Peter, James, and John realized it.

While they prayed, a glory settled upon Jesus The effect was so powerful that Jesus' very appearance was changed. Luke doesn't tell us the nature of the change, but he does say that Jesus' garments became "dazzling white." Suddenly two men were talking with him — Moses and Elijah — about a specific subject: What Jesus was to accomplish at Jerusalem. As Moses and Elijah were ready to leave, Peter broke the silence. His statement was typical of Peter — well-meaning and earnest, but just missing the point. "Master," he said, "it is good for us to be here; let us make three dwellings, one for you, one for Moses, and one for Elijah" (v. 33).

Then it is as if heaven corrected Peter's plan. "This is my Son," the voice said, "my Chosen; listen to him!" (v. 35). The Holy Spirit seemed to be saying, "Moses and Elijah are fine, but don't think of building three equal tabernacles. There is one voice, and one alone, to whom you should listen — the voice of my Son, my Chosen."

Then, just as suddenly, there was no one there with the disciples, but Jesus. Something about the occasion was so special, however, that Peter, James, and John said nothing about it to their fellow disciples.

This is a key story in the life of our Lord. Luke points out that it was set between two special events. It came, he says, about eight days after Jesus had charged his disciples to remain true to him even in the face of persecution, promising that some of them would not taste death before they had seen the kingdom of God. Apparently Luke looked upon this event as a sampling of the kingdom of God; it was the unique moment when Jesus' glory was revealed.

It was also preparation for Calvary. Moses and Elijah had apparently come to discuss this event with Jesus. From this point on, Jesus was headed relentlessly toward Calvary.

Why did the vision include Moses and Elijah? First, because they symbolized the law and the prophets — the two great segments of the Hebrew Scriptures. Additionally, perhaps because they were both described in the scriptures as being spared by God from the actual experience of death.

But the voice from the cloud made clear that they were in no way to be compared with Jesus. Peter fumbled with the idea that they could build three tabernacles to honor them all; there could be no such equal honor. Jesus was the beloved Son, the Chosen One, utterly different from Moses and Elijah.

As much as the disciples loved Jesus, I doubt that they saw his uniqueness. If anything, Peter may have felt he was stretching a point when he suggested three tabernacles, thus putting Jesus on a level with Moses and Elijah. Something in him may have said, "The Master will be pleased that I honor him so." It's always so difficult for us to estimate the greatness of someone near at hand, particularly when compared with notable historic figures. But even more so when they were looking upon one who was in a completely different category from all their previous judgments.

Some Bible scholars feel that perhaps this incident is actually a resurrection story which somehow became misplaced in ancient manuscripts. I can understand why they came to such a conclusion, because this event is so out of the ordinary. I think they miss the point, however. This transfiguration is, rather, a kind of preface to the resurrection. It is as if the Spirit of God were giving the disciples a basis for receiving the resurrection when it happened. Peter, James, and John were thus given an insight into the glory of their Lord which prepared them for the climactic event of Easter.

The key phrase in this story is in verse 32. I particularly like the language of the New International Version: "Peter and his companions were very sleepy, but when they became fully awake, they saw his glory and the two men standing with him." Their realization of the glory of our Lord came to them, not when they were in a state of dullness or of stupor, but in a moment of heightened consciousness: "when they became fully awake." And ironically, when Peter became logical — or as logical as he could manage to be, when he didn't know what he was saying — he offered an inadequate statement.

It is popular in our time to discredit religious experiences. We assume that people receive such experiences when they are not in full possession of their powers. Or perhaps, when we take a posture of intellectual superiority, we reason that such things happen only to basically unstable people.

We should be properly cautious regarding ecstatic religious experiences. There have been innumerable instances where people have done irrational things on the basis of presumed visions or revelations. But we shouldn't rule out or downgrade the true and transforming occasions of religious insight just because there are frauds. Indeed, the best proof of the worth of any matter is that it inspires counterfeits.

The glory of God comes to us when we are most "fully awake." A list of the half-dozen or more true geniuses of human history would surely include the name of Blaise Pascal — the seventeenth-century French philosopher, mathematician, and scientist. In his brief 39 years, he made scientific discoveries which are basic to a great amount of our most significant contemporary knowledge.

But with all his ability in logic and all his commitment to tough-minded scholarship, Pascal found the greatest assurance in his experiences of faith. On the evening of Monday, November 23, 1654, he felt the reality of Jesus Christ in such intensity that he wrote:

> *God of Abraham, God of Isaac, God of Jacob.*
> *Not of the Philosophers and Scientists.*
> *Certainty, Certainty, Feeling Joy, Peace.*
> *God of Jesus Christ*

He copied on parchment the full witness of his experience and sewed it into the lining of his coat, where it was found by his servant after his death nearly eight years later. For Pascal the greatest reality was not what he discovered in laboratory experiments, but what he found in his communion with God, through Jesus Christ. It was at such a time that he was "fully awake."

Most of us are too quick to downgrade our faith perceptions. We seem to feel that the things we can touch and handle are the only realities; and we are instinctively skeptical of that which we get by faith. We always say that love is blind; but a thoughtful woman who was very much in love once replied, "No, love isn't blind. Quite the opposite. It has the ability to see some things others cannot see." The same can be said for faith. True faith does not blind us to the realities of life; it simply enables us to grasp and understand some things which are otherwise beyond us.

The Gospel of Mark has a fascinating contrast in our levels of perception. Mark 5:20 tells us of the miracle Jesus performed for a man who had been violently insane. It says that when people saw and heard what had happened, "everyone was amazed." But in the next chapter, Jesus is in his hometown and the unbelief of the people was such that "he could do no deed of power there," except for a few minor healings. Mark says that Jesus "was amazed at their unbelief" (6:5, 6). The crowds marveled that Jesus could work miracles; Jesus marveled that people could be so possessed of unbelief! The crowds looked upon miracles as out of the ordinary;

114

Jesus thought of unbelief as out of the ordinary. He saw belief and its results as our native state, because he believed that you and I are meant to live "fully awake" to the glory of God.

It is not that some of us are believers and some are not; it is just that we choose to invest our believing in different places. Someone once noted that Coleridge and Shelley visited Chamonix about the same time. Coleridge proceeded to write his grand hymn in the Vale of Chamonix, in which he described Nature as seeming to take one voice which echoed and re-echoed to the name of God. But Shelley wrote in the visitors' book at Chamonix: "Percy Bysshe Shelley. Atheist." Which man, at that moment, was more "fully awake"? And who, by contrast, had so shut his human perceptions that he missed the glory which was all around him?

Early in the twentieth century, Henry Van Dyke, the great Presbyterian poet-preacher, described his time as "the Age of Doubt." In the doubting of God, recent generations are probably much like his. We have conditioned ourselves, with a peculiar intellectual prejudice, against seeing the glory of God in daily life. And we are desperately poorer because of it. Keats cried out in one of his memorable lines, "beauty was awake! / Why were ye not awake?" God may well address that question to us. There is glory all around us, magnificently awake; why are we not awake to see it?

Are there ways that we can help ourselves be more awake to the glory of God? By all means! As surely as we have been conditioned to the sensual, and often to the fearing and the despairing, so we can help condition ourselves to a way of life which is more open to faith — and thus more likely to receive the vision of the glory of God.

Spiritually, as well as physically, we are what we eat. Our contemporary society feeds us a constant diet of that which is secular. We have to put forth special effort to find food which will nourish the deepest hungers of our lives.

Part of the secret is frequent attendance at the house of worship. This is no commercial; it is simply a statement of the facts of life. We are bombarded all week long by voices that dull our sensitivity to God and to the eternal; so we need desperately to take advantage of that special time each week when we can concentrate on hearing another voice.

But Sunday worship is not enough. We must also establish some patterns of daily renewal. We need the lift, day after day, which comes through reading the Bible, and through other devotional and inspirational books and magazines. Equally, we need the special strength that comes through those friends with whom we can share both our faith and our struggles. I could wish no better gift, for you and for me, than that we are blessed with a few special friends who are willing to "talk faith." Such persons can do something for us which sometimes not even the most inspirational book can do.

And in all our searching, let us remember that God is on the side of our quest. We were built for faith, so to speak; it is our native air, and we function best when we breathe it in great drafts. We were not meant to be one-dimensional creatures, who live only by the perceptions of human reason and physical experience. We need to be shaken fully awake, so that we can see the glory of God. God our Father desires such a gladness for us.

So let us seek God in holy expectation. We may not have a moment on a mount of transfiguration with Moses, Elijah, and Jesus. But on our own little mountain, at home, or in our automobile, we can be with our Lord. And in that moment, we will find ourselves as blessed as were Peter, James, and John, so long ago, when they were "fully awake" to God's glory.

J. Ellsworth Kalas

# Sermons On The Gospel Readings

## For Sundays In
## Lent And Easter

### *Salvation At The Skull*

### Frank G. Honeycutt

*For Cindy*
*in thanksgiving for twenty years*

# Introduction

There is obviously much that we cannot know about the mysteries of God. But having said that, there is much we *can* know. Much has been revealed to us. Much has been passed on by faith communities who have preceded us and struggled with what it means to believe and obediently follow in a world like ours.

The longer I am a pastor the more convinced I am that serious disciples *must* be serious students of the Bible. I've never met an exception. There are obvious limits about what we can know about God and even scripture reveals baffling passages that have confounded the most proficient scholars for centuries (see, for example, 2 Kings 2:23-25 for an odd humdinger).

But the Bible is a treasure trove of spiritual guidance for the patient reader who is willing to let a story percolate and gestate, the student willing to set aside our modern obsession with instant inspiration and meaning. "For the Rabbis and Church Fathers," writes Burton Visotsky, "reading the Book was an adventure, a journey to a grand palace with many great and awesome halls, banquet rooms and chambers, as well as many passages and locked doors. The adventure lay in learning the secrets of the palace, unlocking all the doors and perhaps catching a glimpse of the King in all his splendor."[1]

This may frustrate those with little time for nuance. "The Bible may be difficult and confusing, but it is meant to challenge our intelligence, not insult it. It becomes insulting when it is distorted by fanaticism and foolish religiosity."[2] The "authority" of the Bible finally rests not on pompous ecclesiastical pronouncements assuring the faithful that this particular tome is inherently "holy" but rather on the power of scripture to transform and liberate God's people. This is the final test of the Bible's authority in any age:

119

whether we are changed people as a result of reading and living the Word.

The sermons in this collection attempt to reflect the great themes of Lent and Easter: discipleship, sacrifice, death, and new life. I'm hopeful that they might be helpful to other preachers in preparing their own sermons for these important seasons. The reflections here may also be read devotionally or in small groups for those seeking to follow Jesus more faithfully in an era where the church is tempted to water down the demands of Christian discipleship in order to attract new members.

Blessings upon your journey these Forty Days and the Great Fifty that follow.

Frank G. Honeycutt
Abingdon, Virginia
Easter 2002

———————

1. Burton L. Visotsky, *Reading the Book: Making the Bible a Timeless Text* (New York: Schocken Books, 1991), p. 18.

2. Thomas Merton, *Opening the Bible* (Philadelphia: Fortress Press, 1970), p. 14.

# Escape From The Island
# Of Spiritual Sloth

I was noodling around on the internet not long ago, doing some research on the "Seven Deadly Sins," and came upon what has surely been an overlooked theological resource in explaining the mysteries of what Gregory the Great, in the sixth century, called "a classification of the normal perils of the soul in the ordinary conditions of life."

There is quite a bit of material out there referring to the deadly list of seven but by far the most intriguing theological website was one I discovered titled, "The Seven Deadly Sins of Gilligan's Island." I am not making this up. Seven characters on the island. Seven sins. You're welcome to look it up for yourself.

The Professor obviously represents the sin of *pride*. What else are you going to feel after rigging up a ham radio with wire and two coconuts? Mary Ann? Oh, she's an easy one. *Envy*. Always envying the glamorous Ginger. And it doesn't take a rocket scientist to discern that Ginger is the living embodiment of *lust* on the island. (I still have dreams about Ginger after all these years.) Thurston Howell, III, is an easy candidate for *greed*. After all, asks the webmaster of this site, "What kind of person takes a trunk-full of money on a three-hour cruise?" The Skipper merits two deadly sins, *anger* and *gluttony*. He always seems to be furious with Gilligan, forever whacking his "little buddy" with his hat, not to mention gorging himself with papayas.

Gilligan himself is not assigned a deadly sin. He plays the role of *Satan* who forever keeps the other six trapped on the island. And that leaves *sloth* to Mrs. Thurston Howell, III. According to the

121

same webmaster, "She did jack (expletive) during her many years on the island and everybody knows it." Well, I hope that's helpful for you. There are many fine books describing the theological mechanics of the seven deadly sins, but you might discover how sin really works by watching a few re-runs.

And so we come to "sloth." There are many proverbial sayings in the King James Version that warn of slothfulness and its outward aftermath. "By much slothfulness the building decayeth; and through idleness of the hands the house droppeth through" (Ecclesiastes 10:18). "Slothfulness casteth into a deep sleep" (Proverbs 19:15). "Thou wicked and slothful servant, thou knewest that I reap where I sowed not and gather where I have not strawed" (Matthew 25:26). But "sloth" is largely an archaic-sounding word we no longer use. To my knowledge it appears only once in the NRSV. But even in the newer translations there are delightful allusions to slothfulness. One of my favorites is from Proverbs: "Go to the ant, you lazybones; consider its ways and be wise ... How long will you lie there, O lazybones? When will you rise from your sleep? A little sleep, a little slumber, a little folding of the hands to rest, and poverty will come upon you like a robber, and want, like an armed warrior" (6:6, 9-11).[1]

As the seven deadly sins took shape in the early Middle Ages, the Greek word *acedia* came to describe what we refer to as "sloth." And *acedia* could certainly describe someone who was just plain lazy. But, more accurately, it came to describe a person who was *spiritually lazy*. The Greek word literally means "I don't care." So what forms can this spiritual laziness take in our churches today?

Well, spiritual laziness might mean coming to worship services on Sunday, listening to what a priest or pastor tells you week after week, but never really taking time to reflect upon and study the teachings of the church for yourself. Spiritual laziness might mean giving lip-service to the importance of the Bible in our common life together but really never reading the Bible on a regular basis. Spiritual laziness might mean that a person *sings* "What A Friend We Have In Jesus" but really never spends enough time with Jesus so that a friendship with the man is truly constituted.

122

"Sloth," in the original list of seven deadly sins, describes the state of a Christian who remains in an embryonic, beginning state of discipleship, year after year after year. The leaders of the early church assumed that one's *eternal* life was a gift from God. They also assumed that one's *internal* life required discipline, study, commitment, and a lot of hard work. *Acedia*, sloth, spiritual laziness, whatever you want to call it, is a crippling problem for the modern church in America. As Peter Gomes, chaplain at Harvard University and an Episcopalian, puts it: "It's startling how many adult Christians walk through life with a second-rate second grade Sunday school education." So how do we move away from sloth, from spiritual laziness? (And it afflicts all of us, even the clergy, by the way.)

After pulling a muscle on a bike ride, I once jokingly complained to a doctor friend that I was getting older. My friend replied, ever the clinician, "You're not getting older, you're rotting." A nice, comforting thought, don't you agree? But, in truth, a helpful thought if taken seriously. As is this: *Remember that you are dust.* That's why we're here tonight, isn't it? To remind each other that the worms will go in and out soon enough. *Remember that.* Even have somebody rub your nose in it, smudge a black cross on your brow with a couple cups of ashy flakes vacuumed from last year's palms. That's why we're here. So, all together now: How do we, Christ's church, who all exhibit from time to time the spiritual slothfulness of Mrs. Thurston Howell, III, on our little congregational island, keep a faithful Lent? Here's the truth: *We* cannot keep a faithful Lent and *we* cannot even *begin* to rid ourselves of spiritual slothfulness.

But Christ can in us. Not by magic. And not with a wiggle of his divine nose. Christ needs room to change us. "One of the greatest deceptions in the practice of the Christian religion," writes Dallas Willard, "is the idea that all that really matters is our internal feelings, ideas, beliefs, and intentions."[2] Let me tell you something. We have bought into that hook, line, and sinker in the mainline church. "Faith is what I believe in my head," we say. And yet for my money one of the most devastating things Jesus ever said to would-be disciples was this: "Why do you call me 'Lord, Lord' and do not do what I tell you?" (Luke 6:46).

So if we are serious about moving from spiritual slothfulness towards Christian maturity then we will see the Christian life primarily lived through an old, old set of habits that do not "save" us (please don't confuse this) but rather give Jesus room to work. Things like almsgiving to the poor and regular prayer and even fasting, the very things Jesus mentions tonight, and a host of other habits. Churches of grace, wishing to avoid legalism, have usually perceived these disciplines as optional for Lent and life. But Jesus doesn't say, "If you *choose* to fast, pray, or give alms, be sure to do it this way." He doesn't say, "If you get around to it, this is the way it's done." No. Jesus says, "When." "When you fast ... When you pray ... When you give alms." Not "if." Spiritual disciplines are what disciples destined for death do to keep our inner lives in shape. Somehow we have accepted the notion that although it takes hours of sweat and discipline and hard work to maintain a healthy exterior, our interior lives need no such maintenance. We'll gladly pass out on the ThighMaster, we'll spend hours in search of washboard abs, but we squawk loud protests when the church suggests fasting or tithing as a means to mature spiritually. In so doing we betray an interest in health that is only *skin* deep.

We are rotting away, destined to become the ash that adorns our brows tonight. We will face suffering and crises and pain and horrible forks in the road, sooner or later. No one is exempt. It's part of what it means to be human. And in my mind there are only a couple ways to handle what's coming or even what you might be going through right now. There are two basic types of human response in my experience. First, we can ignore what's coming and be surprised and shocked when suffering arrives and ask, "Where is God? Surely my faith in God protects me from this."

Or, we can take another approach. Instead of asking, "Where is God?" we might reflect upon God asking a question of us: "Where are you?" It's the old question God asks of a wayward Adam and Eve in the garden. "Where are you? Where have you been? Where are you going?" It's hard to answer God's questions without a few spiritual habits that allow God to claim more and more of our interior lives until we are wholly and completely the Lord's. And when that happens it really will not rattle us if death occurs thirty years from now or tomorrow. *Without* disciplined spiritual habits, we face death with only our intellects and emotions. We'll get through it, but I can promise you it will be hellish.

I recently read a story of a father whose daughter, as a teenager, was plagued by terrible bouts of acne. Her face became so ravaged that at times she could not bring herself to leave the house. She was in such anguish. One day her father led her to the bathroom and asked her if he could teach her a new way to wash. He leaned over the sink and splashed water over his face, telling her, "On the first splash, say, 'In the name of the Father'; on the second, 'in the name of the Son'; and on the third, 'in the name of the Holy Spirit.' Then look up into the mirror and remember that you are a child of God, full of grace and beauty." It was a practice that the girl took into adulthood.[3]

Martin Luther once said, "You cannot stop the birds from flying over your head, but you can keep them from building a nest in your hair." Death will come to us all. In fifty years or so, less for some and more for others, it will seem like we've been vacuumed from the premises without a trace. How shall we face this reality? How shall we prepare?

In one of his classic tales of Narnia titled *The Silver Chair*, C. S. Lewis describes a young girl named Jill Pole who is about to undertake an arduous journey fraught with many perils. Aslan the lion, who serves as the Christ figure in these tales, appears to Jill before she departs. He says, "Remember, remember, remember the Signs. Say them to yourself when you wake in the morning and when you lie down at night, and when you wake in the middle of the night. And whatever strange things may happen to you, let nothing turn your mind from following the Signs ... know them by heart and pay no attention to appearances. Remember the Signs and believe the Signs. Nothing else matters."[4]

1. The first three biblical references in this paragraph are all from the King James Version. The fourth is from the NRSV.

2. Dallas Willard, *The Spirit of the Disciplines: Understanding How God Changes Lives* (San Francisco: Harper and Row, 1988), p. 152.

3. Stephanie Paulsell, "Honoring the Body," in *Practicing Our Faith: A Way of Life for a Searching People*, edited by Dorothy C. Bass (San Francisco: Jossey Bass Publishers, 1997), p. 19.

4. C. S. Lewis, *The Silver Chair* (New York: Macmillan Publishing Co., 1953), p. 21.

# On Defeating The Devil

At every baptism in the Lutheran church an old question is asked. A question used at countless baptisms all over the world. A question that is almost as old as the church itself. Just before water is splashed in the threefold name, I look at parents and sponsors and sometimes adult candidates across the pool and ask: *Do you renounce all the forces of evil, the devil, and all his empty promises?*

To tell you the truth, I've been waiting for somebody to laugh at the question. Who really believes in the devil anymore? We've left him behind with the Easter Bunny and the Tooth Fairy, relegating "evil" to more manageable and explainable psychoses that can be named and catalogued within the human heart. There's nothing wrong with Hitler, Pol Pot, Timothy McVeigh, Osama bin Laden, and even the fictional Hannibal Lecter that a little pharmacological therapy can't fix, right? I remember approaching my systematic theology professor in seminary and asking, "Do I *really* have to say that line about the devil and all his empty promises?" I'll never forget his response. My professor smiled at me and said, "Spend twenty years in parish ministry and come back and ask me that question again."

Well, it's been fifteen years. And although I certainly don't believe in the existence of a red-suited man with a pitchfork who can be cornered, named, and thereby avoided, I have seen enough darkness, in my own life and in various other situations, to re-think my theological arrogance. Maybe this so-called "outdated" line in the baptismal liturgy is not so outdated after all. *Do you renounce all the forces of evil, the devil, and all his empty promises?*

Malcolm Muggeridge, the late British journalist, converted to Christianity in mid-life after years of agnosticism. "Personally," he once wrote, "I have found the Devil easier to believe in than God; for one thing, alas, I have had more to do with him."[1] *Do you renounce all the forces of evil, the devil, and all his empty promises?*

People usually say, "I do," when I ask them this question. It's relatively simple to make a vow — whether a marriage, confirmation, or baptismal vow. Do you promise? Do you pledge? Do you give your word? "I do." No sweat. The harder thing, as we come to discover, is living out a specific vow in a family or certain community of people. I don't care what you call "the devil and all his empty promises." But I've come to believe that the naïve person isn't the one who believes evil is real, but rather the one who believes evil can be rationally explained away. *Do you renounce all the forces of evil, the devil, and all his empty promises?* If we say, "I do," then how does one live out such a vow?

Today's Gospel story offers us a few hints. Jesus sends the devil packing in this story. But how? There's a haunting line at the very end of the story. The narrator reports that "when the devil had finished every test, he departed from him until an opportune time." This will be an ongoing battle for Jesus, which is a rather interesting idea if you think about it. One theologian has noted: "Being committed to the way of God in the world does not exempt one from the struggle. In fact, it is those who are most engaged in the way of God who seem to experience most intensely the opposition of evil."[2] This is not a one-time shot for Jesus in the wilderness. The battle is ongoing. "He departed from Jesus until an opportune time." The narrator, with these words, seems to suggest that the battle is ongoing for us all.

Let me say here that the Bible never describes the appearance of the devil. Rembrandt made a pen and brush drawing of this scene in 1650 and the devil is graphically shown as a skeleton with a tail and bat wings.[3] But nowhere is the devil described in this story. Instead, the devil comes to Jesus as a tempter. And, to tell you the truth, offers Jesus three things that look pretty good. There doesn't appear to be anything horribly wrong with the things he offers Jesus. Bread, wealth, and power. The American way, come to think of it. In other words, the devil isn't offering Jesus things that look really bad, things we normally associate with the dark side and point to as horrible social ills. Instead, the devil is offering Jesus things that look, well, quite good. In the Bible and in life, the devil is rarely obvious. That would be too easy. Avoid everything that looks patently evil and we're home free. But the devil doesn't work that way in this story. The devil offers Jesus things that look quite appealing, not things that look obviously bad. As someone once put it, the devil often dresses in drag.

But Jesus prevails. He renounces the devil and his three empty promises. And so let's return to that question of a moment ago. *How?* How does Jesus renounce the devil dressed in drag? There are two ways he renounces the devil, as far as I can tell. Maybe you've picked these out already.

First, Jesus encounters the devil in the strength of forty days of fasting. And I use the word "strength" in a way that has surprised me this Lenten season. "I have always thought," writes Mark Buchanan, "that the devil was coming to Jesus at his weakest moment: Jesus gaunt, raw-boned, wild-eyed, ready to scavenge any moldy crust of bread or scrape any meat shreds off a lamb's bone ... But I'm not so sure anymore. The more I learn from fasting the more I see that Jesus actually stood at his strongest when his belly was empty. Jesus is in peak condition, a fighter who has been training hard. When he steps into the ring, his opponent doesn't stand a chance."[4] So that's the first way that Jesus sends the devil packing. He is spiritually strong as a result of spiritual disciplines as he heads into the encounter with the devil.

Second, watch how Jesus answers the devil's very enticing temptations. Does he toss out some magic totem? Dos he rely on strong mental resistance? Does he ask God to rescue him in some impressive way? No, on all three counts. *Jesus quotes scripture.* Jesus is so utterly bathed in holy scripture that he is able to bring the story that is centuries old *forward* into his own life. These references are all from the book of Deuteronomy and the wilderness wanderings of his spiritual forebears. But Jesus recasts the words into his own wilderness encounter with the devil. The words are not magic, but they are enough to send the devil packing.

Jesus lived in a world of story. There was, of course, the dominant story of Roman rule. But there was also a minority story. And because the people who told the story were twice enslaved for long periods of time and persecuted for much of their history, special care was taken with the story's transmission. Some people wonder why Jesus' ministry didn't get underway until his thirties. My guess is that he was being shaped and formed by the stories of his religious community. It is true that at age twelve he impressed the rabbis with his knowledge of Torah in the Temple. But Jesus wasn't born in Bethlehem with the Ten Commandments on his lips. He wasn't *that* precocious. His ministry was formed by a story told long before he was born. He saw himself *in* the story, not outside of it.

So it behooves the church to recall that one of the parental promises at holy baptism is this: "As they grow in years, you should place in their hands the Holy Scriptures and provide for their instruction in the Christian faith." The stories of the Bible give us the gumption to resist a devil who usually dresses in drag. It will be difficult for us to resist such temptations on our own.

Martin Luther, in his classic hymn, "A Mighty Fortress," makes the same fantastic claim that this temptation story makes today: "One little word subdues him." Jesus would be lost without this Word, without these scriptures.

Will Willimon, chaplain at Duke University, was reflecting on a "Men's Soul-Making Weekend" offered near campus. The publicity poster described the event as "a time for men to recall their boyhoods, become animals and heroes, and honor their ancestors and elders." Willimon's reflections fit the spirit of today's temptations in the wilderness: "If I ever invite you to join me for a $200 weekend to beat drums ... and tell you how deeply significant it is for me to be a white male, act bored. Then remind me that all of that is ultimately uninteresting. Tell me again the story of the Jew from Nazareth who reached beyond race and gender to summon a new people by water and the word, and call me a Christian. My little life has significance only within his light."[5] Our personal stories need a much broader scriptural story in order for us to find meaning, purpose, and the inner resources to resist evil. We need a story that was being told long before we were born and a story that will be told long after we return to ash and worm castings.

So, let me pose the question again. *Do you renounce all the forces of evil, the devil, and all his empty promises?*

Maybe it's a question you're still laughing at, intellectually, deep down. Maybe it's a question you didn't give a whole lot of thought to when you said, "I do," at the font back there.

But if you're beginning to suspect what is truly at stake here, then Jesus gives us some hints as to how to send evil packing. Two things, really. Spiritual disciplines and an immersion in holy scripture. That is what made Jesus strong enough to resist.

And that is what will make you strong enough in this wilderness we wander in today, where "hordes of devils fill the land, All threatening to devour us."[6]

---

1. Malcolm Muggeridge, *Jesus: The Man Who Lives* (New York: Harper and Row, 1975), p. 51.

2. Fred Craddock, *Luke* (Louisville: John Knox Press, 1990), p. 55.

3. Hidde Hoekstra, *Rembrandt and the Bible* (Weert, Netherlands: Magna Books, 1990), p. 298.

4. Mark Buchanan, "Go Fast and Live: Hunger as Spiritual Discipline" *The Christian Century* (February 28, 2001), p. 16.

5. William H. Willimon, "Not for Men Only" *The Christian Ministry* (March-April 1998), p. 39.

6. Martin Luther, "A Mighty Fortress Is Our God" *Lutheran Book of Worship* (Minneapolis: Augsburg Fortress, 1978).

# Jesus, Desirous

In the powerful movie, *Ulee's Gold*, Peter Fonda plays a tired man who is a beekeeper by day. He runs the old family business of collecting and selling the golden honey that pays the bills. It is exhausting work for a man now in his late sixties. Ulee does most of it by himself because he cannot afford to hire someone to help him. He maintains and moves the hives, gathers the trays, separates the honey from the wax, spins the final product into jars, and ships it off to market. He worries about the ebb and flow of money offered by his distributor and doesn't sleep well at night. You can almost watch the spirit drain out of Ulee as the movie progresses.

But what really causes Ulee to worry is his daughter and her children. His daughter is in and out of drug treatment facilities and long ago left three children with Ulee and his wife. Now that his wife is dead, it's only Ulee. His daughter phones about twice a year. I recall one scene where the oldest girl, around sixteen, is about to leave on a date with her older boyfriend. A rather fresh argument still hovers in the room. Ulee has worried about her for weeks, not knowing exactly what to do, remembering his own daughter's rebellion at about the same age. A car is honking in the background. Ulee is slumped down in a chair, exhausted from a fourteen-hour day. Before she steps through the screen door, Ulee says, "Remember — curfew is 12 o'clock." His granddaughter stops at the far end of the living room, turns, and says with a face that is half sneer, half smile, "I'd like to see you *make* me get home by twelve." The screen door slams behind her and Ulee knows she is right. He is powerless to make her do much of anything anymore.

One of the popular images of Jesus in many religious circles is that he is a man who can do anything. Walk on water. Turn a couple fish and a few loaves into a feast for thousands. Even raise the dead. "That's our Jesus, he can do anything."

Today's Gospel lesson is a rather loud refutation to that popular claim. Jesus can do many impressive things. I'll not argue that. But one thing he cannot do is make us love him. He cannot legislate love nor control human will. "How often have I desired to gather your children together as a hen gathers her brood under her wings, and you were not willing." Jesus cannot do just anything. He has tried to gather this particular flock many times. "Often," he says. It's a strange thing to say out loud, but Jesus failed at that. Struck out. He'll walk out of a tomb in a few days, but apparently he can't walk into our hearts without permission. "How often have I desired to gather you and you were not willing."

I suspect Ulee knows exactly how Jesus feels. I suspect anyone who has loved someone deeply and knows they can't shelter them from harm's way understands the pain in Jesus' lament over the city. Jesus can do a lot of amazing things. But he can only watch as his sons and daughters go through the screen door saying, "I'd like to see you *make* me." His will cannot overpower our wills. He is off the chart with a lot of things. But Jesus is powerless at that.

Unrequited love is tough enough one time around. Jesus was about this "often." I daresay he still is. It's tough to put any type of love on the line and have that love rejected. I remember this woman: a blond co-ed at Clemson University in the winter of 1977 who attracted my attention and infatuation like no other that year. I was smitten.

At first I was subtle: smiles in the lunch line, hellos on the way to class. And then bolder: a phone number was secured, we dated a few times. And then overbearingly mushy: on a park bench in the middle of campus, on Valentine's Day almost 25 years ago, I nauseatingly poured out my heart in a speech that rivaled a Shakespearean sonnet. It even makes *me* gag when I think about it now. Well, it was not to be. I got the drift eventually. She was never home when I called. We never passed each other on the way to class anymore. Word got back that she was dating someone else.

Unrequited love for a nineteen-year-old is as close to the end of the world as one may ever come.

Jesus' desire for us, no doubt, is a bit different than my desire for that young woman. But it is similar in this regard: Jesus is willing to make a fool of himself to get our attention. He likens himself to a hen. To a chicken. Out of all the animals that Jesus could have chosen, a veritable Noah's ark of biblical metaphors, *he chooses a chicken*.[1] He could have chosen the powerful eagle of the book of Exodus (19:4). "I bore you on eagles' wings." There is a cagey leopard prowling through the pages of Hosea (13:7). God is likened to a lion elsewhere. But a chicken? Really now, what kind of confidence does a chicken instill? When we send our children out the screen door to face the perils of this world, wouldn't you prefer "God the ravening lion" at your child's side rather than Jesus "the mother hen"?

"How often have I desired to gather your children together as a hen gathers her brood under her wings." What kind of chance is this hen going to have against the likes of a fox such as Herod? Some friendly Pharisees warn Jesus this morning that Herod wants to kill him. No surprise there. Herod has already chopped off the head of John the Baptist at a wild party where anything went. A chicken's head won't matter much. Put it on the chopping block and be done with all this squawking about peace and poor people. How annoying. Herod, by the way, was a character with a notorious reputation for bizarre immorality and rather raunchy party-going. The very last person you'd want your daughter to date. Curiously, the Greek word for "fox" that describes Herod is here rendered in the feminine, which, according to Frederick Buechner, "may or may not be an allusion to some of Herod's more exotic proclivities."[2] Jesus probably bugged the living heck out of Herod.

But this is the world we live in. Foxes have always had a certain allure over God's children, in this or any century. They may not be quite as bizarre and murderous as Herod, but foxes still slyly woo away the hearts of God's brood. And this is the thing: *Jesus is powerless to stop it*. He can walk on water and raise the dead, but he cannot make us love him. He desires such love, but he cannot force it. Cannot keep us from slamming the screen door in his face, defenseless against the many Herods waiting in the shadows. One of the hardest things in life is loving someone you know you can't shelter or protect.

So what is Jesus' plan? What's he going to do now? Strangely, his plan is to keep offering the love of a mother hen. Keep spreading his wings. He will offer his life to Herod on our behalf. He will follow us into the darkness we have chosen for ourselves, over and over again. He will place *himself* between that darkness and us.

And if you look closely at this man hanging on the cross, his arms eternally outstretched, the span of his reach on that wood will begin to resemble the loving wings of a mother hen, gathering up her chicks in a love that doesn't make sense but breaks our hearts if we look long enough.

Jesus does not count on the world ever seeing or understanding such love. And even as he hangs there with wings nailed to a tree, he cannot make us love him. Cannot make us accept his love.

But his desire for us is there. Always, eternally there. "How often have I desired to gather your children together as a hen gathers her brood under her wings, and you were not willing." He said that 2,000 years ago. He says that today.

Jesus was a powerful teacher. A worker of miracles. A prophet who shook this world to its foundations. But you know what? I've decided that he is not all-powerful. That may sound shocking and even unorthodox, but he's not. There is one little thing that Jesus needs of you. One thing that he desires but cannot (or will not) control.

He desires your will. Your proud, defiant control over your destiny. To relinquish that is both the hardest and the sweetest thing we'll ever do.

Every day we start again.

---

1. I am indebted to Barbara Brown Taylor for pointing out the curious choice of this metaphor (given other biblical options) in "As a Hen Gathers Her Brood" *The Christian Century* (February 25, 1986), p. 201.

2. Frederick Buechner, *Peculiar Treasures: A Biblical Who's Who* (Harper-SanFrancisco, 1979), p. 54.

**Lent 3**
**Luke 13:1-9**

# Headlines And Holiness

Imagine for a moment that Jesus is watching television with his twelve disciples. They're on furlough from teaching and healing, taking it easy in the living room of Peter's mother-in-law, doing a little mindless channel surfing. Maybe they catch a little of an NCAA Tournament game, March Madness. These are *guys*, you know, just relaxing from a demanding schedule.

But eventually the evening news comes on. They put down the popcorn and listen intently to the day's tragedies. One disciple says, "Hey, Jesus, that horrible bombing over on the West Bank where that guy drove a bus into a crowd of people. Do you think that because these Palestinians suffered in this way they were worse sinners than the rest?" It was a popular question in Jesus' day. Still is. If something bad happened, it must have been for a reason. Jesus scratches his beard for a moment. "No, they didn't die because of anything they did. It was a purely random thing. But let me tell you something. Unless you guys clean up your acts, you'll die just as tragically."

There is a low murmur in the room. The disciples look at each other like Jesus has missed his morning medication. As two begin to leave to find a bathroom, the newscaster reports another catastrophe, this one halfway across the world. Jesus pipes up this time. "Hey, guys," he says, "those people over in El Salvador. What about them? The earthquake that hit there killed hundreds of people. Does that mean that these Salvadorans were worse sinners than their neighbors in Guatemala?" Jesus waits for his question to sink in. "No, the tragedy had nothing to do with their morals. Those people just got in the way." The disciples breathe a sigh of relief, gladdened to know that God doesn't work that way. But then Jesus looks at them all. "Let me tell you something, though. Unless you people start going in the right direction, you will share a similar fate as those Salvadorans and it will seem like a building falling on your head to crush the life out of you." I believe somebody got up and changed the channel after that.

Am I getting these details right? For my money, this story of Jesus and the day's headlines is as strange and befuddling as any in the Gospels. What was Jesus thinking? His followers were clearly concerned about the news events of the day. Both reports are about atrocities visited upon innocents. One news story describes a case of evil devised by intentional malice. Pilate gruesomely kills some Galileans as they knelt at worship. The other story describes suffering by random chance. Eighteen people over near the pool of Siloam are crushed because they happened to be at the wrong place at the wrong time. These two headlines pretty much cover the waterfront of any modern headline that deals with suffering. Any sad news report. A bad person caused it *or* someone was in the wrong place at the wrong time — malice or chance, take your pick.

Whichever you choose, the followers of Jesus want to try to make sense of suffering. A popular response was to try to find purpose, some reason, for the events of the day. "Were these *worse* sinners, Jesus?" Behind that question was an underlying assumption: *these people must have done something really, horribly bad to cause God to abandon them in this way.*

Such assumptions are still very much with us. Many well-meaning Christians, uncomfortable with saying, "I don't know," need to produce a reason for everything that happens. For example, people get AIDS only because they are sexually promiscuous. Little children die because it was time for God to call them home. This catastrophe is happening to you now because of what you did thirty years ago. Christians are often uncomfortable with ambiguity, so we often concoct a preposterous reason to explain things. Certainty is a false god that brings comfort to many. Thankfully, Jesus parts ways with these assumptions. "Were these *worse* sinners, Jesus?" Twice, he says, "No."

But watch what Jesus does. He does indeed part ways with those who want to say bad things happen only to bad people. "No, I tell you, it doesn't work that way," he says. But neither will Jesus spend much time with the faith-shaking, all-time favorite question of "enlightened" Christians. Why do bad things happen to *good people*? I get asked that all the time. In fact, I ask it all the time myself. We pick up the newspaper, listen to the evening news, and ask, *Where is God? Could God not have prevented this tragedy? Was God asleep or something?* And our real unspoken question is perhaps this: *Does God even act in the world today at all? Is this whole life simply an exercise in randomness?* Theologians today say that the number one question facing young people in this country is not atheism, whether or not God exists, but rather the question of meaninglessness,[1] whether there's any real purpose to anything at all.

It's rather peculiar that Jesus doesn't really tackle our favorite questions in this story. He doesn't go there, even though he could have, even though we wish he would indulge us at least for a moment. Here's a perfect opportunity to talk about the very thing that troubles us: *Where is God? Why doesn't God do something?* Endlessly interesting questions for most of us. Instead, Jesus does a rather shocking thing.

They are all sitting around watching the evening news, stories of malice, stories of chance, and Jesus says the unthinkable. "No, I tell you; but unless you repent, you will all perish just as they did." Jesus, Mr. Compassion, said that. The gentle man who frolicked with children and bunnies. "Turn yourself around or you can count on a building collapsing on you some day on the way to work." What *is* that, anyway? Wouldn't you love to have Jesus at your hospital bedside? Wouldn't Jesus make a great teacher of pastoral care? "Pastor, did I get this colon cancer because of anything I did in my past?" "Heavens, no," is Jesus' pastoral response. "Where'd you get that idea? Don't give it another thought. But before we pray, let me share this little tidbit with you. Unless you clean up your act, my friend, it's curtains for you." The gospel of the Lord.

What is Jesus doing here? I'll tell you what he's doing. He is slyly shifting the conversation away from God's responsibility and

139

toward us. We love the God question. *Where was God when this happened?* It may be our all-time favorite philosophical question. One of the real classics. Not only that, it is also quite easy to watch the evening news and point out examples of really evil people and really evil events. The nation breathed easier, for example, when Timothy McVeigh was finally executed. One less atrocious human being in the world. It's easy to spot people like him. We are far *less* comfortable, however, discussing our own role in the suffering and injustice of this world.

And we may say to Jesus, "Look, I never slit anybody's throat. I never designed a shoddily constructed building that collapsed on anybody." And you would be right. But Jesus is saying today, at least in part, that the headlines that grab our attention and raise our moral revulsion are finally a smokescreen for the more subtle sin that is in each of us. And who is to say that such collective sin does not do more damage — more damage to the ecosystem, more damage to the hope of eradicating global poverty, and more damage to the widening racial divisions in our country than a *boatload* of evil villains and a *century's worth* of natural disasters?

It is far easier, you see, to locate evil in somebody or something else rather than in ourselves. Far easier to rant and rave at the evening news rather than ask what I'm going to do about that or consider how the way I now live may, in fact, be contributing to the problem.

Today Jesus will not allow his followers to blame others or God. He turns their philosophical gymnastics squarely back on them.

Jim Wallis, one of the founding members of the "Sojourners" community in Washington, D.C., writes these pointed words:

> *Many think conversion is only for nonbelievers, but the Bible sees conversion as also necessary for the erring believer, the lukewarm community of faith, the people of God who have fallen into disobedience and idolatry ... [Our task] is not to make the gospel easy but to make it clear ... evangelism should call for (and expect) a radical change in behavior and lifestyle.*[2]

140

It is easy for Christianity to exist in a vacuum, shouting condemnations of what we are "against" in the world. It is quite easy to talk back to the evening news and rail about the world's problems. Exponentially more difficult is being honest about the sin in ourselves.

Jesus knows something that we often forget. It isn't the headlines that define the world's problems. It's us. We're all the problem. "For three years I've come looking for fruit on this tree, and still I find none."

Ultimately, our obsession with headlines is just a diversion from the real territory Jesus wants to enter. There are bloody tragedies every day across our country and world. I don't deny that. But perhaps our focus should return to the spilt blood of the cross, sown into our lives at Lent.

More fruit will be harvested there than from a lifetime of watching the evening news.

---

1. See, for example, Douglas John Hall's excellent book, *Why Christian? For Those on the Edge of Faith* (Minneapolis: Fortress Press, 1998), especially pages 35-62.

2. Jim Wallis, *The Call To Conversion: Recovering the Gospel for These Times* (HarperSanFrancisco, 1992), pp. 7, 17.

**Lent 4**
**Luke 15:1-3, 11b-32**

# The Waster

We live in a world where the concept of fairness is nearly elevated to a level of worship. If you live or work with children on a regular basis then you will recognize that most squabbles erupt from this very old emotion of feeling somehow slighted or mistreated. *He got a tablespoon more Moose Tracks ice cream than I did. No fair! Why does she get to stay up a half-hour later than I do? That's not fair! She got to sit in the front seat last time. It's not fair that I always have to sit in the back. Sally's curfew is 1:30. Why do I have to be home at midnight?* I've decided that if you're going to be an effective parent in the twenty-first century then you might consider enrolling in law school first. A parent needs the wisdom of a judge and the memory of an elephant. Wisdom to hand down rulings on a moment's notice and a memory to recall past court cases so that at least a semblance of fairness might be projected to all parties involved.

If you think we outgrow this obsession with fairness, think again. It's as old as Eden and so deeply imbedded in our collective marrow that most people take it to the grave. I've seen adult strangers argue over their place in line at Wal-Mart. I've seen loving family members get in a tiff after a funeral over who gets what in the will. All over issues of fairness. And you might say to yourself, "Oh, I would never do something like that." I was coming back from the hospital the other day, waiting patiently as interstate traffic funneled down to one lane, and here came a teenager in a sports car, blowing past those in line, looking for a place to sneak in. What did I do? Hey, I tried to cut him off. He wasn't getting in front of me. It wasn't fair.

According to the dictionary, the word "prodigal" is an adjective that means "recklessly wasteful." "Prodigal" is derived from the Latin word *prodigere*, which is translated as the verb "to squander." Therefore, a prodigal son is literally a wasteful son, one who throws away opportunities recklessly and wastefully.

The younger son in this famous parable is a waster. He is one of the most famous rogues in the entire Bible. In our soap opera imaginations we can read between the lines and pencil in all the sordid ways he must have wasted his inheritance. He had a good case of the "gimmee's." "Give me the share of the property that will belong to me." He takes the money and blows it on "dissolute living." The story actually doesn't go into detail here about what such dissolute living entails but a vast panorama of fanciful options stands before a wasteful young man with a pocketful of change.

In 1636, Rembrandt painted a suggestive portrait of a jaunty, saucy, debonair Prodigal with a pencil-thin moustache. He wears a hat with enough plumage to take flight while hoisting a large flute of ale, itself over a foot tall. There is a young lady on his lap enjoying the fun while (in the original painting) another lass sans clothing plays a mandolin in the background. A peacock pie on the table suggests the arrogance of the scene. In *Rembrandt and the Bible*, a note says that the great painter used himself as a model for this particular canvas[1], which might tell us more than we'd like to know about how parables are supposed to work.

We know this story well. We know all about this Prodigal, this waster. And what we don't know, our imaginations are more than happy to provide. And we know all about the father, too, who takes back his rogue of a son even before the confession gets completely confessed. The father runs across the field and smothers his son with kisses, a robe, a ring, and a huge party. Come to think of it, many would call him a "waster" too. For who would spend so much so foolishly? Especially on somebody who doesn't deserve it? I don't know what you'd call it. I'd call it a huge waste.

But even though you may have sown a few wild oats in your past, grateful to be taken back and forgiven, my guess is that you

144

probably identify most with the older brother in this old story. Jesus definitely wants his listeners to see the folly in the older brother's behavior, but, darn it, slip into his shoes for just a second and see if you don't sympathize.

What has the older son been doing as the sun is setting in this story? In short, he has been working his hind end off all day. Make that all month, because he's been doing his own work plus that of his brother for weeks now. He is exhausted, his boots smell of cow manure, and he could certainly use a shower. And then he hears it — music and dancing. The Greek word here for "music" is interesting. The older brother hears the *symphonia*. Not just a fiddle and a banjo player. He hears a "symphony" of instruments, a veritable orchestra of merriment.

Befuddlement is not the right word to describe the older brother's reaction. He knows his old man doesn't throw parties on weekdays. Someone finally breaks the news. It is too much to bear. Robe, ring, and fatted calf — an unbelievably excessive trinity of welcome for someone's who's been a royal jerk. "Father, give me the share of the property that will belong to me," said the younger son before he left. I don't know whether you noticed, but he was asking his dad to execute the will before the old man stopped breathing. In effect, the younger son was saying, "Drop dead, Dad."

So tell the truth. Had you been in the older brother's shoes, working double shifts while your younger brother lived it up, would you have gone in to the party? A tongue-lashing, yes. Some clearly-defined way to make up for all the heartache, yes. A definite period of visible remorse, yes. *But a party?* Be honest. There is something primitive and basic afoot here that tweaks our sense of moral outrage. I'll tell you why you probably wouldn't have gone in: *it simply wasn't fair.*

There are many theological nuggets to mine in this old story. But this is perhaps the most basic: *God isn't fair.* Sorry. God doesn't play by our rules, see life the way we see it, or keep score the way we keep it. God isn't fair. And if we're honest, we won't be tickled pink by that. Why? Because it is precisely a sense of fairness that floats most of our ethical boats.

145

God isn't fair. And not only that: God has an ongoing love affair with sinners. He throws a party of rich food and drink to get their attention. He invites the undeserving. Dances with ne'er-do-wells. Slips a ring on their finger. Curious word: "ring." It appears only here and one other instance in the entire New Testament. Perhaps the implication is that Jesus is eternally "wedded" to sinners.

So let's step back outside with the older brother, still in need of a shower, arms folded across his chest, the moral high road. "But when this son of yours came back ... you killed the fatted calf for him." He cannot even bring himself to acknowledge his brother with a name — "this son of yours." A sense of unfairness, as you know, can turn venomous rather quickly.

So where are we at parable's end? Are we inside the party celebrating? Or are we standing outside with our arms folded, refusing to come in? Jesus will not tell us how this story will end. The father passionately invites the older son inside, "pleads with him" to join in the welcome. Curiously, however, we are never told what the older brother decides to do. The story ends but it doesn't end. You can almost hear the voice of Walter Cronkite saying, "YOU ARE THERE." Will we RSVP to a party thrown by an unfair God? Or will we stubbornly remain outside?

In a world where God does not play fair, this parable forces us to make a choice. Who is the real "prodigal" here? Who is the real "waster"? From the beginning Jesus says that this is a story about two brothers. Which one is the authentic prodigal? Which one has yet to come home to the Father's extravagant love?

We can waste our lives keeping score and complaining about unfairness. We can harbor grudges to the grave. We can completely misunderstand what Jesus is all about even as we worship every Sunday. We can waste life waiting for apologies, waiting for people to act decently and fairly, waiting for others to earn our forgiveness and acceptance. Jesus waited on none of those things. As I recall, his words as they nailed his hands and feet, his words as they rammed the crown of thorns over his brow until the blood trickled were *not*: "You'll get yours, sucker." Remember? "Father, forgive them; for they do not know what they are doing" (Luke 23:34). He too has a gracious dad who welcomes sinners.

Every Sunday, God throws a party for sinners. Some of us have recently been in a "far country" and we are making our way back home. And others, perhaps working hard in the fields of the Lord for years, have slipped into a Christianity that is more about controlling God's love than celebrating it. An orchestra of voices, a *symphonia*, a communion of saints, calls one and all to the table. The judge of the world presides. But let me warn you. He is not fair. Will not play favorites. But clearly likes to throw a party.

So who is the real prodigal? It's not the one with a shady past. It's the one who stays outside. The one who could not bring himself to forgive. "This brother of yours was dead and has come to life; he was lost and has been found." The one we usually call "prodigal" is alive. Found. That means the dead one, the lost one, is the one who stubbornly chooses to remain outside the Father's party.

What a waste.

---

1. Hidde Hoekstra, *Rembrandt and the Bible* (Weert, Netherlands: Magna Books, 1990), p. 337.

# Costly Extravagance

"Why was this perfume not sold for three hundred denarii and the money given to the poor?" Well, it's not a bad question. Judas may have been a thief and informant, he may have embezzled money from the common purse occasionally, he may have had other motives besides the high moral road he seems to project, and he probably really didn't give a fig for the poor. But isn't he basically right? Couldn't the pound of expensive perfume dumped on Jesus' feet have been used for a better purpose? I must admit that I wish Mary had chosen the less expensive Oil of Olay or maybe just a bottle of good old English Leather. Nard was imported from the Himalayas, for crying out loud! Couldn't the money have been used to buy food for a starving family or improve the miserable housing in Jesus' neighborhood?

Just how much did Mary's generous act cost anyway? Judas, who probably knew more than most the going rate for such a Nieman-Marcus extravagance, suggests that the perfume could have been sold for 300 denarii. A footnote in my Bible reports that a denarius was "a day's wage" for most people. You can do the math. Figure a six-day work week with the Sabbath off and you're basically looking at close to a year's salary. A year's salary on Jesus' *feet*? Translate that to today's economy and, conservatively, we're talking about $30,000 poured onto Jesus.

Why did Mary do such a thing? Did his feet smell that bad? Jesus suggests that the perfume has something to do with his upcoming burial. But Mary couldn't have known that. And even if she did, doesn't she go a little overboard with the funeral expenses? She reminds me of those people who choose the most expensive casket possible only to have it buried in the ground. That's essentially what happens to this perfume. It's wasted. A year's salary could have helped a lot of needy people. That's Judas' point. And if you ask me, it's not a bad point, even if he was a thief.

But Jesus says, "Leave her alone." The fragrance of the perfume was absolutely permeating every nook and cranny of the house, a veritable olfactory circus in your nose, and Jesus says, "Get off her case." And then he says something that sounds a mite confusing, if not downright callous. He says, "You always have the poor with you, but you do not always have me." Now what does Jesus mean by that? That the poor can go fly a kite? Is he giving the green light to garish narthex statues given to glorify God by wealthy benefactors across the world? This verse has been used to justify more than one massive church building program. What does Jesus mean by these words?

Twenty years ago I used to teach school in Camden, South Carolina. It was a classroom for educable mentally-handicapped children and most of my students were very poor. I remember a little girl named Natasha in my class who brought me a Christmas present that December just before the winter break. She was plump and very shy and hardly ever spoke. After the bell rang for the bus on the last day before vacation, she came up to my desk and handed me a present. A very nice present I might add, a present that I'm sure cost more than her family could afford. I didn't need the gift and was reasonably sure her mom and dad could use the money. Natasha was so proud standing there. Her family was grateful that I'd taken an interest in their daughter. They didn't need to buy me a gift. But they were so very grateful. What could I do but hug that little girl and say, "Thanks"?

John Vannorsdall tells the story of the first congregation he served, a country church where many of the members had gardens. A parishioner asked, "Would you like some carrots, pastor?" He answered, "A few would be nice." The next day a bushel of carrots appeared on the parsonage porch. Vannorsdall recalls wondering,

"A bushel of carrots for two people? Were they crazy? Not at all; just grateful to God, just happy. A bushel of carrots for the pastor was an exuberant way of returning thanks. We ate what we could."[1]

You might ask, "Well, if Jesus accepted a $30,000 foot massage, would he also drive a Lexus? Would he ski at Aspen? Would he stay at the Hyatt Regency? Would he always choose Ben and Jerry's?" To ask these questions is to miss the point. The record is clear that Jesus was a friend of the poor. The evidence is so overwhelming in the Gospels that we hardly need to mention this friendship.

Recall the setting of this story. This particular night he was eating dinner with a grateful family. Do you remember what happens one chapter earlier in this Gospel? Two sisters meet Jesus a few days after a funeral, completely overwhelmed with grief for their dead brother. They even get sort of testy and uppity with Jesus. "If you had been here, Jesus, our brother would not have died." Usually when a funeral is finished the mourners gather for a meal. The strange thing about this meal is that the deceased is present and even bellied up to the table. This very brother Lazarus now sits with Jesus, eating fried chicken and sipping sweet tea. How grateful are the sisters? We aren't told the specifics about Martha but she has a track record in the Bible for whipping up some marvelous meals. I've no doubt that the table was set impeccably. And I'm sure that a plate of her award-winning biscuits graced the feast that night and certainly one of her desserts she cranked out only for the most special occasions. She was a grateful sister. Her brother was back.

We know more about Mary's impetuous response. She too was grateful and brought out what could have been a nest egg for the family, maybe their life savings, and anointed the feet of the one to whom she owed everything. Maybe she overdid it. Maybe she got carried away. Should Jesus have scolded her for wasting such an expensive gift in such a foolish way? "Leave her alone," he said. This is a dinner where two grateful sisters give thanks to Jesus for restoring a once-dead brother. Was the response extravagant? Did Mary overdo it? Probably. But how could Jesus have done anything except receive the gifts of two grateful sisters who brought him presents from their once-broken hearts?

So Mary anoints Jesus' feet. I find it interesting in the Gospel of John that in the very next chapter Jesus is *washing* the feet of his disciples, an action that clearly points to service in the world. John seems to be saying that there is a connection between honoring Jesus and serving Jesus. Between loving God and loving neighbor.

Maybe Mary goes overboard in honoring Jesus. Maybe she overdoes it. That is not really our modern problem, though, is it? Our problem is usually *underdoing* it — a paltry, miserly response. Taking Jesus for granted. Going days without consulting him in prayer, assuming he's aware of our gratitude and thankfulness. Rightly seeking to help and serve poor people but neglecting the primary relationship with Jesus that keeps sending us into the world to wash feet. Giving lip-service to the importance of honoring the man in order to get on with the real business of the church.

You know, as I look closely at this story I don't think it's about frugality or money at all. Not centrally, even though it seems to be. This story is mainly about gratitude and recognizing what Jesus has done in our lives. And whether you're rich or whether you're poor, there is a common call to stop, slow down, and give thanks. There will be time to serve the poor. As Jesus says, they are always with us. Never has that call been more pressing or obvious for the world's Christians.

Our honoring of Jesus may not involve money or perfume at all. But the act itself, like Mary's, will "fill the house" (read: the church) with a certain fragrance. It is the fragrance of love, devotion, and gratitude for one who has loved us so lavishly and in such a costly, costly way. Three hundred denarii can't begin to touch it. How do you honor and say thanks to someone who has saved your brother's life? Indeed, saved your own life?

Mary's gift was both "costly" and extravagant, even lavish. She was overcome with joy and thankfulness. Maybe she overdid it. On a Friday afternoon so many years ago, Jesus offered his own costly and extravagant gift. Pray that we will not "underdo" it as we seek to honor him in our lives this Lent.

152

Jesus brought life into Mary's world of death and she was grateful.

Our move.

---

1. John W. Vannorsdall, "Elephant Blessings and Other Extravagance" *The Lutheran* (January 4, 1989), p. 18.

# Salvation At The Skull

I remember pulling into a gas station once when I was sixteen years old and just learning to drive in Chattanooga. The tires were squealing badly on 90-degree turns and I didn't know a lot about cars but knew enough to know it was time to find an air pump. Somehow I'd missed the lesson in proper tire inflation but had seen people do it and was reasonably confident that I could handle the job with no problem.

So I pulled in, unscrewed the little caps on the valve stems, and grabbed a hose, ready to inflate to the required pressure. Kneeling down, I squeezed the trigger on that hose expecting air, but out shot a rather fast stream of water, soaking my pants in the process and reddening my face. I was very shy at sixteen with little self-confidence and quickly surveyed the parking lot to make sure no one had witnessed this bone-headed act. Sort of like when you fall down in public and quickly look around to see who's watching.

Well, there they were. Four older guys across the parking lot had seen it all and were having a grand old time at my expense. I remember one of them almost falling out of the car with laughter. I was mortified, completely humiliated. I had also purchased gas at the station but almost drove away without paying for it. It would have been easier to face the police. I had to walk right past them. One of them made that unmistakable dopey laugh like Walt Disney's "Goofy." It seemed like an eternity before I finally got out of there. There they were in my rearview mirror, still slapping their knees and having a ball. I do not recall the exact wording of my prayer of vengeance that day. But my beseechings to our Lord were quite inventive, colorful, and creative. "Smite them, O God, as you did your enemies of old." I took a 90-degree right out of the parking lot and can still hear the squeal of those under-inflated tires that never did get air that day or maybe that month.

Jesus hangs on a cross today at a place called "The Skull" and three sets of people take turns mocking him: the religious leaders, the soldiers, and even one of the criminals who hangs there beside him. They mock him and laugh at him and tack a funny sign over his head. It said, "King of the Jews," but if somebody had replaced it with a sign that said, "Goofy," I'm sure there would have been no objections.

The mockery heard by Jesus comes from different angles. But did you notice that the gist of the humiliation is very similar from all three perspectives? The leaders say, "He saved others; let him save himself!" The soldiers chide, "If you are the King of the Jews, save yourself!" A crucified criminal mocks, "Aren't you the Messiah? Save yourself and us!"

*Save yourself.* Well, why not? He fed 5,000 people with a few fish and some scraps of bread. He walked on water, even turned it into wine. He healed a blind man with a bit of mud and a promise. He even raised a family friend from the dead! Why did Jesus just hang there and allow it to happen? Why didn't he *do* something? Why didn't he show those wiseacres a thing or two? "Smite them, O God, as you did your enemies of old." That's the prayer we'd expect from Jesus. Instead we get this goofy prayer: "Father, forgive them; for they do not know what they are doing." What sort of prayer is that? "Save yourself," say all three. "Show us your power." Why *didn't* he show them?

Flannery O'Connor, the late American fiction writer who was also a devout Roman Catholic, once said this about the demise of the modern novel: "People without hope not only don't write novels, but what is more to the point, they don't read them. They don't take long looks at anything because they lack the courage." What O'Connor said about the novel is also true about the cross.

It is hard for us to look at the cross for very long. Indeed, it is hard for many Americans to take a "long look at anything" except maybe the half-hour sit-com where the problem is both introduced and solved in the span of thirty minutes, including commercials. Our modern response to the cross is remarkably familiar. "What are you doing up there? Save yourself, for heaven's sake." We turn away. We refuse to take a long look. Church attendance figures in congregations across the country don't lie. Exponentially more people attend services on Easter Sunday compared to Good Friday. We want Jesus off the cross and raised. "Save yourself and us!"

I don't trust statistics much, but here are some interesting ones. In the year 1900, Christians in Europe and North America comprised 77 percent of the world Christian population. Over three-quarters. The figure in 1998 was 38 percent. By 2025, estimations project the number will shrink to 27 percent.[1] Here's an interesting little twist. American churches used to send missionaries to the far, dark reaches of the world to share the gospel. We still send some. But now the trend is that those far, dark reaches of the world are sending Christian missionaries to America. Now isn't that rich? The upshot of this is that the cross, sacrificial dying on behalf of others, does not hold much appeal for many, many Americans and Europeans. But in developing nations that struggle with widespread poverty and suffering, Christianity is booming.

"Save yourself!" they shouted. Isn't that our national anthem of sorts? "Save yourself! Show us some power, some fireworks, some glitter." All three voices in the story are essentially saying the same thing. They cannot imagine that the cross means anything other than "Goofy" is dead. They cannot look long enough at the cross to take it seriously for their lives. So they glance and shake their heads in common derision.

But one man does look. He senses the mysterious paradox in the death of this innocent man who "has done nothing wrong." He looks at Jesus hanging there — powerless, humiliated, silent before his tormentors. And maybe that man with a shady past looked a long time that long afternoon. And he saw something in Jesus that the others didn't. "Remember me," he said. "Remember me." He didn't say, "Save me." He didn't say, "Get me out of this, will ya?" He just said he wanted to be remembered. To have Jesus recall his life. It's interesting. That's what Jesus asks of us, too. To remember him. "Do this in remembrance of me. Look at my body and not turn away."

On some days it would be greatly satisfying to have a God who would rescue us from all calamity and danger; a God who smites bullies at the gas station and saves us from all humiliation, pain, and suffering. A "Mighty Mouse" God who flies from the heavens singing, *"Here I come to save the daaay!"*

But that is not the Christian God, unfortunately. Or maybe fortunately. The Christian God invites us to look long and hard at the cross. Occasional glancing won't cut it. In fact, if you think you've got the cross figured out, that's a sure bet you probably haven't. Refusing to avert our eyes, we hang there in our own crucifying moments and slowly drink in the life that is Jesus. "Remember me," we say. "Remember me when you come into your kingdom."

Many, many years ago, at a place called "The Skull," other dominant voices rang out. "Come down from the cross. Are you not the Christ? Show us then! *Save* yourself and us!"

By staying there, he has.

---

1. These figures are from an article by Darrell L. Guder, "Missional Theology for a Missionary Church" *Journal for Preachers* (Advent 1998), p. 3. He is citing work from the *International Bulletin of Missionary Research*.

# Pilate Pops The Question

I ran across a story recently of a pastor from South Africa who had just finished his first year of ministry as a pastor in the United States. He had served congregations in two countries and gotten a pretty good idea of the challenges facing the church in both places. When asked to compare and contrast the two settings, he had this to say: "I am still trying to come to terms with a culture where Mother's Day and Father's Day are more obligatory days of church attendance than is Good Friday."[1]

*Where are you from?* I was in Boston several years ago for my brother's wedding. My older brother walked into a convenience store and asked for something in his thick Tennessee accent. The cashier audibly laughed, physically turned, and yelled toward the stockroom, "Hey, Marge! Come on out here and listen to this guy talk!"

*Where are you from?* When a son or daughter brings home the first boy or girlfriend from college that's about the first thing parents want to know. "Where's she from? Where'd he grow up?" We want to know all about this person's family — who their people are, what they do for a living.

*Where are you from?* After studying genealogy research techniques with the Mormons in Salt Lake City for several Elderhostel sessions, my mother can now tell her children all about their lineage and background and all the darkness and light down through the generations of our family. For example, my great-grandfather, for whom I'm named, was once the sheriff of Cabarrus County in North Carolina during the early part of last century. He was against

159

capital punishment but in December of 1908 presided over the last legal hanging in that county. I daresay you've got strange stories rattling around in your past, too. The tales reveal our origins, our odd assortment of forebears.

*Where are you from?* Our answer to that question is no small source of family pride or perhaps even pain. The answer has to do with homeplace, geography, generations, momma, daddy, family. Most of us can answer the question with a fair degree of accuracy. If truth were told, it's probably why we hold up Mother's Day and Father's Day with all the honor of a high liturgical holy day. Maybe more if that South African pastor is right.

Pilate asks Jesus a very straightforward question today. "Where are you from?" Now Jesus could've told Pilate about his own family tree. Bethlehem, Nazareth, Joseph, Mary. He could've gone way back and named King David as his great-great-great (and then some) granddaddy. But he chose not to do that. "Where are you from?" asks Pilate. And Jesus says not a word.

Now *we* know the answer to that question. Jesus has already answered Pilate once. "My kingdom is not from this world. If my kingdom were from this world, my followers would be fighting. But as it is, well, I'm not from here." Pilate, as you may recall, got a little huffy with that first answer. By the time Jesus' final sentencing rolls around, Pilate isn't put out with Jesus at all. He's downright afraid of him. The text says, "more afraid than ever." So Pilate returns to his headquarters in the middle of the night and locates Jesus once more. *Now where'd you say you were from?* Pilate is as nervous as a caged cat.

Have you ever noticed in John's Gospel how downright calm Jesus seems to be as he faces his execution? After sassing the high priest, he's as cool as a cucumber when a policeman slaps him so hard you can hear the echo. Jesus never once questions his purpose in John or has even a hint of internal angst about his mission. You won't find the words, "My God, my God, why have you forsaken me?" in this story. In the other three Gospels, somebody carries Jesus' cross for him. In John, Jesus himself lifts the lumber. Even though the authorities eventually kill him, Jesus still seems to be completely in control of the proceedings. Remember back in the

160

garden, when the soldiers come to get him? He never once resists. "When Jesus said to them, 'I am he,' they stepped back and fell to the ground" (18:6). In the Greek he actually says, "I am" to the soldiers. The divine name from Exodus, the name revealed to Moses at the burning bush, is found here on the lips of Jesus. "I am," he says to the powers that arrive with darkness. And the soldiers hit the deck. These same powers do indeed execute Jesus eventually. But please note: they are never in control. The one hanging on the cross, in apparent weakness, is paradoxically in charge. *Now where'd you say you were from?* Pilate asks, "more afraid than ever."

Now we the tellers of this story, we the insiders who are aware of the outcome, know exactly where Jesus is from. And, people of God, he ain't from here! He's from a kingdom that makes Pilate's domain look like adult bullies playing with tinker toys. Pilate and his cronies have no power over Jesus and we know exactly why. "My kingdom is not of this world." Don't we know this? Nobody can touch Jesus. Not *our* Jesus. Not even the most well-managed evil, the most heinous suffering, the most brutal jabs and taunts in the world. "Where are you from?" Pilate asks. And we know the answer to that question that makes Mr. High And Mighty Muckety-Muck, the model of decorum and control, so nervous. *See who's sweating?* See? Not Jesus. Never once is he out of control in this story. He knows where he's from; knows who his real daddy is. Jesus is in handcuffs before Pilate, but who has the real power?

We know this answer and get an "A" every Good Friday, every Easter. This day gets a little more complicated, however, when we realize something. We know where Jesus is from and why he triumphed over the power of evil, but we are mired in something of an identity crisis in the twenty-first century church nonetheless. Why? Because we forget where *we* are from. Or else we pretend we don't know. In a prayer that Jesus prays just before those soldiers arrive, he says to God, "Father, I have given [my followers] your word, and the world has hated them because they do not belong to the world, just as I do not belong to the world" (17:14). Did I hear the man correctly? *They do not belong to the world.* He's talking about us.

161

"Where are you from?" Pilate asks Jesus. But the question is also our own. Must be our own. If we are his disciples, his followers, we will have a fairly good idea how to respond. And how we answer, truly answer, will have everything to do with our commitments, how we spend our money and time, whom we name as descendants on our family tree, and how our allegiance to God is lived out concretely in the here and now. Our answer will determine how we face evil and temptation, how we handle suffering, how we maintain quiet confidence in the midst of crisis, how we bear our own crosses, and how we relate to people of ill-will who wish to harm us.

Jesus knew his true origins. "My kingdom is not of this world." People of God, we are baptized into this same homeland. Our true citizenship is elsewhere. This doesn't lessen our responsibilities here. In fact, it may heighten them. Such a confession surely clarifies why we're here in the first place.

The church faces myriad challenges in a new century. To face them we must first come to terms with a little question Pilate posed to Jesus so long ago. It also our question.

*Now where'd you say you were from?*

---

1. L. Gregory Jones, "Evil and Good Friday" *The Christian Century* (April 12, 2000), p. 432.

**Easter**
**Luke 24:1-12**

# Resurrection And Remembrance

Down through the centuries there have been various and sundry attempts to try to discredit the resurrection of Jesus — some amusing, some rather outrageous. The "stolen body" hypothesis is perhaps the most popular among the many explanations. This theory supposes that grave robbers tampered with the tomb and moved the corpse of Christ in the middle of the night. Some suggest the robbers were disciples. Others maintain it was Pilate in an attempt to squash a movement that was born anyway.

Then there's the "wrong tomb" theory. The women just got turned around in the dark on that first Easter morning. When they come to the wrong tomb in the early a.m., they see a couple of gardeners who say (and this is biblical), "He is not here." What they meant to say was, "He's really *over there*. He is not here." But the women flee in panic and the rest is history.

Have you ever heard of the "lettuce" theory? Also known by some scholars as the "salad" theory? In this scenario, the gardener gets so ticked at curiosity-seekers trampling his new lettuce garden that he physically removes the body of Jesus and plants it elsewhere. I am not making these up. These are bona-fide historical theories.[1]

And there's really no time to mention the "rapid-decay" hypothesis where in Palestine's hot, muggy climate the body simply decomposed at a rather alarming rate. Or my personal favorite, the "twin brother" conjecture. You can probably figure out the gist of that one on your own. One of the latest explanations, offered by John Dominic Crossan at DePaul University, is that Jesus' body was probably eaten by dogs like most of the other criminals crucified at that time.

I find each of these theories rather laughable. They each come at Easter from a rational, scientific angle that attempts to enter the tomb with a test tube. "The facts just don't add up, Mr. Watson, so it can't be true." Presto, resurrection disproved. Others, you may have noted, have entered the tomb through another door, also with a test tube, trying to *prove* the resurrection. The Shroud of Turin comes to mind, which is somewhat similar to the misguided search for Noah's Ark. "I've got the DNA, dated the carbon-14, Mr. Watson. So Easter, we can all rest assured about this, is really true after all." Trying to prove the resurrection is a little like trying to prove the existence of God. The truth of Easter, like the truth of the Creator, is not deduced through experiments. Resurrection is an enterprise of faith. And faith, I have come to know, is an exercise in remembering.

*Something* happened in the lives of the first disciples that transformed them from cowardly, frightened, timid followers at Jesus' death to bold, courageous advocates of the Word who risked life and limb for Jesus in the book of Acts. Most of the disciples were martyred for their faith. Myths are important and powerful windows to the truth. But myths do not make martyrs. I doubt that someone would die defending the salad theory.

I want you to notice something with me this morning. *When* does Easter happen for these women in Luke? They come down the path to embalm the body of Jesus. They see a stone rolled away and even enter an empty tomb. Does that do it for them? That's fairly strong Easter evidence. But no, an empty tomb does not do it. "They were perplexed about this," but no Easter.

How about the angels? The two guys in dazzling clothes? Now that's pretty impressive. One could believe a lot (right?) if visited by a pair of angels. Angels are all the rage these days. Is this enough to initiate belief? Something utterly paranormal? No, it is not. The women were "terrified" but Easter hasn't happened for them yet. There is this modern mantra about Easter that goes something like this: "If I had only been there and seen it with my eyes like those first disciples, then I could maybe become a follower of Jesus."

164

But these women were right there. They could feel the stone where Jesus' warm body had rested only hours before. They saw the folded grave jammies. They interviewed some angels. But still no Easter. So what caused Easter to happen in the hearts of Mary Magdalene, Joanna, Mary the mother of James, and the rest?

Look closely at the text from Luke. The angels don't come at these women with test tubes and various theological hypotheses. They don't try to talk them into Easter at all. "Remember," they say. "Remember how he told you." Verse 8 is short, but on it turns the reality and truth of Easter for these women. *Then they remembered his words.* Right there. Easter happens for these women right there and not a moment sooner. And Easter happens, please note, not because they were intellectually argued into it, but because they *remembered.* They remembered the words of Jesus. *Easter happened then.* And not one moment sooner.

What implications does such an Easter story have for modern Christians like us? Well, lots. We tend to want to prove it. Or disprove it. *Long live the intellect!* But what if Easter doesn't happen that way, not just for these women, but for anybody? What if Easter happens largely through remembering the words of Jesus, living the words of Jesus, being so thoroughly familiar with the words of Jesus that they're more important than our next breath? *Then they remembered his words.* But what if we don't know those words? What if we've forgotten them? Theophan the Recluse, a nineteenth-century Russian spiritual master, once wrote: "Everywhere and always God is with us, near to us, and in us. But we are not always with him, since we do not remember him." *Then they remembered his words.* Our forgetting the words does not cancel the reality of the risen Christ in the world. But our lack of memory severely restricts Easter happening in us.

And we are on the verge, as Christians here in America, of forgetting the words. We have a memory problem. We are inundated with 64 channels worth of words. We are bombarded with a "world wide web" of words. But the serious student of the Word of God is increasingly rare in our churches. We have stopped telling the story in our homes, stopped reading the Bible on a regular devotional basis.

Theologian Ellen Charry pointedly asks: "Unless our children know Jesus, what will protect them from hurting themselves and others?" (I might also ask that question of adults). "Accepting guidance from any source but the self — and especially looking for guidance from God — is looked upon as a sign of weakness [in our culture]."[2]

So how will resurrection happen among such a proud people? How will resurrection occur in rocky marriages? In friendships that have soured? In family squabbles? How will resurrection happen in a world struggling with addiction, poverty, and racism? How does Easter leap off the calendar and into our hearts? Well, how did Easter happen for the women at the tomb? *Then they remembered his words.* It behooves us to ask this Easter: *How many of Jesus' words are portable for us? What words of Jesus can we take into the tombs of this world, of this community? Are we truly allowing the words of Jesus to bore into our proud hearts?* Here in America, we undeniably have a memory problem.

You may have noticed the article in *Newsweek* magazine about the explosion of Christianity in developing nations.[3] The author of the article, Kenneth Woodward, spent three weeks traveling around the African continent. His car broke down twice and then a third time in a remote part of Nigeria. It was Sunday morning and Woodward was worried. "We had to fetch a village mechanic before he went to church," he says, *"because we knew he'd be there for hours."* In Africa, Latin America, and Asia, particularly its poorest pockets, the church is thriving. Here in the West, with notable exceptions, expressions of Christianity are severely compromised and weakening. The next pope, according to Woodward, will most likely be a wonderful man from Nigeria. And the dark "pagan" places where the American church once sent Christian missionaries are now sending their own missionaries to evangelize people in the United States! They have been sent, I think, to jog our memories. The center of the Christian world is shifting. And that may not be a bad thing for the American church, which has largely lost its way. It will cause us to focus once again on mission for a whole generation of marginally connected people.

*Then they remembered his words.* Maybe I'm missing something in the story today. But isn't *this* how Easter happens for these women? Isn't *this* how resurrection becomes real for them? Jesus' words come alive in their hearts in the context of a tomb. You are welcome to try to prove or disprove Easter with a test tube. But to tell you the truth, I'm not sure your findings will matter that much one way or the other.

Resurrection happens in our lives when we choose to cultivate a healthy Christian memory. When we remember his words. It behooves the American church, perhaps more than ever before, to teach and discover those words, daring to take them on the road into the tombs of our community.

Easter happened 2,000 years ago. But how does it happen today? When we remember his words.

---

1. Most of the theories discussed here are described in detail in Paul L. Maier's book, *In the Fullness of Time: A Historian Looks at Christmas, Easter and the Early Church* (HarperSanFrancisco, 1991), pp. 189-96.

2. Ellen Charry, "Raising Christian Children in a Pagan Culture" *The Christian Century* (February 16, 1994), p. 166.

3. Kenneth Woodward, "The Changing Face of the Church" *Newsweek* (April 16, 2001), pp. 46-52. The quote from the sermon appears in the "Bylines" section of the magazine (p. 6). The emphasis here is mine.

# Bearing The Scars

I remember taking my first real high school date to see the movie *Jaws* — that summer blockbuster from the mid-'70s that brought sharks as big as houses into the national imagination. I also recall fantasizing that perhaps my date would need to depend on a masculine shoulder in the face of such marine carnage. The truth of the matter is that my hands never stopped gripping my own armrests throughout the movie. She may not have been safe at the shore that summer, but she was certainly safe from me that night.

One of the few funny scenes in the movie is where Richard Dreyfuss and his companions begin comparing boating accidents and shark and barracuda bites, around the table one night. They begin showing each other their scars. A shirt is pulled up. A sock is tugged off. Pants are pulled down. These old sailors reveal more and more of their gouged flesh, their old, dated scars, utterly engaged in the art of one-upmanship. More and more clothing falls to the floor until they're standing in little more than their underwear. They finally look at each other, throw back their heads, and laugh. I think a shark bumps the boat right after that.

The resurrected Jesus makes several Easter appearances in our Gospels. Usually, though, he is hidden at first. Mary Magdalene mistakes Jesus for a gardener and not until our Lord speaks Mary's name does she finally recognize him. On the Emmaus road, Jesus walks along with two admirers. Neither has a clue who he might be. Not until he breaks some bread is Jesus' identity revealed. Another time, Jesus is on the beach one sunny morning and calls out

169

to the disciples who have returned to fishing. They don't recognize their Lord until he instructs them to cast their nets on the other side.

In today's reading, Jesus again reveals himself to the disciples. But once again they can't tell it's him. They are together on that first Easter evening, behind locked doors in fear. And who can blame them? Crucifixions in those parts were contagious. Mary has reported the fantastic, farfetched events of the morning. Suddenly Jesus stands among them and says, "Peace be with you." But they don't put two and two together. Not just yet. I don't know what they thought they were looking at, but they weren't thinking "Jesus."

Then he lifted up his shirt and pointed to the scar on his side. Then he pulled back the sleeves on his robe and showed them his palms (an ironic contrast to the "palms" waved only a week earlier). Maybe he even pulled off his sandals and showed them his feet. At any rate, he revealed how the Romans had roughed him up. The text reports these words: *"Then* the disciples rejoiced when they saw the Lord." Not a moment sooner. *Then*. Here's an important detail for latter-day followers: Those early disciples did not have a clue who was standing before them until Jesus showed them his scars. Only then did they rejoice.

Near the end of Homer's epic, *The Odyssey*, Odysseus finally returns home after many years of travel. But when he comes home, he is disguised as an old man. The aging family nurse, Eurycleia, begins to bathe the man she thinks is nobody more than some old stranger. Only when she sees Odysseus' old hunting wound, inflicted by a boar in his youth, does she come to recognition. Homer writes: "This was the scar the old nurse recognized; she traced it under her spread hands, then let it go, and into the basin fell the lower leg ... sloshing the water out ... her eyes filled up with tears; her throat closed and she whispered ... *'You are Odysseus!* Ah, dear child! I could not see you until now.' "[1]

Jesus showed them his wounds. The disciples rejoiced when they saw Jesus. They could not see him until then.

This easy-to-overlook detail has a lot to say to us modern church members. Here we have a risen Jesus, safe and sound in the bosom of his Father, past the trauma of Good Friday, nothing but good times ahead, and his friends haven't a clue who he is until he shows them his scars. There is a profound connection between the risen Christ and the scars of Christ. Easter does not totally negate Good Friday.

"Jesus will always bring you peace and joy." Ever heard anyone say that? "If you're a real Christian, you'll always have peace in your heart." Well, what if you feel great sadness? Does that mean you're not a real Christian? People bear real and traumatic scars from a real and traumatic past. But when Jesus comes, we are sometimes led to believe, then everything is rosy and gay. Not only do I think that's hogwash, I'm also fairly certain that *Jesus* feels it's hogwash. "He showed them his hands and his side." It wasn't a heavenly cloud that brought those Easter disciples a sense of peace and recognition. It was a scarred Jesus who dared to show them his wounds. Even Easter does not erase scars. "The problem with so many modern Christians," said Flannery O'Connor, "is that they want faith to be a warm electric blanket, when of course it is the cross."

So what does this story say about the modern church? What does it say about all of us who carry around scars and old wounds? It means, I think, that we are to find a way to show our scars to one another. To stop pretending they don't exist and stop believing the lie that good Christians with the right sort of faith don't have such scars. Perhaps the true test of an authentic church is to follow Jesus' lead. "He showed them his hands and his side." How will we show one another our wounds?

Perhaps this is what the doubting Thomases among us are really looking for. Authenticity. Do they doubt Jesus? Or his body, the church? Church is not about starched people who assemble for an hour each week, knowing little about one another. Church is about gathering around a *scarred Lord* who profoundly touches our *own scars* and unites us in community with precisely what we have in common: not our potential, not our social standing, not even our denominational theology, but primarily our woundedness. Perhaps we want an explanation for those wounds. Perhaps we want more than this story offers. "The only 'answer' [the Bible] gives to creaturely suffering is Jesus ... God's response to human suffering and to the 'groaning' of the whole creation is not theories *about* Jesus, but Jesus himself."[2]

And so he stands in the middle of the community. "Peace be with you," says this Jesus with palms outstretched, wounds wide open for examination. And when *we* say it to each other before Holy Communion each week, it is far more than a way of saying, "Good morning." It is sharing profound hope with another human being. It is offering the promise that Christ knows about your wounds, that peace is discovered in the healing bath and welcome table. Easter has a heck of a lot to do with Good Friday.

"Ah, dear child," said the old nurse Eurycleia upon discovering the wound. "I could not *see* you until now."

"He showed them his hands and his side. *Then* the disciples rejoiced."

It's a great comfort to me that Jesus' wounds were openly presented to his followers that first Easter evening. It is precisely how the disciples came to know that it was truly Jesus.

And perhaps that is still true. Perhaps others will come to know that Jesus is alive when his church dares to show their scars to one another and say, "Peace be with you."

"Unless I see the mark of the nails in his hands, I will not believe," said Thomas.

Jesus bore scars even on Easter. So must we come to terms with our own. Our scars are a large part of who we are. As we share them in community, perhaps Christ is saying: "Ah, dear child. I could not see you until now."

1. *The Odyssey*, translated by Robert Fitzgerald (New York: Anchor Books, 1963), p. 368. I am indebted to William Willimon for pointing out the connection between this passage and the Thomas story.

2. Douglas John Hall, "Suffering — God's Answer" *The Lutheran* (March 22, 1989), p. 6.

# The Gotcha God

There is the embarrassment of getting publicly caught. Private sins are bad enough but to be exposed red-handed before others, your picture on the front page of the newspaper, is something else entirely. *Gotcha.*

I once heard a story[1] of a gambling casino in Lake Tahoe that has a women's room at the top of a long flight of stairs. This bathroom is in full view of diners sitting at a handful of tables down below. Only one person at a time can use the facilities. Why am I telling you about a bathroom in Lake Tahoe? Well, this particular bathroom supposedly has a tasteful painting of a man who is wearing nothing but a strategically located fig leaf. And this very fig leaf in question is conveniently hinged, lift-able. You can probably guess where this is leading. Restroom users who are curious enough to peek under the hinged fig leaf set off a series of flashing lights, bells, and whistles down below in the restaurant. The restroom user, of course, emerges red-faced to a standing ovation and takes what is probably one of the longest trips of her life down a staircase. *Gotcha.*

Today's Gospel lesson is largely about a very old pair of questions. First question: How are disciples supposed to behave when they believe no one else is watching? And second question: What is the nature of our God who knows everything we do and sneaks into our lives unannounced? *Gotcha.*

The story opens with seven disciples sitting around talking, and, to tell you the truth, I sense they're a little bored. We know about Judas' demise, but that leaves four others unaccounted for and there seems to be this feeling afoot that it's tough to hold things together since Jesus has departed. "I don't know about you guys," says Peter, "but I'm going fishing." One of the things we lamentably miss in the Gospels is voice inflection. How do you think Peter announced his fishing intentions? Maybe he announced his plans with an exclamation point, much like an eager young boy ready to dig worms, throw some dirt into an old coffee can, and attach a red and white bobber onto the frayed line of his old attic Zebco. *Hey, guys! I'm going fishing! Who's with me?* But I somehow doubt Peter said it like that. I'm guessing that the tenor of Peter's voice resembled something approaching resignation. A return to routine. *There's nothing else to do, might as well go check those nets.*

Jesus has given the disciples clear instructions. But they return to their old jobs as if nothing has changed. "Jesus is gone. Get over it. Get on with your life. Our time with Jesus was interesting, but we've got work to do. I am going fishing." Peter's resignation has long been a problem for the church which suspects that Jesus is really gone. Easter for many is a charming historical event that we re-enact each spring. We have a hard time, therefore, sustaining the excitement of Easter. The crowds return home, back to the routine, largely unchanged.

Of course, the disciples catch nothing. They fish all night with slack nets. It is notable that in the Bible, the disciples, professional fishermen, please remember, who probably could have had their own fishing show, never catch a single fish without Jesus. Not a perch. Not a minnow. Not a guppy.

A hint of light starts to sliver on the horizon. Some guy on the beach has a fire going. We know the guy. They don't. "Children, you have no fish, have you?" I asked this about Peter, but what tone of voice do you think Jesus uses here? Well, it could be a smart-aleck voice, dripping with sarcasm. *Sort of struck out, kids, didn't you?* Jesus could be back to check up on disciples who had very clear marching orders to spread good news and catch people. That man on the beach could be saying, *Gotcha.*

There are a lot of people in the world who believe in a "Gotcha" God. A God who virtually exists to catch us doing wrong things in bad places at bad times. There are a lot of people who have been

174

raised in such a religious environment, who were taught to fear this God who would catch us, expose us, shame and then punish us.

I'm convinced that's why Peter acts so erratically in the boat. I'm sure he's excited to see Jesus and all, but I'm also betting he thinks he's been caught. In the commentaries, historians virtually trip over themselves explaining this line about Peter being naked in the boat. "Well, he was hot. It was how fishermen dressed so that their loose clothing wouldn't get caught in the nets. He was actually wearing some underwear. Etc. Etc." But the text plainly says that he was naked. As a jaybird. And because John's Gospel never misses an opportunity to shine truth through symbol or metaphor, I'm suggesting that Peter's posture in the boat that morning says everything about this idea of *gotcha*. He was exposed before Jesus. The fig leaf had been raised and bells and whistles and sirens were going off in his head. The poor boy had literally been caught by God with his pants down, ashamed to be found doing the same old thing he'd been doing before Jesus walked into his life. From *Peter's* perspective, he'd been busted by the Jesus police. Flashing lights and wailing sirens on the beach. Peter stands up in the boat, fully exposed, and squints his eyes. "Who? What? It can't be." What Peter wouldn't give for a fig leaf just about now! He pulls on his pants, dives into the water, and flails for shore. Maybe there's some way to explain, to rationalize, to clarify things for Jesus.

Well, maybe you've never heard the story this way and maybe you think I'm stretching the interpretation just a bit, but I truly think Peter is swimming furiously because he thinks he's been nailed, exposed, caught. Squirming like a fish in a net. Peter washes up on the sand, probably ready with a thousand explanations. But the man on the beach is not waiting with accusations and reprimands. He is not waiting, after all, to spring out into the waves and say, *"Gotcha."* Did you notice that about this man?

Peter may have been caught red-handed but Jesus offers him some red snapper. "Come and have breakfast." It's one of the most tender things Jesus says to disciples in all of the Gospels. "Come and have breakfast." He could have said a lot of things to those guys. Instead they have breakfast around a fire on the beach.

You knew this already: there is the embarrassment of getting publicly caught. Jesus will always discover us doing things we shouldn't be doing — catch us with our metaphorical pants down, embarrassed because we're doing exactly the *opposite* of what he taught us. Holding grudges, hoarding money, ignoring the poor, fearing illness and the grave. We simply cannot sustain Easter excitement on our own.

But it is hopeful for me to discover in this story that Jesus does not really return to "check up" on the disciples. He returns to feed them. He returns to let them know that Easter *can* be sustained even in the mundane, predictable routine that you and I face every week. He feeds us at the table of grace ("for you and for you") and sends us out to start again, resurrected and thankful. Jesus is no cosmic snoop, no *gotcha* God.

Some fine day in the future, when we all get to heaven, there will be a corner of that expansive place where all the nations of the world are gathered — people of every race and situation, people who have suffered and laughed, and especially people who have gotten caught, which, in truth, is all of us. A virtual sinner's reunion.

We're at the beach together; staying at this ocean-front mansion that somehow accommodates everybody. Some are gathered on the porch at first light, sipping coffee. And others are squinting towards the water.

There is a man in the distance grilling fish over a fire. He is wearing a chef's cap. And he is waving and calling, "Come. Come and have breakfast."

No one will have to tell us. We'll just know.

We'll know it is the Lord.

---

1. Martin E. Marty, "Who's Watching?" *The Christian Century* (April 1, 1992), p. 351.

# Believing And Belonging

Jesus is taking a walk today. It is winter, December, a little chilly. He's out for a stroll in Solomon's portico, which was a covered walkway of sorts on the east side of the Temple. Maybe he needs a break after a morning of teaching. People have just questioned his sanity (10:20). Soon they will try to stone him (10:31). So he heads out for a walk. It is winter and his reception has been rather wintry. Maybe he's wearing a windbreaker.

There are lots of people in Jerusalem around this time of year. It's time to celebrate the festival of the Dedication, better known as Hanukkah, sort of a Fourth of July for Jewish people who gather to recall the liberation of the Temple by Judas Maccabeus almost 200 years before Jesus takes this chilly stroll. Judas violently drove out the pagan interlopers who had desecrated the altar and made a mockery of the ways of God. This bit of history is not lost on Jesus or on those who closely follow him on his walk. He doesn't get very far before the questions start to fly.

Let me quickly say at this point that Christians need to be very careful in telling these old stories not to make Jewish people the proverbial whipping boys in the death of Christ. Recently a professional born-again basketball player was quoted as saying the Jews "had the blood of Jesus on their hands." I'm not the first to point out that it was inevitable that *somebody* would kill Jesus for the way he lived and taught. To tell the truth, it's not beyond the realm of possibility that Christians would kill him were he to walk our streets in the flesh today.

But back to the story. Jesus tries to get away for a walk. But several people block his path from a side door. Others hurry and catch him from behind. Soon they have him completely surrounded there in the walkway. A circle of cool questions and wintry stares. "How long will you keep us in suspense? If you are the Messiah, tell us plainly." In other words, *if you are here to liberate us like Judas Maccabeus once did, then stop speaking in riddles and cut the nonsense.*

Jesus turns and looks at his accusers and gives them two answers. Both, in my opinion, seem infuriatingly evasive. First answer: "I've already told you once and if I tell you again nobody would believe me anyway." Second answer: "You don't believe me because you're not one of my sheep." I'm sure this circle of scholars simply threw up their hands in exasperation at this point. Jesus is just talking nonsense. And so the porch gets chillier. And seconds later when he makes the audacious claim, "The Father and I are one," well, it's just too much. To claim to be on par with God is blasphemy. Jesus' fate is sealed from this day forward.

Today I want to look closely at this second answer of Jesus: "You don't believe because you're not one of my sheep." And I especially want to look at his answer not from the historical reality of first-century Judaism but from the perspective of the modern American theological mind. Another way of stating Jesus' answer is to say that our ability to grasp the truth of Jesus depends on whether we're in the flock or out of it.

Now this statement presents something of a problem for modern people in that so many modern seekers are not really sure they want to be part of a flock or a church or organized religion or whatever you want to call it. They prefer to learn from the outside and maybe read the teachings of Jesus in a college textbook or perhaps pick and choose what fits them from a much wider smorgasbord of options, crafting a homemade religion with a little Jesus here, some Buddhism over there, and a bit of Confucius on the side. Please do not think I'm judging such a salad bar approach to theology. At the very least, such people are searching and that is good.

What I am saying is that Jesus makes the rather strange claim today that he cannot be understood in this fashion. He cannot be understood and people cannot come to belief by watching and learning about him from the outside. "You do not believe," he says, "because you do not belong to my sheep." This is a dilemma for modern people, to say the least. We have been taught to learn about truth in the mind, intellectually. Jesus says, "No, you learn about *my* truth by becoming part of a people, a flock." It's tricky and almost impossible to convince someone of this. It's as if Jesus hangs a sign around his neck that says, "DISCIPLES WANTED: (Belief To Follow)."

Apparently, according to Jesus, we do not talk ourselves into belief or will ourselves into faith. We *practice* ourselves into belief. This frankly goes against the very way we've been taught to learn. Usually we study, think, reflect, and then act. But Jesus insists on the opposite. He says first one is to associate with the flock. And *in the going,* with a group of others, the voice of Jesus becomes clearer. To be honest, I've found this to be true, exactly how it works. I've never run across a person, for example, who is growing in their understanding and following of Jesus apart from their participation in a flock of other followers. Maybe you know someone in this category. I haven't met them.

Timeout for this clarification: I am not talking about church membership here. At least not in the way we've come to know it. Church membership is important but church membership does not *necessarily* mean one is a sheep. A sheep is a person who sticks with the flock and listens with other sheep for the voice of Jesus; a person who trusts that Jesus will lead and guide the flock. Church membership can often degenerate into a religious individualism every bit as pronounced as a secular home-made religion. One theologian has observed, "Christians were [once] taught that worship was preeminently their opportunity to be 'fed.' But it was rarely recognized that to be fed is to be infantilized. To say I go to church to be fed is the same as saying, 'I go to church so I can act like a baby.' "[1] Of course, this is not what Jesus has in mind when he calls us to be disciples.

"You do not believe," says Jesus candidly, "because you do not belong to my sheep." I suppose this could be true of people both inside and outside of the church, as we know it in America. But here's my main point. These words of Jesus present a real dilemma for modern people who are used to figuring out truth for themselves. And a real challenge for congregations serious about evangelism and sharing the good news of Jesus. So much evangelism is about convincing people of certain theological facts.

"Can't you see the truth?" shouts the evangelist on the street corner. "The evidence is crystal-clear, my friend! Believe this or else!" If I'm reading Jesus correctly today, this is not the way to do evangelism in this or any century. It's not just that a person *won't* believe in Jesus apart from a flock of others; it's that they *can't*.

Stanley Hauerwas, in his book *After Christendom?*, puts this very well: "To become a disciple is not a matter of a new or changed self-understanding, but rather to become part of a different community with a different set of practices." He then goes on to give two examples of what he means by this. "In short, we do not believe in God, become humble, and *then* learn to pray, but in learning to pray we humbly discover that we cannot do other than believe in God." Hauerwas even makes the bold claim that "we must be trained to be a sinner. To confess our sin, after all, is a theological and moral accomplishment."[2]

"You do not believe," says Jesus today, "because you do not belong to my sheep." Effective evangelism, according to Jesus, is not when you've got a preacher or group of doorbell ringers trying to talk people into the truth of the gospel compellingly with intellectual maxims that just can't miss. No. Jesus says belief and discipleship happen in the context of community, a flock. And being part of a flock that is serious about following Jesus is how people learn about the man and come to follow him themselves.

Long ago, Jesus took a wintry walk. He didn't get very far. He was surrounded by people who were confused by him, befuddled by his pronouncements, and longing for just a little straight talk. Jesus replied to them in rather stunning fashion. He said they would never understand him from a distance; never believe in him by looking in from the outside.

What if the same is true today? If it is true, and I think it is, then we don't first see how many articles of the Apostles' Creed we can get people to agree to and we don't first make sure every question is correctly answered for precise theological orthodoxy. We instead invite people to trust in the power of Christian community, and trust that in time what is found here is nothing short of life-giving, transforming.

In Jesus we have found One who is one with the Father. One with God. So we invite. The questions newcomers bring are good. And the suspicions are all part of it. And the intellect will surely be an ally to the love of God and neighbor in the long run.

But more than anything, it is being part of a flock, like this one, that will help another into the arms of Jesus and will strengthen your own trust in the man.

"You do not believe," he once said, "because you do not belong to my sheep."

---

1. Rodney Clapp, *A Peculiar People: The Church as Culture in a Post-Christian Society* (Downers Grove, Illinois: InterVarsity Press, 1996), p. 95.

2. Stanley Hauerwas, *After Christendom?* (Nashville: Abingdon Press, 1991), pp. 107-108. The emphasis in this quote is mine.

# Just Like That

"Just as I have loved you, you also should love one another."
Perhaps more than any other single verse in the New Testament,
this one should cause us to rise up from the pew, run out the church
doors, and never come back.

Just before he died and just after he washed feet, Jesus shared
some advice with a community in crisis. A community that would
soon be without a leader. "Love one another," he said.

Now on one level, that's no sweat. Think nice thoughts, do an
occasional good deed, and center your life around the tenets of
Hallmark. Love. We know how to do that because we are generally
pretty nice people, right?

But wait a minute. Jesus doesn't stop there. He also says, *"Just
as I have loved you."* Now that's the part I often run from. And I
wouldn't blame you if that's what you decide to do. I'm okay in
the love department and think it's a pretty good idea. But Jesus
doesn't say to love just any old way. But rather *his* way. Just like *he*
did. Just like a cross. You can die loving his way. Loving his way is
not safe. But that's his advice. Check that. Actually it's a non-ne-
gotiable *command* for those who choose to follow. But we won't
quibble.

Jim Wallis of the "Sojourners" community in Washington, D.C.,
once wrote that the American church has a huge credibility problem. "Our Scriptures, confessions, and creeds are all very public,
out in the open. Anyone can easily learn what it is supposed to
mean to be a Christian. Our Bible is open to public examination;
so is the church's life. *That is our problem*. People can read what

our Scriptures say, and they can see how Christians live. The gulf between the two has created an enormous credibility gap."[1]

Jesus goes on to say today, "By this everyone will know that you are my disciples." Exactly *how* will others know this about us? By our ability to articulate the Apostles' Creed from memory? From the way we're able to reel off the 66 books of the Bible in order? Nope. Jesus suggests that others will detect our discipleship to the extent that we love as he loved. We sometimes miss how huge of a claim this teaching of Jesus really is. And what exactly is at stake when we do see it.

Immersed in a culture that has largely given up God, the credibility of the American church is *contingent* upon the church's ability to produce disciples who love as Jesus loved. Jesus says that the only way others will know you're a disciple is through the extent his love has a place in all you do and say. "By this," he says, "others will know." This entails more than getting the liturgy right each week or listening to a preacher hand down helpful spiritual advice.

It means knowing intimately the teachings of Jesus and taking them on the road in public. It means living Jesus' way in a culture that wants to kill him again. It means loving not when we feel like it or on our own terms, but *as he did*, in all things. The life of a disciple will begin to look like, well, a cross. "Love one another," he says. But in a certain, prescribed way. "Just as I've loved you." If that little word "as" does not put the fear of the Lord in you, then you need to go back to Bible 101 and look closely at exactly how this man loved. Even upon the one thousandth reading it's hard to believe he says some of the stuff he does.

The teachings of Jesus are not so hard to stomach in the abstract. It's when we try to apply them to the concrete stuff of life that problems arise. Timothy McVeigh's death several years ago was on one level simply the execution of justice applauded by millions. You don't blow up children and get away with it.

But here's my question: Does such a response square with the teachings of Jesus? And I would have to say, "No." In fact, I defy you to find a place in the Gospels where Jesus responds to violence with more violence. You may support capital punishment and I will listen respectfully to you. But you will have a tough time finding support in *our Lord's teachings* for such an action. And there's the rub. We are to love *as he loved*, not based on our opinions or feelings of justice at the time. You may say, "Well, Jesus lived in a less complicated time." And I say baloney. He died for what he believed. I'd say that involved a fair amount of complication. And you may say, "Well, he's the Son of God." And I say that you are a *child* of God, in baptism a disciple not even once-removed. And you may say, "Well, such a life just isn't practical." And I say touché. There's not a blessed thing practical about being a disciple of Jesus. Who told you that? If you want to get practical, then join Kiwanis.

It is decidedly *impractical* to love as Jesus loves. It's amazing to me that we church people aren't mad at Jesus more than we are. For his teachings challenge much of what we hold so dear. If you read the Bible closely, prepare to be bothered. Maybe that's why modern Christians have largely given up Bible reading as a daily discipline. What Jesus teaches compared to how we live is often too much to bear. "Love one another," says the man. "Just as I have loved you." Do I really love *that* way? Or want to?

And that's a dilemma for us, isn't it? Realistically, how *do* we love as Jesus loved? Do we simply decide one Sunday morning that from now on, by golly, I'm going to try my darndest to love this way? Is it a matter of willpower? Or do we perhaps try to scold people into loving as Jesus did? Tell them things like, "Well, you *ought to* love like Jesus loved after all he's done for you, you ungrateful wretch." One of the things I find somewhat simplistic about the "What Would Jesus Do?" movement is that presumably one is to discover WWJD and then just do that very thing. I recall those Michael Jordan commercials where young adolescents were invited to "Just Do It" — just get in there and be Michael, you can do it, forgetting the years of practice and toil it took to become such a basketball player. It's like telling a young person to sit down at a piano keyboard and play Chopin before he or she has taken the time to learn the scales.

I'm unconvinced that individual willpower or authoritarian scolding will teach children or adults very much about loving as Jesus loved. These, by the way, are the historic routes taken by the liberal and fundamentalist wings of the church from last century. A) Pretty much leave people alone and let them find their own way, basically making up the morality they need as they go along; or B) "Guilt" people into change by telling them how worthless they are. Such tactics will usually create either very puny or very resentful disciples.

So again the question: How *do* we teach people to love as Jesus loved? The love of Jesus is too strange, too much at odds with popular culture, too divinely whacky for a person just to up and decide one fine day to live this way.

One unusual feature of the Gospel of John is that there is no Passover meal. In every other Gospel, Jesus makes precise preparations for such a meal. And then during the meal Jesus institutes the Lord's Supper. "This is my body. This is my blood." But in John the details are very different. In this Gospel, Jesus eats a meal with the disciples, but it isn't the Passover. In John they gather well before Passover occurs. And Jesus really never institutes Holy Communion here. Look high and low and you'll never find him saying, "This is my body" while holding up some bread. In John chapter 13, Jesus stoops to wash the feet of his friends, and then begins a long, unbroken four-chapter speech: a kind of last will and testament for those who will carry on his ministry. It is not until chapter 19 that the Passover is finally mentioned by John, the same day that Jesus is crucified at high noon. Lambs were traditionally slaughtered at this hour in preparation for the Passover meal.

John may be different, but he's not subtle. In his Gospel, Jesus does not *eat* the Passover with his followers. Instead, he *is* the Passover. He becomes the Passover Lamb who takes away the sin of the world. We sing of this promise each and every time we share the Lord's Supper. *Lamb of God you take away the sin of the world, have mercy on us.* We wipe his blood on the doorposts of our lives and we are freed from death. Passed over. Jesus doesn't eat the Passover in John. He is the Passover. He's the main meal. Like in no other Gospel, John forcefully suggests that we are saved as Jesus dramatically dishes up his body for the salvation of the world. Jesus' life is sacrificed for the nourishment of all humanity. For God so loved the planet. Jesus offers himself for our well-being, not to appease some demanding God who wants blood payment for our sin, but rather to show us truly how to live. For others. "As I have loved you."

At the heart of our attempts to love as Jesus loved is this meal where Jesus has offered his very life. If indeed "you are what you eat," perhaps our eucharistic celebrations should come with warning labels. Over time, dining with Jesus will transform us more and more into his likeness.

The phone rang some time ago. It was a friend whose daughter had been murdered in a nearby state — incredibly painful and tragic. On a hike once this friend told me that he eventually wanted to visit his daughter's murderer. Well, that day arrived. That's why he was calling. He and his wife had been to the sentencing. "You know, Frank," he said on the phone, "we talked to him and offered him our forgiveness." There was a silence for awhile. Somehow I wasn't expecting this. "And you know," he went on, "it looks like we'll be visiting him from time to time. We went down there thinking there would be some sort of closure to the trip, an end to all this pain, and here it seems God is opening up a new chapter in our lives."

A long time ago, as he hung on the cross, Jesus the Lamb of God prayed for the very people who were killing him. "Father, forgive them for they don't know what they're doing."

"Love one another," he said.

Just like that.

---

1. Jim Wallis, *The Call To Conversion: Recovering the Gospel for These Times* (New York: Harper Collins, 1992), pp. 18-19. The emphasis here is mine.

# Moving In

Philip Yancey, the best-selling author, once holed up in a mountain cabin for two weeks during a Colorado winter. His intent was to bring a stack of books and do some work on several writing projects. What happened instead is that he opened only one book: the Bible. He began at Genesis and read straight through as the snow fell, six feet of fresh powder in all. By the time he reached the book of Revelation, Yancey had to call someone to clear the driveway. "The combination of snow-muffled stillness, isolation from all people, and singular concentration changed forever the way I read the Bible."

What struck Yancey the most was that our common perceptions of God simply do not square with the way the Bible actually portrays God. For example, we tend to perceive God as all-powerful but also rather aloof — mighty and eternal, but also rather emotionless. Yancey instead discovered a God who was "not a misty vapor but an actual Person. God feels delight, and anger, and frustration. Again and again he is shocked by human behavior." Yancey was reminded that the God of scripture cannot do just anything. "The Bible shows God's power to force a Pharoah to his knees and reduce mighty Nebuchadnezzar to a cud-chewing lunatic. But it also shows the impotence of power to bring about what God most desires: our love."[1]

Today Jesus is going away. He is preparing his disciples for his departure. And in John he takes almost four chapters of unbroken speech to do it. One of the disciples asks a very understandable question. "Lord, how will we know you after you leave?" There's more than a hint of separation anxiety in that question. Jesus tells the truth. "Those who love me will keep my word, and my Father will love them, and we will come to them and make our home with them. Whoever does not love me does not keep my words."

*"We will make our home with them."* Isn't that a great expression? Earlier in this same chapter (14:2) Jesus said, "In my Father's house there are many dwelling places." It's a verse often read at funerals. Jesus has plans for us. He will take us to a "dwelling place" when we die. And between now and then he will also "make his home" with us right here if we keep his word. What we don't see in English is that these are the exact same words in Greek — "dwelling place" and "home." We will indeed "go home" one day. But Jesus decides to rent a room in our hearts right now, long before we get there. The idea all through the Gospel of John is that heaven begins right here on earth. But there is a condition attached. Jesus will move in with us now only if we are keepers of his word.

"The weirdest corruption of contemporary American Protestantism," wrote William Stringfellow in 1967, "is its virtual abandonment of the Word of God in the Bible."[2] Is that too harsh? Over thirty years later is it fair to say that the modern church has "virtually abandoned" the Word of God? "Those who love me will keep my word," says Jesus. "Whoever does not love me does not keep my words." Let's go a step further. What if you don't know the words to begin with?

On a recent week-long bicycle trip on the Blue Ridge Parkway, I carried a small New Testament and a collection of Wendell Berry poems among other much heavier things like peanut butter. One of the poems, titled "The Snake,"[3] kept playing theological tag with the daily lectionary readings from Luke and Romans. The poem is set in late fall and the narrator comes upon a swollen snake, almost completely disguised in the dead leaves, whose belly is "thickened with a mouse or small bird." The snake is so engaged with the basic act of digestion that he hardly takes the trouble to flick his tongue. The narrator picks up the snake and holds it a long time, "thinking of the perfection of the dark marking on his back" and the "death that swelled him." When winter comes, the snake is remembered. Berry writes:

*Now the cold of him stays*
*in my hand, and I think of him*
*lying below the frost,*
*big with a death to nourish him*
*during a long sleep.*

It's been a while since I've read a poem that has so thoroughly jarred me awake. *That's me*, "lying below the frost," where I spend so much of my emotional time. *That's us*, "big with a death to nourish him." *That's us*, gathered at the communion table week after week, feasting on the death and life that will finally awaken us from the cold. Perhaps Berry doesn't intend these theological images. It doesn't matter. When our experience, even an innocent walk through the woods, rubs up against the story of Jesus, something amazing happens and we catch our collective breath because we see for the first or five hundredth time that we're in the story and not just listening in. "Those who love me will keep my word, and my Father will love them, and we will come to them and make our home with them."

I read recently of an Episcopal congregation that had gone through a building program and experienced some problems with the installation of new carpet. The carpet built up this huge charge of static electricity either due to dryness in the air or some odd propensity of the rug itself. During the liturgy, the pastor intoned the words of blessing, lifted the chalice to the lips of an assisting minister, and watched in horror as a sudden electrical discharge knocked this man flat on his back. My source goes on to report, "In fact, parishioners were so consistently shocked that it became customary to serve an acolyte first and let him or her absorb the initial and most charged jolt. The acolytes, in turn, would draw straws to assign this somewhat sobering duty."[4]

Beyond the rather bizarre similarities to child sacrifice in this story is a parable of truth for congregations like ours. Perhaps Holy Communion should be more like a jolt of grace than a sweet sip of kindness. Perhaps the Eucharist should knock us on our duffs because it is attempting to re-arrange our priorities and introduce us into the story much like Saint Paul was thrown to the ground one fine day on the way to Damascus.

191

In the Parkway campgrounds on our bike trip, the bathrooms were referred to as "Comfort Stations." That amused me somewhat because that phrase pretty much describes the central paradigm for the American congregation. Are we a "Comfort Station" that dispenses sympathy, kindness, friendliness, understanding, accommodation to the culture, and little else besides comfort? Is that what a church is for? Or is there more to it than that?

Many are familiar with the various biblical gaffes from Sunday schools across the nation making their way around the internet these days. You know — "Noah's wife was called Joan of Ark," "The seventh commandment is thou shalt not admit adultery" or "When Mary heard that she was the mother of Jesus, she sang the Magna Carta." A professor of Bible at a Lutheran school recently wrote: "Nearly all the students in a typical undergraduate class at a church-related college consider themselves Christians, and most come from families more or less active in a church. Nevertheless, the world of the Bible is a mostly foreign land."[5] I find those words both sad and alarming. To use again the words of William Stringfellow, is it off-base to admit to the "virtual abandonment of the Word of God in the Bible" in our churches today?

In holing up in a cabin for two weeks during a snowy Colorado winter, Philip Yancey discovered something about the God of the Bible. God's power, though obviously impressive, cannot bring about the very thing God most desires: our love. Jesus wants to make a home with every human being. But being in church on Sunday can't ensure this. And your name on a membership roll is not really what the man is talking about. Jesus needs room. "Those who love me will keep my word."

One of my candid confirmation students recently told me that reading the Bible was so confusing that it was like listening to a foreign language. There is a lot of truth in that statement. For those of us with children, we have a couple of options. We can, for example, try to force church, Bible, and God down the unwilling throats of the young while we still have time. Writer Anne Lamott was once asked why she made Sam, her young, resistant son, go to church. "I make him because I can," she said. "I outweigh him by seventy-five pounds."[6] What parent hasn't fought this battle?

192

One of the best ways to teach a new language to children, however, is to become conversant with the language yourself. And so here are a few suggestions: *Turn off the television. Read the Word daily. Study the Word faithfully. Help shape the Bible curriculum for adults and children here in our congregation.* One does not learn French or basic piano scales all at once. We must begin. We must continue. We must re-commit.

People of God, so much is at stake. In fact, if I'm reading this lesson correctly today, everything is at stake. "Those who love me will keep my word, and we will come to them and make our home with them. Whoever does not love me does not keep my words."

*We will make our home with them.*

Our attention to the word will determine whether Jesus has moved into our lives to set up house, even down below the frost. Or whether he has slowly been served with an eviction notice while we weren't looking.

1. Philip Yancey, *I Was Just Wondering* (Grand Rapids, Michigan: William B. Eerdmans, 1998), pp. 153-55.

2. Bill Wylie Kellerman, ed., *A Keeper of the Word: Selected Writings of William Stringfellow* (Grand Rapids, Michigan: William B. Eerdmans, 1994), p. 167.

3. Wendell Berry, "The Snake" *Openings* (New York: Harcourt Brace Jovanovich, 1980), p. 9.

4. Rodney Clapp, *A Peculiar People: The Church as Culture in a Post-Christian Society* (Downers Grove, Illinois: InterVarsity Press, 1996), p. 112.

5. Frederick Niedner, "Ground Zero: Forming Students Through the Bible" *The Christian Century* (April 18-25, 2001), p. 16. Both the quote and the anecdotal sayings are from this article.

6. Anne Lamott, *Traveling Mercies: Some Thoughts on Faith* (New York: Pantheon Books, 1999), p. 100.

**Ascension Of The Lord**
**Luke 24:44-53**


# Now What?

The Ascension of Jesus into heaven is one of those strange Bible stories that Cecil B. De Mille would've enjoyed filming. Charlton Heston would play Jesus, of course. He would give the apostles some final instructions and then say with just the right touch of divine resonance, "STAY HERE IN THE CITY UNTIL YOU HAVE BEEN CLOTHED WITH POWER FROM ON HIGH." Charlton/Jesus would take the next cloud to heaven in proper cinematic flourish. I picture it as an escalator-type effect, slow and lingering but with a decided trajectory, just the right light but without the stairs. Maybe some cherubim music, but clearly within the bounds of proper taste.

Finally, the camera cuts to an overhead shot of the apostles — dazed, mouths agape, like Gomer Pyle looking up at a skyscraper for the first time. Shazzam, he's gone. Someone once playfully suggested that as Jesus departed into heaven, the disciples finally saw the "sole" of Jesus. S-o-l-e, the bottoms of his shoes. Anyway, they all stood there looking up as if visiting Cape Canaveral for an Apollo space shot. "Now what?" we can almost hear them all say. "Our leader is gone. Now what?"

The Ascension of Jesus is a great story. Like the parting of the Red Sea, or the sling-shotting of Goliath by David, or the feeding of the 5,000, you can see the Ascension in your mind. You can use your imagination and fill in the details. My childhood King James Version devoted a full-color plate to the Ascension. Yours probably did, too. Rembrandt's version of this scene, painted in 1636, is a classic.[1] The disciples are in the shadows looking like they want to grab Jesus' feet and keep him on earth (like trying to tether an escaping hot air balloon) while the little child angels sans underwear are pushing him up and away towards the light. There's a devilish little angel over in the corner (actually more resembling a Munchkin from Oz) who's making a face directly into the gaze of the viewer of the canvas as if to say, "We've got him up here now. You don't. Now what are you going do?"

It's easy to imagine the Ascension in your mind. Pick an impressive cumulus some fine afternoon and you're halfway home. This is dramatic, spine-tingling scripture. A great story. It's too bad Cecil B. De Mille died in 1959. Less clear, though, is the actual meaning of this event.

For example, why did Jesus have to ascend to heaven in the first place? It seems like someone who went to all the trouble to be killed and rise from the dead would want to hang around longer than a mere forty days before taking the first flight home. (And this is the traditional period of earthly post-resurrection time. Luke maintains that the Ascension occurred Easter evening!) Anyway, didn't Jesus have more to teach the disciples? Wouldn't his ongoing crucified and risen presence win a few more converts to his side? Couldn't Christianity use someone even today like the Dalai Lama who would speak truth and ooze wisdom for the masses? Jesus seems to be leaving the whole show to a group of guys who frankly do not have an impressive track record for theological insight or fidelity to his teachings. What was Jesus thinking? Why did he leave them there so alone in some field outside of Bethany? Better yet, and this is the question we'll ask if we're honest: *Why did he leave us?*

I clearly remember my first day of college. In 1975 I chose a school where I did not know a single soul. It seemed to be a great idea at the time of acceptance, but when my parents drove me four hours to a campus of 10,000 strange faces, I wasn't so sure. We piled my stuff into the dorm, walked around a little, had lunch, and said good-bye. I remember watching their license plate until I could see it no longer, knowing I would not be going home until Thanksgiving. It was a tough transition for me, going from the very familiar to the utterly unknown. I was homesick for what once was. I turned and headed to my room, alone. I imagine the disciples felt a little like this as they watched Jesus until he was out of sight.

Jesus loved his disciples. Why did he leave them? He leaves them, I think, because if he stayed around they would never be able to grow in their understanding of God and their understanding of their own mission in the world. If Jesus had stayed, we would always be looking to him — for the miracle, for the right word, to touch the hem of his garment. If you recall in the Gospels, Jesus never tried to draw attention to himself. His concern was for the disciples and their growth. For that to have a chance of happening, Jesus had to remove himself bodily. He loved his disciples, but he wanted them to grow up.

We all know families, and it's painful to see them, where the parents linger so close and for so long in the lives of their children, well into adulthood, that the children aren't given room to be themselves. "After all I've done for you, the least you could do is ..." When a parent says this, the family has failed. A primary purpose for a family is to allow enough room for the children to grow and become what God is calling them to be. There are families whose members simply will not let each other go. It is good to be close. But each family member also needs room to fly and let God's spirit fill their wings.

Jesus knew this with his disciples. And I frankly think this is one of the main theological functions of the Ascension. It was time for the disciples to be out on their own. Out of Jesus' nest. The disciples surely must have asked each other: "Now what?" It's a good question to be *allowed* to ask. Many people never get to ask it because all the decisions are made by someone older and wiser or with more authority. *That's* why Jesus ascended. That's why he got out of the way. To help disciples everywhere discover that Christian mission is in the hands of his witnesses now. We might say, "Please, Jesus, stay with us like you were. Pull all the miracles. Comfort us when we're confused. Be our Big, Safe Teddy Bear. Take all of our tears away." No. The ball is in our court now. "Why do you stand looking up toward heaven?" the men in white robes want to know (Acts 1:11).

197

Nevertheless, remember this. After Jesus ascended, the disciples' relationship with Jesus has changed, but it's important to know they aren't alone. "I will not leave you orphaned," he once said (John 14:18). The disciples weren't alone any more than a freshman college student whose parents leave their son in a strange place with new decisions to make. What's important to see here is that Jesus loves us enough, has enough faith in us, to be his witnesses and carry off his mission in this world.

There will be plenty of times when we shake our heads, look up in the sky, and ask, "Now what, Lord?" Be glad that you can ask such a question. Be glad that someone has given you room to answer it.

---

1. Hidde Hoekstra, *Rembrandt and the Bible* (Weert, Netherlands: Magna Books, 1990), p. 435.

# Listening In

Sometimes I think it would be so much easier to be a disciple if Jesus walked among us in the flesh. If he would drop by the office here from time to time and we would chat and maybe go grab a cup of coffee or go for a walk and spend the afternoon together. He would tell me what was going well and not so well here at church and then perhaps confront me with the glaring inadequacies and shortcomings of my own life and I would say, "Yeah, I know. You're right about that. I'll try and knock that off." Just an occasional face-to-face visit would be helpful. Maybe once a quarter. Heck, I'd even settle for once a year.

You know it's not easy to be a disciple of Jesus. It was hard enough for those twelve who followed him around for a couple of years or so — those who could touch him and argue with him, pray with him, and stand in awe of him. But if you put 2,000 years between then and now it gets even harder. A friend of mine calls us "disciples once-removed,"[1] but in truth we are disciples many times removed. More and more people in our culture are calling us hopelessly naïve, praying to a Lord we cannot see, trusting in stories that have been passed down by dubious means, living a promise that can never be proven. It's tough to be a disciple in today's world. And I suspect it will be even tougher for generations yet to come.

John 17, the entire chapter, is a long remarkable prayer. In chapter 18, Jesus is arrested by soldiers in a set-up that leads to his trial and crucifixion. I find this to be a rather remarkable sequence. Jesus must have known that he was about to be arrested and yet he *prayed*! He prayed a lingering, unhurried prayer that night at precisely the same time the soldiers were in route, plotting their ambush. I believe I would have considered a handful of other activities than prayer, such as running, maybe hiding.

But Jesus prays. He prays this beautiful chapter-long prayer that resembles the surface of a pond after throwing a stone into its middle. And we get to listen in. First, Jesus prays for himself. That's the first ring of the splash. He knows what's about to happen this night. "So now, Father, glorify me in your own presence with the glory that I had in your presence before the world existed" (17:5). These two have been on speaking terms, apparently, for some time.

Then Jesus prays for the twelve men who have been his companions in this ministry, asking that God might protect them and keep them strong in the face of adversity. "I am not asking you to take them out of the world, but I ask you to protect them from the evil one" (17:15). That's the second prayer ring on the surface of the pond.

And then Jesus prays for another surprising group. "I ask not only on behalf of these [disciples], but also on behalf of those *who will believe in me* through their word." In other words, Jesus is praying for us! That's the third ring in the pond. On the night that he was betrayed, with the soldiers waiting in the garden hedges, Jesus peeks into the future with this prayer and sees disciples just like us. Jesus is praying for people of every time and place who try to follow him without the benefit of direct physical contact.

Hey, we've made it into the Bible after all, come to think of it. Jesus is kneeling and pouring out his heart to God and suddenly stops and says, "Father, I do not pray for Peter and James and John and Andrew and Bartholomew *only*, but I also pray for Mary Jane and Ernie and Linda and Lukas and Velma and Kat and Jill and Christopher and David ... and (*insert your own name*)." Isn't it incredible that Jesus would be able to squint into the future with his prayers and remember us long before we were a wiggling zygote, long before we were a gleam in our parents' eyes, long before our great-great-great-great grandparents went to Sunday school? "I ask not only on behalf of these, but on behalf of those who will believe." It's remarkably comforting for me to know that Jesus understands how hard it is for me to be a Christian.

Jesus has loved us for so long. He has been praying for us for so long. And I'm convinced he is praying for us still, ceaselessly interceding. Jesus has loved us for so long and his love is so much deeper and stronger than any other love, that we are able to rest in confident assurance regardless of the predicament we are facing. The man knew the soldiers were coming for him, and yet he calmly prayed! That same peace is available to each of us! How might our prayer lives change if we sat quietly each day knowing that we not only pray *to* this man of peace but also begin to understand that Jesus has already been praying *for* us all this time, such a very long time?

Next week we celebrate the coming of the Spirit at Pentecost. And do you recall one of the gifts brought by the Spirit to the church? "Likewise the Spirit helps us in our weakness; for we do not know how to pray as we ought, but that very Spirit intercedes for us with sighs too deep for words. And God, who searches the heart, knows what is the mind of the Spirit, because the Spirit intercedes for the saints according to the will of God" (Romans 8:26-27). Wow! Before we open our mouths in petition, *we are being prayed for*. Perhaps our devotional lives would be enriched if we regularly got quiet and became confident that Jesus has already been praying for us all through the day and night before we thought to open our mouths to ask him about something.

What might such a spiritual consciousness mean for young people, for example, who are fearful of the future and worried about what to do with their lives? What might such a spiritual awareness mean for couples whose marriages are in trouble? For older people who face illness and uncertainty about what the coming year might bring? For pastors who lose sleep worrying about the churches they serve? For any of us who wonder from time to time what Jesus is up to in the world? "I do not ask only on behalf of these," said Jesus, "but also on behalf of those who will believe." What is Jesus up to? I'll tell you what Jesus is up to. Jesus is praying for us. For disciples once-removed and a thousand times removed. It has become wonderfully liberating for me to believe that he is still at it.

I want to close this morning with an old prayer from the Danish theologian, Soren Kierkegaard, who died in 1855 at the age of

201

42. He struggled with the meaning of faith as deeply as any theologian in recent Christian memory. "Father in heaven! You have loved us first. Help us never to forget that You are love so that this sure conviction might triumph in our hearts over the seduction of the world, over the inquietude of the soul, over the anxiety of the future, over the fright of the past, over the distress of the moment. You have loved us first, O God, alas! We speak of it in terms of history as if You have only loved us first but a single time, rather than without ceasing. You have loved us first many times and every day and our whole life through."[2]

---

1. Pastor Ron Luckey, Faith Lutheran Church (Lexington, Kentucky).

2. Cited in Richard J. Foster and James Bryan Smith, *Devotional Classics* (HarperSanFrancisco, 1990), p. 107.

# Sermons On The Gospel Readings

## For Sundays
## After Pentecost
## (First Third)

## *When The Wind Begins To Sing*

## Stephen M. Crotts

*To Elizabeth Aiken Crotts,*
*my mother.*
*Seventy-four years have shaped her,*
*and she has shaped me.*

# Introduction

Martin Luther wrote, "The Bible is a manger in which the Christ child is laid."

Theologian Emile Brunner wrote, "The Bible is like a very old and scratched phonograph record, but if you put it on, the music is still there."

Manger bed of straw, phonograph recording — I prefer wind!

Jesus preached to Nicodemus, a devout Jew and Torah scholar of his day. He said, "The wind blows where it wills, and you hear the sound of it, but you do not know from whence it comes, or wither it goes" (John 3:8).

The wind is invisible. I am hard put to define it, but wind is a powerful factor in our lives.

It makes my neighbor's wind chimes sound. It causes a flag to snap at attention atop a pole. It hisses through the pine forest, whips up white caps on the bay, and wuthers around the eaves of my house. The wind spreads pollen, carries the drenching rain, and carves dunes. It even propels the sailboat along.

So with God's Word. The wind of God's Spirit blows through the pages of scripture. It warns, soothes, informs, corrects, inspires! And *preaching*, God's *then* word made *now*, is a big part of God's plan in applying this word to our lives.

In each of these texts, I believe I have heard the wind begin to sing. And I offer the music to you in Jesus Christ. For *When the Wind Begins to Sing*, the good Lord is shaping his creation.

Stephen M. Crotts
Innisfree
Burlington, NC

# Who's Afraid Of
# The Holy Ghost?

Ellen Ann is a pretty little six-year-old who has grown up in a lovely home that is next door to a town cemetery. In her few years, Ellen Ann has witnessed dozens of funerals from her backyard swing. One day her mother found her in the graveyard burying one of her broken dolls. The child scooped out a hole, put the dolly in, covered it over with sod, and stood up to reverently intone, "In the name of the Father, and of the Son, and in-the-hole-he-goes!"

Maybe that's all you know about the Holy Spirit. And if so, you are not alone. Today God the Spirit is the forgotten person of the Trinity. Like the people of Ephesus, when asked, "Did you receive the Holy Spirit when you believed?" we, too, must honestly answer, "No, we have never even heard that there is a Holy Spirit" (Acts 19:2 RSV).

But did you know that the Holy Ghost is not optional? In fact, Christ commands us to live the Christian life in his power! "Receive the Holy Spirit," he says in John 20:22. "Walk by the Spirit" (Galatians 5:16 RSV). "Do not grieve the Holy Spirit" (Ephesians 4:30). "Do not quench the Spirit" (1 Thessalonians 5:19). Jesus said, "And I will pray the father, and he will give you another Counselor, to be with you for ever, even the Spirit of truth, whom the world cannot receive, because it neither sees him nor knows him; you know him, for he dwells with you and will be in you" (John 14:16-17 RSV).

So, let's take a few moments to study the Holy Spirit, to learn his ways, and make a decision about receiving him into our lives.

## Power

In Acts 1:8 Jesus said, "But you will receive power when the Holy Spirit has come upon you...." The Greek word for power is *dynamis*. We derive our words dynamite, dynamo, and dynamic from it. And Jesus is saying we shall receive this sort of power when the Holy Spirit is accepted into our lives.

Take Peter as an example of the Spirit's enabling power. Before Pentecost, before he had received the Holy Spirit, he was by Jesus' side and he made all the right sounds, "Lord, I will follow you even unto death." But Peter could not live out his creed. In the Garden of Gethsemane he slept. When the soldiers came he lashed out in anger and fled into the night. Then following at a distance, when a servant girl accused him of being a Christian, he cursed and swore he never knew the man Jesus. Yet after Pentecost when Peter had been filled with the Spirit of Christ, he threw open the doors of the upper room and boldly preached Jesus as risen Lord. And throughout the subsequent pages of scripture we see Peter growing and manifesting the power of God as a healer and as a man overcoming his racial prejudices, becoming an author (something out of character for a rustic fisherman), and finally refusing to deny Christ and run away as he was crucified upside down on a cross in Rome.

If you are a Christian, this same life-changing power is in you. But you say, "I am a Christian. But I certainly do not feel so powerful right now! Where is this strength?" And the answer is: down inside you. Deuteronomy 33:25 explains, "As your days, so shall your strength be" (RSV).

My car is sitting in my driveway right now. It does not seem to be powerful in any way. I can go out and sit in it, turn on the parking lights, and listen to the radio — but it still seems to have no real power. When I start the motor and idle down the driveway and along the neighborhood streets, it still does not impress me with power. Yet when I pull out on the expressway and need to go 55 miles per hour, the exact power I need is there. And that is the way the Holy Ghost operates in the life of the believer. "As your day so shall your strength be." The power to love, to forgive, to witness, to suffer, to discipline, to be patient, to create — it's all there as needed, adequate power for daily living.

## Point Out Sins

In John 16:7-8 Jesus said the Holy Spirit does more than empower. He said, "Nevertheless, I tell you the truth: it is to your advantage that I go away, for if I do not go away the Counselor will not come to you; but if I go, I will send him to you. And when he comes, *he will convince the world concerning sin and righteousness ...*" (RSV). In other words, the Holy Spirit will point out right and wrong in our lives.

Consider an experiment. Imagine the room where you are seated to be full of light. There is no way to turn any more lights on. The room simply has all of the light it is going to get. But, does the light have all of the room? No, it does not. For there are shadows all about.

What if one by one you removed every object that blocked the light's presence in the room — a table, a chair, a trashcan? When you finished, would the room have any more light in it? No. It's just that the light would have more of the room.

The Holy Spirit works like that in the Christian's life. He is a person and he enters our lives totally at conversion. One does not receive an arm and a leg of the Spirit. And later come his head and his hands. He is a person and he enters us fully or not at all. So, the question is not: "Does the believer have the Holy Spirit?" The question is: "Does the Holy Spirit have the believer?" As the Spirit enters our lives, he begins to point out our sins one at a time. Maybe he begins with our pride, encouraging us to confess it and in God's power put it aside. That done, he may point out unforgiveness, then lust, poor financial management, disrespect for authority, impatience, and so on and so forth. As we walk in the Spirit, grieve not the Spirit, quench not the Spirit, we are changed day by day into the likeness of Christ.

The key principle to remember here is that you the believer first get all of the Spirit you are ever going to get. And then, little by little, the Holy Spirit gets all of you.

**Teacher**

In John 16:12-13 Jesus further explained the Holy Spirit's work in the Christian's life. Standing before the twelve disciples, he said, "I have yet many things to say to you, but you cannot bear them now. When the Spirit of truth comes, *he will guide you into all the truth*" (RSV).

Imagine that! Twelve persons who'd given it all up to follow Jesus 24 hours a day for three years. They'd heard his every saying, watched him minister, and witnessed his frequent miracles. And still Jesus called them to his side and announced, "I have yet many things to say to you, *but you cannot bear them now*." Wow! That would have hurt my feelings! And it must have hurt theirs! But the point is this: If Jesus said it to the twelve, how much more must he be saying it to us today?

We are so ignorant. Not a one of us knows it all yet.

But the Spirit is here to teach us. Jesus promised, "When the Spirit of truth comes, he will guide you into all the truth."

When I was a teenager, my father bought a Lincoln Continental town car. He never really used it for road trips. He was content to ride out for ice cream with the family, take it to church, and the like. And, of course, my father never bothered to read the owner's manual.

We teenage boys, however, thought that car was fantastic! And we learned everything about it we could. And that made life interesting when Dad and my brothers were in the car together.

My brother Paul would adjust the electric seat to a new position and my father would say, "How'd you do that? I didn't know that button was there!"

We'd raise the car antenna with the electric switch and, amazed, my dad would say, "Gee! Would you look at that!"

Over the years we showed my father all sorts of things about that car — cruise control, automatic light dimmer, an 8-track tape system, the switch to open the trunk from the glove compartment, and more.

Dad had simply bought more car than he had yet realized! And we were leading him into all truth!

The point is this: Jesus Christ has bought us more salvation than any of us can yet imagine! And it is the task of the Holy Spirit to teach us more and more all that we are and can do in Christ.

Little by little, day by day, as we study the Bible, live among Christians, think and experience the Christian life, the Spirit teaches us about prayer, being single or married, friendships, witnessing, the second coming, ecology, justice, suffering, stewardship of time, fear, doubts, the sacraments, and so much more.

I like to say that the Holy Spirit is here to take off of you everything that sin and Satan have put on you and to put on you everything that Christ wants you to have. He takes away sins and gives to us truth. He removes our weaknesses and puts on us his strength. He gives and takes away according to his good pleasure.

### Talent

And now yet another exciting work of the Holy Spirit in the believer's life. 1 Peter 4:10 teaches, "As each has received a gift, employ it for one another, as good stewards of God's varied grace" (RSV). The Greek word used for gift is *charis*. We get our word charismatic from that. And the Bible is saying, "Each has received a charis." So every Christian is called to the charismatic dimensions of the Christian life. But what does that mean?

I asked a Sunday school class once, "What are the gifts of the Holy Spirit?" There was a great deal of silence and finally someone nervously volunteered, "Gold, frankincense, and myrrh." Such is our ignorance of basic Bible facts.

You'll find the gifts of the Spirit listed in places like 1 Corinthians 12, Romans 12, and Ephesians 4. There it becomes clear that the gifts are actually talents for ministry like administration, showing mercy, teaching, evangelism, helping, discernment, knowledge, prayer, healing, encouragement, and more. And the Bible says, "As each has received a gift (or talent) employ it for one another...."

James Oglethorpe, the founder of the state of Georgia, was a Christian involved in a small group Bible study in London. A friend's senseless death from fever in a squalid English debtors' prison caused him to run for Parliament, win, and launch a panel reform movement.

Then the idea struck him! Why not take good men serving prison time for debt and let them work by helping colonize the New World for England? He was given money, equipment, ships, and permission to take convicted debtors to America to form a new colony called Georgia.

Upon their arrival in the new land, each colonist was put to work — some farmed; others built, soldiered, or fished. But each colonist was made to serve some useful purpose so that the colony would progress.

And all of this history is but a parable of how it is in the kingdom of heaven. You see, Jesus is our Oglethorpe who has freed us from our debts of sin, transported us to a new colony of God, the church, and given us each some ability, some special talent that we might make ourselves useful. Some of us teach. Others help, show mercy, or evangelize. Some pray. Some give. Some administrate. And all of us together build up the community. The church then is nothing but a group of Christian colonists doing the various jobs of ministry so that the world can see the kingdom of Christ lived out in community right in our midst.

Hence 1 Peter 4:10. "As each has received a gift, employ it for one another as good stewards of God's varied grace" (RSV).

**Character**

And now a final mission of the Holy Spirit in each believer's life. Galatians 5:22 explains, "But the fruit of the Spirit is love, joy, peace, patience, kindness, goodness, faithfulness, gentleness, and self-control" (RSV). In other words, the fruit of the Spirit is *moral character.*

Many ask, "If I open myself to the power of the Holy Ghost, if I let him point out my sins, teach me, and call me to useful involvement in the church, what will happen to me? What will my life be like?" And all I can say is, "The fruit of the Spirit is love, joy, peace, patience, and the like."

Notice it does not say, "The blossom of the Spirit is love." It says, "The fruit." And that is the final product of a tree. So the fruit or final product of the indwelling Spirit is not power or truth or spiritual gifts or correction from sin. The final product is character, moral maturity described as love, joy, peace, patience, kindness, goodness, faithfulness, gentleness, and self-control.

A few years ago a major American magazine polled its readership, asking, "What do you most want out of life?" And the three major answers were: I want love, I want to be happy, and I want peace. And those are the first three fruits of the Spirit! So it is abundantly clear that what we most want out of life is what the good Lord is most eager to give!

**Conclusion**

Would you like to receive the Holy Spirit? Galatians 3:14 explains we "receive the promise of the Spirit through faith." So, if you are willing to turn from your sins, to trust Christ as your redeemer, and invite by faith the Spirit's presence into your life, it can happen right now.

You may not feel anything.

You may not understand it all.

But nevertheless, he will come to you. And you will receive all of him there is. And over the next days and years of your life, he will receive all of you — your mind, your will, your emotions, your talents, your relationships. He will do this as you walk in him, quench him not, grieve him not.

Imagine a pipe open at both ends and stuck vertically in the river bottom. It is as full of water as it can get. But since it is at odds with the river current the water in it is not moving. Take that same pipe and rest it horizontally with the flow of the river and it is still no more or less full of water. The difference now is that the water is pouring through it.

And that is how life in the Spirit works for the Christian. In Jesus we are each filled with the Spirit. And when we refuse to live at odds with him, to grieve or quench him, we walk by the Spirit.

That means we are teachable as he shows us more and more who God is.

It means we are not self-reliant, but God-reliant as we seek his strength.

It means we receive his spiritual gifts and his talents, and we become involved in the church so as to make ourselves useful.

But most of all, it means our character is changed as we become more and more like the most beautiful person who ever lived — Jesus Christ.

**Holy Trinity**
**John 16:12-15**

# You Ain't Seen
# Nothing Yet!

Before Christopher Columbus, the Spanish flag bore the motto, "No More Beyond." Spain was a mighty empire rich in art, religion, commerce, and science. And as a sign of pride in their accomplishments, the Spaniards took on the motto, "No More Beyond." They were quite certain that Spain and the western world were all there was. Then came the year 1492 and Christopher Columbus' encounter of the New World. Suddenly a vast new continent opened up and the Spanish motto was changed to agree with the facts. Instead of the "No More Beyond" slogan, their motto became, "More Beyond!" Today, the scripture is saying the same thing to the church of Jesus Christ. "There is more! More beyond!"

**No Know-it-alls Yet!**
Today's text tells us that none of us knows it all yet. Jesus looked at his disciples, as he is looking at us today, and he said, "I have yet many things to say to you, but you cannot bear them now." His saying must have hurt the original disciples deeply. They had given up everything to follow him. For three years they had been his students. They had walked with him, eaten with him, prayed with him, questioned him, and hoped with him. All this, and Jesus was saying, "There's a lot more beyond! But you're not ready for it yet."

Which of us has been as close to Jesus as one of the twelve apostles? Have you given up everything to follow him? Where is the church member today who has been there when Jesus preached, healed, prayed, died, and rose? Certainly none of us can boast such a relationship with Christ. So if Jesus could say what he said to the

215

twelve apostles, how much more can he say it to each of us today? "I have yet many things to say to you, but you cannot bear them now."

Christians who really know the Lord have always readily admitted their spiritual ignorance. It is only those young or immature in the faith who act like know-it-alls. Saint Paul, as wise in the ways of the Lord as he was, said of his faith, "Now we see in a mirror, dimly" (1 Corinthians 13:12). Job, in his wisdom, admitted, "Lo, these are but the outskirts of his ways ... but the thunder of his power, who can understand?" (Job 26:14 RSV).

Christians are like a group of blind children who regularly visit the Louvre Museum in Paris. Their teacher takes them there on an educational outing each week. Whenever they stand before some art treasure, the teacher takes each child and guides his fingers over it and describes its appearance. Can you imagine a blind, thin, spindly-legged little child reaching out to feel the famous *Gladiator* sculpture? There is the blind and weak reaching out to embrace the likeness in marble of perfect physical manhood! We Christians are like those blind students touring the Louvre. We do not see it all. We do not know it all. Yet regularly our Teacher, the Holy Spirit, guides us to Jesus Christ, the Perfect Person, the Maximum Man. And there as we glimpse him through a glass darkly, as we grope our way to him and feel his presence, we learn something more of his nature.

Viewing ourselves like blind children touring the Louvre is a humbling experience, is it not? But to see ourselves as such is to see ourselves as we truly are. Did not Jesus say, "Unless you humble yourselves and become as a little child you cannot enter the kingdom of God" (Mark 10:15)? Jesus said this so that none of us would become puffed up with self-importance. He wanted us to see that even the world's most educated man has no reason for vain conceit. "Be like a child," Jesus said. A child is humble. He is inquisitive. He is, most of all, teachable.

Are you teachable as a little child? Or are you like a Pharisee, unteachable and a know-it-all? To the church today Jesus says, as he said to his disciples, "I have yet many things to say to you, but you cannot bear them now."

## We Have A Teacher

Next, the scripture brings us a word of good news. God does not leave us in our blind ignorance. He gradually educates us. He gradually opens our eyes. Christ said, "I have yet many things to say to you, but you cannot bear them now. When the Spirit of Truth comes, he will guide you into all the truth." Here, the Lord is promising that the Holy Spirit will come to us and teach us what we do not yet know.

Notice that the text says, "He will guide you into all the truth." The phrase, "he will guide you," reveals that this will take place over a period of time. It is a process. In other words, it does not happen all at once.

Have you ever been stumbling around in your house in the dark when suddenly your wife turns the lights on? Your eyes, accustomed to darkness, struggle in flutters against the light. Truth is like that too. If God were to enlighten us all at once, we would be unable to bear it. Too much light too soon would be overwhelming! Emily Dickinson wrote, "The truth must dazzle gradually or every man be blind." How true! And did you know that God dazzles us gradually with his truth? The text indicates that our enlightenment from God by the Holy Spirit comes as a process over a period of time. It doesn't say, "He has zapped you with all the truth." It says, "He will guide you into all the truth." I like the way the psalmist puts it. He said, "The unfolding of thy words gives light; it imparts understanding to the simple" (Psalm 119:130 RSV). Elsewhere the psalmist says, "Light dawns for the righteous" (Psalm 97:11).

A generous businessman decided to give $10,000 to a poor aspiring art student. Thinking that much money received at one time might overwhelm the man, he wisely decided to give it to him little by little over a period of time. So the businessman forwarded $100 with a note which read, "More to follow!" After a week he sent a similar check with the same message. At regular intervals he dispatched a third, then a fourth, and a fifth — all accompanied by the same promise, "More to follow!" This went on for several years until the entire gift had finally been received by the fellow. God's truth comes to us like that as well. He doesn't all at once dump it into our laps. That would overwhelm us. It would crush us. Like Jesus said, "We cannot bear it now." God sends us his truth in pieces. He says, "I will freely forgive you — but there is more to follow. I will guide you with my eye — but there is more to follow. Love your neighbor — but that's not all of the gospel. Love yourself — but more follows. Love God with all your heart and mind and soul and strength. More to follow! I will uphold you in the hour of death. More to follow! In my Father's house are many mansions. More to follow!" And so, as the prophet Isaiah predicted, "The word of the Lord will be to them, 'Precept upon precept, precept upon precept, line upon line, line upon line, here a little, there a little' " (Isaiah 28:13).

### The Whole Truth And Nothing But ...

So, verses 12 and 13 have told us two things so far. God has said that none of us knows it all yet. He has said that it is the Holy Spirit's job to enlighten us gradually. And now the text tells us that we shall eventually be fully enlightened with truth. Jesus said, "When the Spirit of Truth comes he will guide you into all the truth." Notice that the verse does not say, "He might guide you into all the truth." It says, "He will!" Notice also that the text does not say, "He will guide you into some of the truth or into your favorite parts of the truth." It says, "He will guide you into all of the truth." If it were left up to us, I'm quite sure we'd only want God to lead us into the easy parts of his truth. "Show us only the parts of thy truth that pat us on the back, O God," we'd pray. Christians have, and probably always will have, the bad habit of wanting God on their own terms. Rather than accepting God on his terms, we accept God on our terms. And a big conflict occurs. But the Holy Spirit is here to teach us God's truth. He is here to teach us all of God's truth about the Bible, prayer, evangelism, holiness, love, and so much more.

If you study the New Testament, you can follow the Holy Spirit's teaching ministry in the lives of the apostles. All his life Jesus taught Peter to put God first in his life. Then at the arrest, trial, and conviction, Peter denied Christ three times and went back to the fishing boats. But Jesus wouldn't let him alone. Resurrected and standing on the beach, Jesus looked at Peter and said, "Do you

218

love me more than these?" Peter said, "Master, you know I love you!" Again Jesus asked him of his love for God. And still a third time he inquired. Three times, one for every denial, Jesus asked Peter if he loved him with all his heart, mind, soul, and strength. You might say Peter was a bit slow like us. We have to have things repeated to us again and again.

Look also at Peter's vision in Acts 10. Not once, but three times the Holy Spirit gave Peter the vision of a sheet being let down from heaven full of all kinds of wild animals. Three times the Spirit said, "What God has cleansed, you must not call common." The Holy Spirit was teaching Peter the truth about racism. "No man is unclean," he said. Jesus had taught this during his ministry. He ate with tax collectors, harlots, and Samaritans. He was the friend of all. And he died for all. But the lesson of loving all people equally went unlearned by the apostles. After the resurrection they still refused to eat with anyone except Jews. Their gospel was only for Israel. So the Holy Spirit had to teach and reteach what Jesus had already taught. Thus Peter was given the vision. And because, like us, he was slow to accept the truth, the vision was repeated three times.

Right here we find clearly one of the functions of the Holy Spirit. He is our teacher. He teaches us again and again the things of Jesus until we accept them and obey him. He teaches us to pray. He teaches us to tithe. He teaches us not to hate but to love. He teaches us to forgive, to worship regularly, to witness. He teaches us to love God completely.

In the days ahead you will discover the Holy Spirit guiding you into more and more of God's truth. He will not overwhelm you, but little by little, line upon line, he will educate you in God's ways. He will do this as you study the Bible. Things you've never seen before will come to light! He will teach you in your experience of trial and effort. As you attempt to learn prayer, he will show you how. He will point out new truth in sermons. Sometimes the truth will hurt. Sometimes you will not want to believe it. But God wants you to know and do all of his truth, so bear with it. Lou H. Evans said that "the purpose of a preacher is to irritate the comfortable and comfort the irritated." So bear with your irritations that you may be comforted! God will also let the Holy Spirit teach you through your parents, through books, your Bible study group, and Sunday school. Your job is to go where the Spirit is teaching. Be humble. Be eager to learn. Be teachable as a little child. God still has so much more to say to us!

A warning here is in order. The Holy Spirit is at work to enlighten you with God's truth. When you receive the light and obey it, you receive more light. But when you reject the light of God's truth and turn away, you grieve your teacher, the Holy Spirit. And that leads to dankness. Jesus said that it was possible to reject God's truth so habitually that one becomes blind. He said, "The people have ears to hear but do not hear. They have eyes to see but do not see" (Matthew 13:13-17). Do take this warning to heart unless you want to become blind to truth. Light from the Holy Spirit accepted and obeyed brings more light. But light rejected brings darkness.

### Will You Be A Learner?

Some years ago I was flying to the island of Haiti. I asked the pilot of the AirFrance jet if I might sit in the cockpit with him and watch him land. He allowed me to sit in the jump seat and observe. After a few moments of high flight, the pilot turned to me and said we were about to fly through the worst thunderhead he'd ever seen. When he tightened his seat belt I tightened mine, too. Within minutes we were bumping and jolting through clouds so thick you couldn't see the tip of the wings. Thunder and lightning groaned and hissed all around us. The pilot said we'd have to land by radar and orders from the control tower. A voice over the radio crackled, "You're now 150 miles from touchdown. Descend to 6,000 feet and come two degrees left." Our pilot obeyed the course corrections. The moments dragged by. Again the voice crackled, "Fifty miles from touchdown. Descend to 1,500 feet. One degree left. You are fifty miles from touchdown." Still the ground was invisible. There was only the fog. I looked at the pilot and he was sweating. I started to sweat, too. Finally the voice over the radio ordered again, "Descend to 500 feet. Cut your air speed to 150 knots. Come one degree right." Moments passed when suddenly through the clouds the airport runway lights became visible and within minutes the aircraft had nestled safely on the ground. We had made a perfect instrument landing.

The Holy Spirit is at work in our lives like that, too. We have been blinded by sin and God is giving us directions through the Holy Spirit and scripture so that we can find our way back to him. In this life he teaches us. He modifies our beliefs. He corrects our course. He speeds us up. He slows us down. Jesus said, "For the gate is narrow and the road is hard that leads to life, and there are few who find it" (Matthew 7:13). But if we listen to the Holy Spirit and obey his truth, we will find our way. We will land safely. We will be right on schedule, right on target with truth.

Jesus said, "Come to me ... take my yoke ... learn from me!" (Matthew 11:28). The church is a place to learn. No, you cannot be just as good a Christian without going to church as you can be by going any more than a man can be a doctor without going to medical school. You must learn the things of God. And one place this is being taught is in church. The Holy Spirit is our tutor. And you ain't seen nothing yet! That might be poor English but it is good theology. We're all still in the school of the Holy Spirit. It is an educational system from which we never graduate. Here we learn and relearn the ways of God in Christ Jesus.

## Conclusion

Albert Schweitzer, in his book *The Quest for the Historical Jesus*, wrote about our relationship with Christ, "He comes to us as one unknown, without a name, as of old by the lakeside he came to those men who knew him not. He speaks to us the same word, 'Follow thou me,' and sets us to tasks which he has to fulfill for our time. He commands. And to those who obey, whether they be wise or simple, he will reveal himself in the toils, the conflicts, the suffering which they shall pass through in his fellowship, and as an ineffable mystery, they shall learn in their own experience who he is."

God bless you with faith and obedience as in the school of the Holy Spirit you learn who Jesus really is.

**Proper 4**
**Pentecost 2**
**Ordinary Time 9**
**Luke 7:1-10**

# Whom Christ Commended

A new soldier, having just completed jump school at Fort Benning, Georgia, stood proudly at attention with his fellow para-troopers. His drill sergeant inspected the line, came to him, and noticed a torn pocket on his uniform. "Soldier, your blouse is frayed," he shouted. To which the soldier retorted, "Sir, this uniform isn't afraid of anything!"

Soldiers can be full of bluster. I've lived near a Marine base and watched them come and go. Jogging along the base roads. Shirts off. Muscles rippling. Tattooed. Swaggering in their uniforms. Full of assurance. Keen-eyed. Pride runs deep.

The text introduces us to a soldier, a centurion. His rank equals that of a sergeant-major in today's army. He'd be in command of 100 men. And he'd be the backbone of Caesar's army.

This soldier has an unusual distinction. He is one whom Christ commended. And for that reason he bears close scrutiny.

### A Sense Of Mercy

Let's face it. Soldiers are taught to kill. It goes with the job. And some enjoy it with a cruel sneer.

Not this centurion, for surprisingly he has a sense of mercy. You see, his slave is sick. In his day a slave was a possession with no rights. He fulfilled a function — no more, no less. Like a toaster, or a bicycle, or a chair. If a servant was no longer useful he was literally thrown out to die.

But this centurion cares. He petitions Jesus for his healing.

During the American Civil War, Federals threw themselves against Confederate fortifications at Fredericksburg, Virginia. Thousands of them were shot dead or left wounded on the field. They cried out in pain, begged for water and first aid, yet none came. Fearful of sniper fire, soldiers on both sides cowered in their bunkers. All except a man in grey, Sgt. Richard Kirkland. He bravely gathered canteens of water, crawled out on the field, and mercifully gave comfort to the blue-coated dying Federals. Sgt. Kirkland himself was killed in action months later at Chickamauga. But years later the Federals refused to forget the Rebel soldier with a canteen of water. "The angel of Marye's Heights," they called him. And today if you visit the killing fields of Fredericksburg, you'll find a monument gratefully erected to his memory.

### A Sense Of Decency

The centurion was an officer in the Roman army occupying Israel. He was their overlord. They were the vanquished. Yet his lips weren't curled in a thinly veiled sneer. His face wasn't that of a killer who enjoyed his work. His visage was softened by mercy. And it was also etched with decency.

The Romans considered all religions as equally true and yet false. They also believed religion to be useful in controlling people. So they were cynical. Like Pilate, who at Christ's trial was to sneer, "What is truth?" As if nobody knew.

This man, however, this centurion, was more than casual with Judaism. He acted respectfully, even building a synagogue for the local Jews. Clearly, he served those he ruled. He was a public servant, a giver, a man of constructive usefulness.

### A Sense Of Humility

This centurion is an extraordinary soldier. He is merciful. He is decent. But look again at his biography in the text. He is also a man with a sense of humility.

He is humble enough to ask Jesus for help. He knows how to kill in battle. But how does one heal? Aye! That's the issue troubling his breast as he languishes over his terminally ill servant. So he sends a soldier to fetch a Jewish friend from the synagogue.

"Would you go to Jesus, ask him to pay me a visit, to heal my servant?" The Jew agrees and goes out to find Christ. But before he can return, the centurion is overcome with humility. He sends word to Christ, "I am not worthy to have you come under my roof."

He knew he was a soldier; Christ was a minister. He was a killer; Jesus a healer. He made war; Jesus wrought redemption. And the comparison left him wallowing in abject humility.

And there is something else here. The centurion, a Gentile, knew the Jewish law enough to know that if Jesus were to visit his post, Jesus would be rendered unclean. And he wished to spare Jesus that defilement.

The New Testament opens with Christ's Sermon On the Mount. And the Sermon On the Mount begins with the Beatitudes, the beautiful attitudes of poverty of spirit, mourning, meekness, and spiritual hunger — all attitudes which find their embodiment in this soldier.

Aye, this is the man whom Christ commended. He is a noble man, a gentleman, with a sense of mercy, of decency, of humility.

### A Sense Of Faith

The centurion also has a sense of faith. He sent word to Jesus, "I'm not worthy to have you come under my roof. Just say the word and my servant will be well. Just as I have men under my command, and I say go and they go, you, too, can delegate this job. Just say the word."

Jesus, hearing this, stopped dead in his tracks, amazed. "Never in all Israel have I seen such faith!" And, lo, the servant was healed.

Now, be very careful to note what impressed Jesus. What drew his commendation for the centurion was not his decency, not his building a synagogue, nor his humility or mercy. It was his faith.

Faith is what Christ is looking for. We do not purchase our relationship with God by offerings of money, mighty deeds, or good character. Healing, redemption, the grace of God come by faith.

Hebrews 11:6 explains, "And without faith it is impossible to please him. For whoever would draw near to God must believe that he exists, and that he rewards those who seek him."

## Conclusion

Maybe you don't have an ounce of decency. Perhaps mercy is alien to your difficult nature. And humility? "Look for it in the dictionary, but not in me!" Yet is there in you a willingness in your desperate life to inquire of Jesus in matters of life and death? When life asks of you more than you have, when you find yourself helpless, will you turn to Christ in faith and call out to him for help? If faith is yours, if Christ is your trust, then you, too, have Christ's commendation.

**Proper 5**
**Pentecost 3**
**Ordinary Time 10**
**Luke 7:11-17**

# Grace Encounters

Several years ago at one of the Lausanne Missions Conferences, something remarkable was decided. Until then the conference had determined two things must be done for effective evangelism to take place. One: the church must create an attractive presence. Two: the church must rightly proclaim the Gospel.

The conference noted, however, that some churches and missionaries had done this for years and absolutely nothing had happened in terms of evangelism and church growth. So they added a third ingredient to the formula: power encounters — that is miracles, healings, surprising restorations of marriages, and the like.

One can see all of these things memorably bundled together in the text, the story of Jesus healing the only son of the widow of Nain. Let's look at each of these points in turn.

**Preach The Word**

The text says Jesus "went to a city called Nain." There he met a funeral procession being led by a widow who was taking her son's body to his grave. And Christ was not mute. He had some things to say about not weeping and the dead rising again.

In John's Gospel, chapter 1, we are told God is not silent, he has a word for all the earth, and "the word became flesh and dwelt among us." Mark's Gospel even tells us, "Jesus came preaching." The content of what Christ preached is found in the Old Testament, the "Bible" of Christ's own day. He learned it so well that at age twelve in the temple he impressed the scholars. And he spoke endlessly of the word being *fulfilled, not broken,* of living by *every word.*

What we have in the New Testament is an accurate accounting of the life of Jesus, his teachings, his death on the cross, and his resurrection, ascension, and the promise to return.

By preaching the word, we mean neither adding to nor subtracting from the message of Christ as contained in the Old and New Testaments.

Many rightly ask how it is we arrive at the conclusion that the Bible is authoritative. After all, how can an ancient book be relevant in speaking with power to us today? The answer comes in what Jesus taught about scripture.

You see, our Christology (view of Christ) can go no higher than our bibliology (view of scripture). If I say Jesus is God but scripture is unreliable even though Jesus said scripture is true, then I say God in Christ was wrong, and so lessen his deity. Either Christ is God and scripture is as he viewed it, truth, or Jesus is only a mere mortal and the Bible is just another book.

Pope John Paul said it well: "We do not make up the faith as we go along." Rather, it is a faith "once delivered" (Jude).

Sadly in our day, knowledge of the Bible is sorely lacking. And preaching is the most neglected art form of the past 100 years. Why, most preachers couldn't make a C- in a high school public speaking class!

Such an abysmal state must be remedied! Pastors must study the word. They must be mentored by the older, talented preachers. Church members must pray for them and give them time to study and bring forth the word in well-crafted sermons. Then, like the text says, we must take the word out into the streets, into every valley of human need, even sad funeral marches where widows walk with no hope but to bury their only son.

Too often we make the church a stained glass foxhole in which we hunker down for the duration. But in the text Jesus shows us how he and his disciples get out and go into the world talking the word, sharing the truth.

Sociologists point out the average person has about fifty significant social encounters per week. That is, we cross paths with

228

around fifty persons weekly and are involved on some level of meaningful relationship. A bank teller who is sad because her sister is dying, a school teacher in the throes of divorce, a client in bankruptcy, a teenager desperately lost in the drug scene. O Lord, make us sensitive! Help us remember we have a sure word of hope!

## Attractive Presence

The second ingredient the Lausanne Missions Conference encouraged is *attractive presence*. This means before we speak Good News, we must be Good News!

I preached the same week this winter during flu season in a dying church and at a flourishing campus ministry. After the church service, an elder got up and suggested we all leave without shaking hands so no one would infect another. It was the coldest crowd I've ever seen, each fearful he or she would get something bad from the other. And as I left, I thought it no wonder the pews were empty.

Then I went to the campus equally devastated by the flu epidemic. There the students announced their plan to take hot soup to the infirm, to pray for the sick, to volunteer to run errands for them, turn in homework, and such. Why, the entire campus was talking about Christians, an attractive presence, a cadre of helpful people amid such miserable flu. And, as I left, I thought it no wonder the chapel was full.

In the text, Jesus was not hiding from the world. He was out in it, striding into the village of Nain, running full head on into a widow, into a mass of weeping, into the knotty problem of an only son's death. He was there with the word. He was there as an attractive presence. Look carefully at the word that describes Jesus' presence in the text: "Compassion." Indeed! Such makes us attractive and welcome in any crowd.

## Grace Encounters

Now we come to the third ingredient, often called the *power encounter*. I prefer to call them *grace encounters*. In the text, Jesus spoke the words, he was a compassionate attractive presence, but he also provided a dynamic encounter with the power of God as he raised the widow's son from the dead.

229

For years, a large segment of the church has labored to proclaim the Bible and maintain a church building brimming full of classes, daycare programs, friendly people, and such. But now a large number of young people are saying, "It's nice to be among such a loving people, and indeed, you labor well in proclaiming the word of Christ, but when do we stop talking and do the stuff? When do we pray and ask God for conversions? For healing? For changed lives? For dynamic power encounters with his grace?"

In my most recent church, we invited people forward at the end of the service. We had trained elders waiting. There we ministered to the failing, the hopeless, the sick, the lost. And, indeed, God did many things wonderful in our sight! There were healings, marriages put back together, conversions, people called out to the mission field, bad habits broken, hoarded money released to missions, and so much more known but to God.

Sometimes we Christians are afraid to lay it all on the line, believing, "What if I ask and nothing happens?" Listen! I learned a long time ago that if God heals, I get no credit for it. All the glory is his! So, why should I take credit to myself if God chooses not to heal in the way I prayed? Clearly, the duty is mine. The results are God's. My job is to be faithful and leave the results to him.

Look at the text. When Jesus worked the miracle, the crowd was awestruck! The text says, "Fear seized them all; and they glorified God." "God has visited his people!" they shouted. "And this report ... spread through the whole of Judea...."

Signs and wonders are the church bells that call people to worship. They are the step beyond presence and talk that show God is real and here and able and willing to do "exceedingly far more abundantly than all we ask or think!"

Now I know some are having trouble here. Why, just this week a fellow pastor said to me, "You act like you believe in miraculous conversion." And all I could say was, "Is there any other kind? When you entered the ministry you entered the realm of the supernatural. You entered the domain of human sin, of amazing grace, of divine intervention, of conversion, change, growth, of uncontrollable and surprising grace encounters."

Robert came to church a desperate man. His third marriage was failing. He'd become sexually addicted. He was lonely. Words of the sermon captured him, gave him hope. He looked around and saw pews filled with worshipers, some bowing in earnestness, others with faces lifted in rapturous praise. He came forward at the invitation, asked for a chance to become a Christian, and immediately felt a weight lifted off his shoulders.

Over the next years his life became different. He began to be kind. He started a small group Bible study in his law office. Fourteen people now attend it.

And the word has gone out across the city that God exists and can change selfish and enslaved divorcees.

Not all miracles, you see, are dramatic. Some come by process, subtly. But they come just the same, grace encounters of Jesus Christ.

### Conclusion

There are over six billion people on the planet today. Yet our churches are so empty! As one pastor put it, "People stay away in droves!"

And the problem isn't getting people to come to church. The challenge is getting the church to go to the world ... with the Word ... as an attractive presence ... believing we can encounter God's grace with power! Yes! Then, indeed, shall the world sit up and take notice that there is a God in Israel!

**Proper 6
Pentecost 4
Ordinary Time 11
Luke 7:36—8:3**

# Incident At A Table

Many of the great events of history have taken place at tables. The Magna Carta, limiting the king's ability to tax his citizens, was signed on a table after the Battle of Runnymede in England. Leo Tolstoy wrote the novel *War and Peace* on the back of a table. The peace treaty ending World War I was signed at table in the palace of Versailles in France. My wife and I fell in love over a dinner table.

The incident described in the text took place at a table. For, "one of the Pharisees asked him to eat with him, and he went into the Pharisee's house, and took his place at the table." And since there is much to be learned from this story, let's turn aside from our busy lives and look closely at what God is saying.

## He Comes Humbly

The Bible makes it clear. Our relationship with God begins with his initiative. For God incarnated himself in Jesus Christ and lived among us. He was born to the carpenter Joseph. He had his nativity in a stable. He was cradled in his mother Mary's arms. He was a Jew. As a boy he lived in Nazareth. He was a brother. He walked beside the sea. And, in the text, he visits a village and accepts a dinner invitation.

As John 1 teaches about Christ, "The word became flesh and dwelt among us." God was saying, "I am here! This is what I look like, what I expect of you."

Years ago, one Christmas morning, the Pope went to visit the inmates of a prison. He sat at their table to eat breakfast with them.

233

And he told the men, "You couldn't come to me so I came to you." Jesus Christ is God doing the same thing for us. We couldn't come to him, so he came to us. We couldn't find God, so he came to find us.

I have watched the high and mighty come to town, eat in the most expensive cafes, insist upon their privacy. Not Jesus. He comes humbly. He is a Nazarene, a Jew, a humble carpenter, and he accepts our invitation to eat with us.

Last summer at a Fellowship of Christian Athletes' summer camp, I was eating with some high school kids at a table in a crowded dining hall. I looked up and coach Bobby Bowden of Florida State University was sitting down at an empty place at our table. The rest of the young men failed to recognize him. Entering easily into our conversation, Coach Bowden and the lads talked of sports, of God, and girls, and politics, even the weather. The young men didn't have a clue with whom they were seated, until later on in the evening I told them.

"He was so humble," one said.

"He was just a normal guy," observed another.

"I can't believe I was that close to the coach of a national championship football team," said yet another.

And in the text, in that long ago incident at table, how many there really understood with whom they were eating? Almighty God! The Deity who shaped the universe took shape among us, becoming what we are that we might become one of his!

### We Come Humbly

Now notice how a lady suddenly crashes the dinner party uninvited.

The very erudite Pharisees are eating with Jesus. They are stiff around him, skeptical of his teachings, clueless as to who he really is. A thin veneer of civility barely conceals their hostility toward him.

Suddenly the door opens and a woman creeps in. She stands behind Christ, seems unsure of herself.

So long she has sought Christ! For months now she's heard of him, talked with those he has healed, forgiven, ennobled. And since

234

there was not much of any of this in her life, she desperately sought him out.

She's kneeling by Christ's side now, her tears splashing his feet. "Oh, I have wet his feet," she realizes in horror. So she unbraids her long hair and dries his feet with her locks.

The Pharisees are incensed. A woman only unbraids her hair at night, in private, for her husband. "This woman is a harlot! And Jesus is no prophet or he'd know what sort of woman is touching him!"

The woman is oblivious to all but Jesus in the room now. She has given herself to so many men, only to be used for a night and cast aside. She has known great sin, great rejection. And now looking up into Jesus' face, she sees unconditional love. And she not only weeps on Christ's feet, drying him with her hair, she humbly kisses his feet with her lips all the while mumbling her prayers of penance.

But that's not all! For while the Pharisees recoil in indignation at both her behavior and Christ's, she opens her hand and pours a bottle of expensive lotion over his body.

One can see in this woman's behavior great humility. As Christ preached in the Sermon on the Mount, the Beatitudes, our relationship with God begins with a sense of our total poverty before God, a deep felt grief over it, a meekness, and a genuine hunger and thirst for righteousness. All this is reflected in the woman's kneeling, in her tears, her hair, and kisses.

### We Don't Come At All!

Jesus comes to us humbly. And we meet him in humility, or we don't come at all. The text says Jesus knew what the Pharisees were thinking. So he put to them a question. "A certain creditor had two debtors. One owed him 500, the other 50. When they could not pay, he forgave them both. Now, which one will love him more?"

Simon, the Pharisee, answered, "I suppose the one whom he'd forgiven the most."

Then Jesus pointed to the harlot. "Since I came she has not ceased to humbly show thanksgiving for my coming, my mercy toward her sins. She's wept, she's dried my feet, she's poured lotion over my body. Simon, she knows she's the bride and I'm her groom in God's covenant of compassion! All the while you've barely concealed your self-righteous anger at me."

Turning to the woman, he said, "Go in peace. Your faith has saved you. You have loved well. Your sins are forgiven."

Then the Pharisees began to yammer all the more. "Who is this, who even forgives sins?"

My, but how pride destroys relationships! Oh, the shallow sophistication of the religious!

I judge myself by my virtues, you by your flaws, and always get such a splendid comparison.

So, I float through life smugly measuring and rating others — "Harlot!" "Spiritual lowlife!" And when I meet Jesus, I feel no need of him, for I can take care of myself, thank you.

I am not poor. I am richly religious.

I do not grieve. I celebrate how much better than you I am.

I am not meek. But I've got a thing or two to teach you!

And I do not hunger and thirst for righteousness. I assure you, I have all I need.

So it is, I can sit at table with Christ Jesus and never know who he is or why he came or how lost in pride I am.

### Conclusion

How many times in church over the past 50 years I've seen this episode reenacted. God is in our midst. And all we can do is look at ourselves in smug self-righteousness and judge others. Measure and rate. "I am pure!" Measure and rate. "Harlot." Measure and rate. "Who does this Jesus think he is?" Measure and rate. "I must say, I throw a nice supper party, even if I do say so myself!" Measure and rate.

But by whose standard? And shouldn't God be the judge?

Yes, this is the text that tells the story. Christ came humbly to table. We, as the woman, join him at table in humility. Or we do not come at all.

236

**Proper 7**
**Pentecost 5**
**Ordinary Time 12**
**Luke 8:26-39**

# The New Man For Our Time

This is the time of the year when new cars are unveiled. The latest models are out and people excitedly inspect the looks, the performance, and the mileage of Detroit's newest automobiles. During this feverous season when many of us are considering the new car for our time, it might also be a good idea to consider God's new man for our time. And here in our text we catch a glimpse of the new person Christ is engineering for such a time as this. This new person is so important his story is told in two pieces — Mark 5 and Luke 8. Let's look carefully at him.

**The God Relationship**

In the text we meet our new man. His name is Legion. You will notice his relationships. Pay close attention to them, for his relationships are the keys to understanding what Christ is doing in our world.

First there is Legion's God relationship. The text says that Jesus drew near the man Legion. And Legion, afraid, threw himself at Christ's feet and cried out, "I beg you, don't torment me." This is the old man. The old man is afraid of God. The presence of the holy for him is a tormenting thing. But in the later part of our text we see the new man. Legion is healed. He is sitting at the feet of Jesus. He's conversing in a relaxed manner. No longer is he fearful of God. He is comfortable in his presence.

In our world today many are like Legion before salvation. They aren't comfortable with God. He is a fearful thought to them. Yet in our society today there are many who are seeking to establish better relations with God.

Just look about you! Notice how religious people are. People are into gurus, transcendental meditation, Scientology, and such kinky cults as voodoo, witchcraft, and drug fests. The very fact that people are searching is proof that they've lost God, for no one seeks for what he already has.

The word "religion" is a Latin word. It comes from the root, "to bind back." Thus, when a man is religious he is attempting to bind himself back to God, to patch things up. But do you realize that the Bible teaches that man cannot by his own work right himself with God? The book of Genesis teaches that there was a time when God and people were close. But man sinned and God moved us from his presence in Eden. And to keep us from re-entering Eden on our own terms, God stationed an angel at the entrance. And this angel wielded a sword to guard the entrance and keep man out. This is how scripture makes it clear that from the human point of view there is no way back to God. Indeed, if we are to be put right with God, God himself must do the work.

A man driving along the highway heard a strange clang, but he ignored it and continued on. When he got home he found that one of his hubcaps was missing. Two weeks later while returning home along that same stretch of highway he spotted his hubcap propped up on the side of the road. Stopping to retrieve it, he found a note attached. It said, "I've been looking for you!" Biblically, the human race is like that lost hubcap. We have no ability to bind ourselves back to God. Unless he comes looking for us, unless he picks us up out of our lostness and binds us back, then there is no hope. And this is precisely the good news of the text. Jesus Christ is God. And he comes looking for the man Legion. He binds him back to God, and now Legion is no longer estranged. He sits relaxed and attentive at Christ's feet.

The new man for our time is a man that God is searching for. He is a man that God has found and bound back by Calvary's grace. And, yes, the new man for our time sits at the feet of Christ.

## The Self Relationship

The text speaks about Legion's relationship with himself: he was nude and unwashed. He bruised himself with stones. And likely he entertained the thought of suicide. But in binding him back, Christ changed all that.

In the later part of the text we see Legion bathed, properly dressed, and begging for a future, a chance to be Christ's companion and disciple.

Many in our world this day are akin to Legion in his self-loathing. A news story told of a British gentleman who committed suicide. True to his class, the man got out his "game book" in which real sportsmen keep a record of every animal they shoot and entered his own name under the category "various." Then he pulled the trigger on himself. Man is a hunted species. And man is often his own predator. U.S. statistics for one year showed there were some 21,000 murders in the United States. But there were 30,000 suicides!

Certainly for every person who kills himself there are thousands of others who at least think about it. And though they cannot work up the courage to slay themselves, they do, like Legion, commit slow self-murder. They "bruise themselves with stones." Ours is a generation of self-inflicted wounds. Overeating, workaholism, smoking, and drinking — these are our killers.

Norman Rockwell has a painting of a little girl seated before a mirror. A movie magazine in her lap is open to the picture of her favorite Hollywood starlet. The child has her hair up like the starlet's. And as she compares what she sees in the mirror with what she sees in the magazine she frowns. So many are like her today. They don't like the way they are. Their face is too plain. Their feet are too big or their figure is too short or tall or plump or skinny.

They feel their talents are not worthwhile. If God were to announce that he would do alterations on people at such and such a time and place, the line would be endless!

Obviously it is not good to go through life disliking oneself. Not only is it depressing to the individual, it is insulting to God! It is to shake an angry fist in his face and say, "You didn't know what you were doing when you made me! You blew it!"

239

In our text, salvation for Legion not only meant a new relationship with God, it meant a new relationship with himself. When God accepted Legion, then Legion began to accept himself. His self-inflicted bruises began to heal.

And the new man for our time? What does he look like? He is a person who loves himself. Because God has accepted him, so he accepts himself.

## The People Relationship

Now let us turn to Legion's relationship with other people. According to the text, Legion once was a kind of town freak. He lived alone in a cemetery, chained there by townspeople who were at their wits' end with how to deal with him. But Christ came and brought deliverance. He changed Legion from a lonely outcast to a friend seated amidst the disciples. And in the end, our Lord sent him home to tell them how much the Lord had done for him. Do you see how Christ's religion bound Legion back, not only to God and self, but to his neighbors as well?

Still, today is the world Legion in its human relationships. Loneliness, crime, war, divorce, injustice, oppression — which of us hasn't felt the blight of such horrors in our dealings with others?

Let me invite you to peer through a microscope for a moment. There magnified is an invisible jungle of creatures! And one of them is the amoeba. He is a clear jelly-like organism with dark spots for a mouth, a shapeless body, and an insatiable appetite. Each amoeba oozes through life, a self-contained little packet. He eats and reproduces, excretes, and eventually dies. The amoeba may travel only a foot or so during its entire life. But that doesn't seem to matter.

Another tiny being in that invisible jungle brought to view under a microscope is the white blood cell. They, too, are tiny self-contained packets of life that eat, reproduce, and die. Yet, unlike the amoeba, they work along with millions of other white blood cells in the body to accomplish a very important goal. They patrol the blood stream cleaning it of any alien germ or infection.

Under the microscope both the amoeba and the white blood cell look very much alike. But in terms of what they do they are world's apart! The amoeba is concerned only with itself. It's only purpose in life is to keep itself well fed and healthy. But the white blood cell has another purpose in life. It is a guardian against infection. And into the battle to keep others well it daily marches.

It seems to me that people are rather like amoebas and blood cells. Except we get to choose our lifestyle. We can be self-centered little grabbers or giving, healing servants. We can be selfish amoebas or servant white blood cells.

In the text we see that Christ's salvation had to do with Legion's relationship with others. Yes, it had to do with God and self. But that was not all of it! Christendom is not just "me and my God," as some are saying these days. It is also "my neighbor, too"! You see, salvation binds us back to our neighbors in servant roles. It changes us from amoebas into white blood cells.

Just as Legion went home and served his neighbors as an evangelist, so God directs his converts to go back into their neighborhoods and serve people with their gifts as well.

The new man for our time has Christ's religion. He is a man bound back to his neighbor by God. He is a man vitally interested in his companion's well-being. He is interested in how government is done. He is interested in human rights, equitable food distribution, evangelism, education, and justice. The new man for our time is like white blood cells. He patrols society on constant guard against the things that harm people.

### The Creation Relationship

A final look at the text is now in order. And here we must notice Legion's relationship to the environment. Legion before Christ was a walking pollutant. He was nude and unkempt. That's visual pollution. He cried out night and day. That's noise pollution. And he must have smelled horribly. That's odor pollution. But after Christ saved him, Legion obviously began to practice better hygiene. He had no doubt bathed, for we see him in the end clothed and in his right mind sitting at the feet of Jesus. His loud, chaotic cries are turned into preaching as he goes home to tell them there of God's grace.

241

Still, today is our world Legion. Our environmental hygiene is poor, for we are polluters. One wag has even suggested that we rewrite, *America the Beautiful* to say,

> *O beautiful, for smoggy skies,*
> *For insecticided grains,*
> *For strip-mined mountains majesty,*
> *Above the asphalt plains,*
> *America, America!*
> *Man sheds his waste on thee,*
> *And crowns thy good with homicide*
> *From sea to oily sea!*

Fifty years ago the Reverend George Buttrick commented on our greedy, you-only-go-around-once, grab-for-all-the-gusto-you-can-get oriented society. Speaking about what we call the "high standard of living," he said, "First of all, it's not high. Secondly, it's no standard. And finally, it's certainly not living!" And his words have proven prophetic. The World Health Organization estimates that up to 85 percent of all cancer in human beings is caused by pollutants introduced into our environment. The National Cancer Institute estimates that between sixty and ninety percent of cancer in humans is environmental in origin. The picture is more and more coming into focus. Our "high standard of living" is killing us.

What are we to do? The answer comes from God's word. Salvation has also to do with our relationship with creation. As Legion began to walk in harmony with the environment, so must we. And for all of us, it will mean that our "high standard of living" is modified, simplified, brought in harmony with God's will. Don't let this alarm you! Less can mean more. Simple can mean better. Years ago John Stuart Mill wrote, "I have learned to seek happiness by limiting my desires, rather than attempting to satisfy them." And if you embark on a more simple lifestyle, I think you'll find yourself happier, too. And God knows, the earth will breathe a little easier.

Some years ago Gandhi met the King of England. As usual Gandhi wore only a loin cloth. And as usual the king was dressed to the chin! "Why don't you put on some clothes?" the King snorted.

"And why don't you take some off?" Gandhi replied. "You've got on enough for three men." And the new man for our time? He is not the man who owns enough for an army. He is not the person who eats enough for three men. His is a simpler lifestyle. His is a life of basic harmony with creation. His standard of living is not set by peer pressure, by the more-is-better syndrome. His is a standard set by God.

**Thorough Conversion**

Back in 1971, I visited Oxford, England. And since C. S. Lewis is a favorite writer of mine, I sought out the college where he used to teach. An old gardener was there and I queried, "Did you know C. S. Lewis?" The man's face lit up and he said, "C. S. Lewis! Sure I knew him. He was one of the most thoroughly converted men I've ever known!" That's the kind of compliment Legion deserves, too. Christ's religion in him brought salvation to his every relationship: God-man, man-self, man-to-man, and man-environment. That's thorough conversion!

Today a great theological debate is going on between the fundamentalists on the one side and the liberals on the other. The fundamentalists say that the gospel is only to get you right with God so you can go to heaven. Liberals say, "No! No! That's all wrong. The gospel has only to do with people and justice!" But I submit to you that they are both wrong! It's not either/or! It's both! The gospel is concerned with both God and people, with both heaven and earth! You can see this so clearly in the great commandment. "You shall love the Lord your *God* ... and your *neighbor* as *yourself*." And here in the text we see salvation at work in Legion's life in each of these ways.

**Conclusion**

Do you recall the nursery rhyme about a crooked man who had a crooked cane, who walked a crooked mile, and who lived in a crooked house? Such is the condition of our world today. It's crooked! It's disjointed, out of kilter. It's broken in its basic relationships. Author Truman Capote once showed up for a television talk show interview bleary-eyed, obviously intoxicated, and claiming not to have slept in 48 hours. He told the interviewer that his anxiety problem caused him to mix drugs and alcohol "like some sort of cocktail." Later Capote confessed for a lot of us when he stated, "I see it as chronic ... there's just something about me ... that doesn't work."

What about you? Are you a crooked man walking a crooked way? Is there just something about you that doesn't work? Let it be a comfort to you to realize that others have been there, too. Legion certainly had been there. But it was the religion of Christ that brought him back! And this same Jesus is here looking to do it all for you today. Do you believe this? Will you call out to him by faith? Will you ask him to thoroughly convert you? Go fall at his feet as Legion did! "What have you to do with me thou Son of the most high God? I beg you! Have mercy on me!"

**Proper 8**
**Pentecost 6**
**Ordinary Time 13**
**Luke 9:51-62**

# Committed To
# The Committed One?

Try this experiment. Turn your radio on. Now dial it to your favorite station. Next, turn the dial just a wee bit more, so that you're still getting the signal, but a lot of static is coming through also.

What's the point? Just as a radio dial must be committed 100 percent to the station to do its job, so must we commit ourselves to Jesus Christ. Yet many of us try to have it both ways. We want to tune into God, yet we also want the world. We want to walk in truth, yet we do not want to discourage temptation entirely. So we get both the music and static.

Jesus said, "No man can serve two masters, for either he will hate the one and love the other or he will be devoted to the one and despise the other" (Matthew 6:24). He said "You shall love the Lord your God with *all* your heart ..." (Deuteronomy 6:5).

Commitment. That's what the text is about.

### God's Commitment To Us

At the center of our Christian faith is a cross. Jesus knew this. The text says, "When the days drew near for him to be received up...." That is, when the time of Passover neared ... when the time for the sacrificial lamb to be slain neared ... when the time for Jesus to be crucified ... to atone for our sins ... yes, that's what the text is saying!

Did you hear about the big tomcat sitting on the fence in the moonlight with his kitty? "I'd die for you, you pretty thing!" he crooned, to which she purred, "How many times?"

Christ was willing to lay down his one life for you.

The text says Christ, knowing what awaited him in Jerusalem, "set his face to go." And along the way there he passed through a Samaritan village. The people refused to hear him. The disciples wanted to call down fire on the people. Yet, again, Christ showed his commitment to mercy, refusing to be harsh. Instead he moved on to the next village.

My, but what a flurry of commitments Jesus reveals in this short episode. He is committed to the cross, committed to finishing his atoning labor in Jerusalem, committed to mercy, committed to correcting his disciples' harsh attitude when he rebukes them, and committed to world evangelism when he moves on to the next village.

This is the Christ! God committed to you and to me, to act in our best interest!

## Our Commitment To God

Now watch what happens in the text. Seeing Christ's resounding commitment, "a man said to him, 'I will follow you wherever you go.'" Yes! The commitment of Jesus elicits from us a commitment of our own.

We are like a man paddling his own little red canoe. He sees Jesus standing on the shore and magnanimously calls out, "Hey, Jesus, hop in and I'll give you a ride!" To which Jesus firmly responds, "What I really want you to do is follow me. Park your little red canoe, and come get in my boat that's parked around the corner and there you can row and take me where I want to go!"

Our commitment in today's church is to invite Jesus Christ into our lives to bless our plans for health ... for wealth ... for fun, and so on. But Jesus isn't interested in our plans. He wants to interest us in his plans.

In *The Cost of Discipleship*, Dietrich Bonhoeffer wrote, "When Jesus calls a man, he bids him come and die." That is, we die to our plans, our dreams, our lives that we might live to his.

Now, in the next few verses, watch what Jesus does. He quickly delineates several things that can hold us back in our commitment. First, He mentions *comforts*.

"Follow me, will you? Foxes have holes, and birds of the air have nests; but the Son of Man has nowhere to lay his head."

Christ was not a nester. He didn't stay holed up in some wallow of comfort. He was on the move, village to village.

I recall lovely Susan Harris 25 years ago. Long blonde hair, single, recent college graduate. Yet there was a call upon her life for Africa. The Sunday night we laid hands upon her and sent her out from the church, she wept. "Here is my home. I am afraid to leave air conditioning. I don't want to have to cut my hair. And I love Dr Pepper soft drinks. And there won't be any where I'm going!" But she went anyway. She's still on the field. She sacrificed her comforts, her hair, her appetites, to go with Jesus to the next village.

Now Christ mentions the next obstacle to hold us back — our *worldly commitments.*

The text says the Lord looked into the face of a follower and beckoned him to come. The man said, "Lord, let me first go and bury my father." But he said to him, "Leave the dead to bury their own dead; but as for you, go and proclaim the kingdom of God."

Yes! We are a people with entanglements. We have parents who care about us. Sometimes they are sick and need care. Sometimes they want us to take over the family business. We have wives to please, mortgages to satisfy, businesses to run. And these things can make us stay put.

I recall a young professional athlete walking forward in a church service, football in hand. Much to my surprise, he placed the football on the communion table and said, "I never want that to keep me from following and serving the Lord!"

Homes, careers, parents, business contracts — these are wonderful things. But when Christ calls they must be set aside.

Finally, Jesus mentions our *comrades.* "Another said, 'Lord, I will follow you but let me first say farewell to those at my home.' Jesus said to him, 'No one who puts his hand to the plow and looks back is fit for the kingdom of God.' "

Yes, *comforts* can glue us to our seats. *Commitments* can cause us to stick. But our *comrades*, our relationships, they bid us stay as well.

So many times in college I would begin a serious relationship with a girlfriend. And inevitably the question would come, "What are you going to do for a career?" When I answered, "Preacher," that usually ended the relationship within the week. One girl actually told me, "I don't think I can marry a preacher. They move around so much. The antiques I will inherit won't fit into just any house."

Jesus says we're working with God, plowing the fields, sowing seed. And we can't be looking back over our shoulders at the comforts, the worldly commitments, and old friendships that would bid us set the work aside. As he "set his face to go to Jerusalem," committed to die for our sins, so must we respond in kind, and set our hearts in faithfulness to do his will.

## Conclusion

Did you hear about the pig and the chicken walking through the impoverished streets of a third world village? The chicken said to the pig, "Look at all these starving people! We ought to do something! Let's cook up some scrambled eggs and ham for them!"

To which the pig replied, "That's only involvement for you, but it's total commitment for me!"

You see, many of us only want to be involved with Christ, not totally committed. But the one who is totally committed to us calls for our full commitment to him.

248

**Proper 9**
**Pentecost 7**
**Ordinary Time 14**
**Luke 10:1-11, 16-20**

# How Good News Spreads!

In 1971 I made a trip to Russia. I was studying literature in England and hitched on to a discount side trip in November. Of special interest to me was the Russian author Leo Tolstoy. I had read his *War and Peace, Anna Karenina,* and *Resurrection.* Knowing of his Christian faith as well as his literary ability, I was drawn to all things Tolstoy.

You can imagine my joy in visiting "Bright Glenn," Tolstoy's country estate. Some of his original manuscripts were stacked in a corner. One, then, could leaf the pages, scrutinize his penmanship, observe his strike overs. I sat at his desk, in his chair, even held his quill pen in my hand. I even fantasized that Leo himself walked into the room, greeted me heartily, and asked me to work with him on his newest novel!

That would be some invitation, wouldn't it? To co-labor with Tolstoy. A commission to co-author the latest Russian classic!

But, alas, there was no risen Tolstoy, no voice of commission. Only silence broken by the shrill November winter winds sweeping across the Soviet plains. And to this day I remain an un-commissioned artist.

There is in my life and yours, however, a genuine commissioning that, if you think about it, far outshines any other possible call to art. It is the Great Commission of Jesus Christ. "Go," God commissions in Matthew. "Go therefore and make disciples of all nations...." In 1 Kings 8:42, it is said of God, "Men will hear of your great name and your mighty hand and your outstretched arm...." God, it seems, wills to work with us to create a people for himself.

249

Genesis chapters 1-2 explain how the Lord creates the heavens and the earth and all life to enjoy it. Then on the seventh day he rested. Somewhere in time humanity sinned and all of life fell to ruin. But God rolled up his sleeves and went to work with a divine redeeming strategy that spanned the years and ultimately included Christ, the cross, the resurrection, and the indwelling power of the Holy Spirit.

This makes today theologically the Eighth Day of Creation. The Lord is at labor setting this abnormal world right again. And he invites us, he commissions us, to co-labor with him in this divine enterprise.

In the text Jesus appointed seventy others and sent them ahead of them, two by two, into every town and place where he himself was about to come. "And he said to them, 'The harvest is plentiful, but the laborers are few.' "

Let's look some at the record of the church and world evangelism. There are four major means by which Jesus Christ has been proclaimed.

**Voluntarily Going**

The first is when God's people voluntarily go. Acts 13:1f speaks of the early church in Antioch. A great host of people had learned of God's love in Jesus and embraced God by faith. A vital church community had formed and matured in knowledge, relationships, and ministry skills.

It was then that the Holy Spirit spoke, reminding the church that there were others "out there," in other cities, in other nations, on other continents that knew not of God nor His ways in Jesus. So it was that Barnabas and Paul were called on to depart the church voluntarily and carry the gospel to regions afar.

The early church didn't hoard the good news. It shared it with breathless excitement. And it did so by sending two beloved men — active, proven, and mature.

In the past, the modern church has sometimes been slack in sending missionaries. And when we do get around to doing so, we all too frequently send under-trained, immature misfits. More than

I care to remember, I have seen untested men, unuseful here, discontented with job, see the mission field as an answer to boredom, a chance to flee their problems, to live the great adventure. And with self-will they head for the third world! And, sadly, their ministry on the field was as big a bust there as it was here.

I spoke with a national pastor in Nepal about missionaries the church sends out. He said, "Stephen, if you won't miss them, don't send them to us!"

The early church sent Paul and Barnabas. They sent their best! We should do no less.

I recall Michael Murray, a bright young freshman at Duke University. He hardly missed a service in the church. He came early and stayed late mixing in with people. When we were short a song leader at the college ministry, he jumped in with his guitar for a whole year. He worked a six-month internship for the church to learn preaching and administration. He got a master's degree in linguistics. He made numerous short term mission trips to China. He married a nurse willing to live in the foreign field. God built Michael very thoroughly. And one cold winter's Sunday night we went as a church out on the front lawn. There Michael and Yolanda Murray knelt down and we laid hands on them sending them out to far regions. And the Murrays today are preaching and living grace among a needy people still to this day.

**Involuntarily Go**

The gospel spreads when we volunteer to go. It also spreads another way — when we involuntarily go.

When Babylon conquered Israel in battle, the year was around 588 B.C. Thousands of Jews were deported 500 miles east as slaves. In their captivity they carried their knowledge of God with them. And many a Gentile thus learned of the Lord.

Psalm 137 was written during this exile. Hear their lament as Jewish slaves living in a pagan land. "By the rivers of Babylon, there we sat down and there we wept, when we remembered Zion. On the willows there we hung up our harps. For there our captors asked us for songs ... How could we sing the Lord's song in a foreign land?"

There have been many led against their will to foreign lands. But they went with Jesus and evangelized the people to whom they were brought captive.

A Welshman named Sucant was abducted by pirates in 403 A.D. The sixteen-year-old Christian lad was taken to Ireland and enslaved for five years by the cruelest of Irish chieftains. Eventually Sucant escaped to join a monastery in Southern France. There he changed his name to Patrick, and intended to live out his years in the orderly monastic life of a monk.

Yet in 432 A.D., at the age of 45, the Holy Spirit called Patrick to return to Ireland and carry the gospel to his former tormentors. This Patrick did, investing the remainder of his life in the Irish. During the next 31 years he baptized more than 120,000 people into Christ!

Still today the Irish say of Patrick, "He found Ireland all heathen. He left it all Christian."

**Voluntarily Coming**

So, according to 1 Kings 8:42, "Men will hear of your great name...." And how shall this be? As we go willingly or unwilling to the nations.

Yet this is not all! For there is still a third way Good News spreads, and that is as others voluntarily come to us.

1 Kings 10:6-7, 23-24, tells of the Queen of Sheba traveling from Africa to Jerusalem to meet King Solomon. Fascinated by his religion and wisdom she came to swill it all in. "So she said to the king, 'The report was true that I heard in my own land of your accomplishments and of your wisdom, but I did not believe the reports until I came and my own eyes had seen it. Not even half had been told me.' "

Roman soldiers on duty in Palestine, men like Cornelius, willingly came to serve in war. While there they inquired of the gospel (Acts 10).

Here in the United States today foreigners are coming in droves to attend our colleges. They are the brightest and best of China, Zimbabwe, Australia, Russia, the Sudan, and beyond. Not counting diplomats, spouses, children, and business travelers, foreign students number well over half a million souls. Eighty-seven percent return to their nations upon graduation. Most assume positions of leadership. And they take with them so much of what they learned here.

Over the nine years I led a Bible study on Elon College's campus I met and had in my home youth from Holland, Israel, Peru, Iran, and Germany. I tell you, the world is coming to our doorstep and we have opportunity to serve them. Perhaps many will convert to Christ and go home like the Queen of Sheba, saying, "Behold, the half of it wasn't told me! For, indeed, there is a God in Jesus Christ!"

### Involuntarily Come

So, we may willingly or unwillingly go. But the gospel also spreads when we willingly come. And, finally, there is a fourth means of missions: unwillingly coming.

Paul the apostle was imprisoned for his faith. Yet in jail he evangelized and mentored soldier converts and wrote much of the New Testament epistles.

I know of a Christian in Brazil thrown into prison on unjust charges. At first he fought to extract himself from such a hell hole. He was unwilling to come to such a place! Then God opened his eyes and he saw 4,000 men with him in the dungeon. And he began to testify and minister. Today, after eleven years in prison, his ministry is fruitful beyond what one can imagine! And no one else could have even gotten into the jail to bring such light! "Things turn out for the best for those who make the best of the way things turn out," he says.

### Conclusion

If you study the history of missions, you find a big push in the early church to evangelize the Mediterranean world between 40 A.D. and 350 A.D. And they did it without radio, television, fax machines, church buildings, cars, phones, and huge budgets.

By 350 A.D. the church had stagnated and grown comfortable in the world. Come 500 A.D. Christianity was actually shrinking in number.

That's when Islam began to spread across Asia, Europe, and Africa. By 700 A.D. it looked like Muslims would rule the world! It was a dark age.

Slowly, however, the church began to reawaken. In 1492 Columbus encountered the New World. In 1517 Luther began the Protestant Reformation. And by 1600 the Colonial era began.

Up until now Christianity was only a Western religion. But now it leapt to a global faith as missionaries carried the gospel to China, India, South America, and beyond.

Schools like Dartmouth College in New Hampshire were founded to evangelize Indians. They took John the Baptizer's motto as their own, "A voice crying in the wilderness."

Still today, however, there are unreached peoples. Fully one half of the world's population hasn't heard the gospel.

In 1930 an American Christian missionary to Japan wrote home to his church alarmed about Japanese militarism. He pleaded, "Send me 2,000 of your best sons as missionaries or in 10 years send me 1,000,000 men as soldiers."

It's chilling, isn't it? If we do not willingly go, God may send us unwillingly.

Make no mistake. God's middle name is "Go." We have been commissioned! As the text says, "Men will hear of your great name!" And by our going and their coming the world will know.

Let this be our truth: that Jesus is the Savior of the whole world. And he is our Lord.

Some of us must go. And some of us must let go of our sons and daughters and friends. Others must help go with prayer and funding. But all of us must get going! For we've a story to tell to the nations!

Proper 10
Pentecost 8
Ordinary Time 15
Luke 10:25-37

# A Show Of Hands

How does one describe love for another person? A Scotsman would say, "Love is an outward inexpressability of an inward all overishness." A teenager might call love "an itching in your heart that you can't scratch." A bride-to-be will likely say that "love is a feeling that you feel when you feel that you're feeling a feeling you've never felt before." And if you ask the poet Carl Sandburg he will tell you that love is "a personal sweat." We could go on passing the microphone around allowing folk singers, politicians, teachers, and housewives to have their say. But there is not enough time. So let us turn to the scriptures, to Jesus Christ, and hear his definition of love for another person.

We find the Lord's definition of neighborly love in the parable of the Good Samaritan. Christ's definition does not come in a song, in feelings or abstracts, in theological sayings or poetry. It comes from a concrete story. It comes in a practical application of human concern. "What is love for one's neighbor?"' we ask Jesus. And his reply, "It's in your hands. Look at your hands! There is where love can be known!"

**Hands That Can Hurt**

When we examine the Lord's parable of the Good Samaritan, we quickly note that the story is something of a meditation on hands. First Jesus tells us about hands that are clenched in fists.

Now hands can do a lot in a clench. They can grip a blackjack, a pair of brass knuckles, or a switchblade. They can squeeze the trigger of a pistol, strike as a fist, or choke the life out of someone.

255

Hands can take and take, and take some more. They can forge checks, steal money, and destroy property.

Obviously, these are the sort of hands the robbers had in Jesus' parable. The text says, "A man was going down from Jerusalem to Jericho, and he fell among robbers, who stripped him and beat him, and departed, leaving him half dead."

Certainly we still have the hands of thieves with us in our world today. Their motto is, "What's yours is mine and I'll take it." Shoplifters, burglars, rapists, murderers — the streets are full of them. But before we pat ourselves on the back saying, "I thank thee, Lord of heaven, that I am not like these thieves," let us examine our own hands a bit more closely.

Our hands can be clenched in fists in many ways. They can be destructive in a variety of fashions. Hands can rob and injure both in what they do and in what they do not do. A school teacher who does not adequately prepare his lesson is robbing his pupils. An attorney who flips through his law books, finds a loophole, and then uses his hands to argue his case fervently in court can rob society of justice. A workman who is lazy and takes shortcuts is a payroll thief. (His paycheck ought to be gift-wrapped each week.) A father is a thief when he does not take time to be with his children. A gossip is a thief who steals a reputation. Then there is the thief who refuses to honor his vows to the church. He deprives the Sunday school of his talents. He withholds his finances. He is destructive by avoiding worship and the therapy therein. And he is being just as destructive to the church as an arsonist or a burglar.

But, I ask you, is this any way to use our hands? I remind you that God showed his hands in this world in the person of Jesus Christ. His hands were gentle hands. They were hands of healing and sharing, praying hands, hands that took up a whip for justice. They were, indeed, saving hands! And aren't those the kind of hands you want?

**Idle Hands**

Yes, hands can do a lot of things. They can rob and beat; they can destroy and kill. But hands are much more versatile than that. Hands can also be idle. They can be folded in the lap or stuffed in a pocket. They can grip tightly, hold fast and firm. Hands can cover the mouth, plug the ears, and shield the eyes from seeing.

These are the kind of hands that the priest and the Levite in Christ's parable had. They were tight-fisted men. Their hands were idle toward human need.

The text says that the robbers left their victim naked and half dead in the ditch. And "by chance a priest was going down that road; and when he saw him he passed by on the other side." No doubt this priest was remembering that according to Jewish law he who touched a dead man was unclean for seven days (Numbers 19:11). From a distance the priest could not be sure, but he feared that the man was dead. And if he touched him he would lose his turn of duty in the Temple. And he refused to risk that, so he passed on. To him religious ceremony was more important than charity. His career was more important than meeting human need. If the robbers' hands were clenched, the priest's hands were tight-fisted. If the thieves' motto was, "What's yours is mine and I'll take it," then the priest's motto was, "What's mine is mine and I'll keep it."

You young people need to guard against this attitude. I am thinking of that little pimply-faced boy in your class. He tries so hard to be included. He is lonely. Do you ever sit with him at the lunch table? Do you offer your friendship to him? Or do you pass by on the other side, not wanting yourself to face criticism and mockery? Do you, too, fold your hands, putting popularity ahead of human need?

A church group asked a minister in Seattle, Washington, to give them a tour of the inner city. "Show us the needs," they asked. So the pastor spent three hours on and off a bus with the church group. He showed them a slum dwelling with its rats and leaky plumbing. He showed them firsthand how the vicious circle of superstition, injustice, oppression, crime, and hopelessness operated. As the bus pulled to the curb back at the church, there was a moment of strict silence as the people sat under the weight of what they had seen. Then the church leader began to thank the minister profusely for the tour. Finishing her statement of gratitude, the woman then asked, "Now before we leave, can you tell us where the best Chinese restaurant in town is?" Not, "I see the need, what can I do?" but, "I feel a need, where can I eat?" And they passed by on the other side.

Another tight-fisted man in the text was the Levite. The text says that he, too, saw the victim. And he too hurried along.

The text seems to infer that the Levite had gone nearer to the man before passing on. Perhaps his heart had immediately gone out to the man. His first reaction was to stop and help. But then he had second thoughts. Bandits were in the habit of using decoys. One of their number would act the part of a wounded man. Then when some unsuspecting traveler stopped over him, the thieves would rush upon him. The Levite possibly thought of all this. Involvement was risky business. And since his motto was, "Safety first," he too, passed by on the other side.

We live in the same kind of world today. Involvement is still a risky business. Helping hands can still get you into trouble. You can still be taken advantage of. And many people have simply stuffed their hands in their pockets and said, "Safety first. What's mine is mine and I'll keep it."

Beckett's play, *Waiting for Godot*, characterizes modern society. In it Vladimir nervously asks, "Well? What do we do?" His friend Estragon hangs his head and mumbles, "Don't let's do anything; it's safer." And so we fold our hands and pass by on the opposite side. It's safer.

You heard about the lady's car that stalled on the expressway. She got out, raised the hood, tied a handkerchief to the aerial, and waited for help. Two hours passed in the hot, blistering summer afternoon. Hundreds of automobiles zoomed past her. You can imagine her relief when a Cadillac full of women pulled up beside her, the electric window lowered, out swept a gush of cool fragrant air, and a lady inquired, "Pardon me. We hate to bother you. But could you tell us where you got that darling pants suit you're wearing?" And so we go through life concerned with our own needs and wants, while blind to the needs of others.

**Helping Hands**

Yes, Jesus said neighborly love is defined in your hands. And hands can do so much! Sure they can gouge and rob and kill. They can be idle, build a fence to hide an ugly view, or stop one's ears. But, thank God, their story doesn't stop here. Hands can also give. They can soothe and lift, offer ministry in any one of a thousand ways. They can give gifts, carry burdens, create, and share.

And in the text Jesus tells us about the hands of a Samaritan he calls good. The text copy says that after the robbers, after the priest and the Levite, after their hands, a Samaritan came to where the victim was. "And when he saw him, he had compassion, and went to him and bound up his wounds, pouring on oil and wine; then he set him on his own beast and brought him to an inn, and took care of him."

Now some interesting things need to be brought out concerning the Samaritan's behavior. The road from Jerusalem to Jericho is the scene of this parable. It was then and still is today a notoriously dangerous road. Jerusalem is 2,300 feet above sea level; Jericho, which stood near the Dead Sea, is 1,300 below sea level. So then, the 21-mile road that joins Jericho to Jerusalem drops nearly 3,600 feet. It is a road of narrow, rocky defiles and sudden turnings. And naturally it was a perfect hideout for bandits. In the fifth century Jerome called it "the red or bloody way." In the nineteenth century it was still necessary to pay safety money to local sheiks before one could travel on it. In Jesus' time people seldom traveled on this road alone. They moved in convoys because of the safety in numbers. Yet the way Jesus told this parable leads one to believe that this traveler had attempted to go it alone. He must have been a foolhardy, reckless fellow. And he ended up victimized and suffering in the ditch. He had no one to blame but himself. Still, the Samaritan had compassion on him. Still, he helped him. Is Jesus saying that we even have to help fools?

Also, notice who it was who helped whom in this parable. A Samaritan was helping a man who was probably Jewish. You will recall that Jews had no dealings with Samaritans, who were social outcasts. So here we find a man who has borne the brunt of a life-long prejudice helping a member of a society that has oppressed him. Today's equivalent would be a black businessman helping a white man who had been mugged by a street gang.

Then there is the fact that the Good Samaritan met the victim's needs. He didn't just pray for the man and walk away. Nor did he give him advice. "The hospital is down this road to the left. Ask anyone. They'll tell you." He took time, muscle, his donkey (while he himself walked), and money, and he got the victim to an inn. There he saw to it that the victim was nursed back to health.

You will also note that the Samaritan met only the man's needs. His purpose was to get the man on his feet so he could stand on his own. Jesus is saying that we are not responsible for a wino's beverage or a bum's cigarettes. If you are a Good Samaritan, you meet a man's needs not his wants or sins. (Welfare take note!)

Also of interest is the fact that we are not told the Good Samaritan's name. He remains anonymous to all. This is in keeping with Christ's teaching on giving: "Do not let your left hand know what your right hand is doing" (Matthew 6:3). The parable is teaching that we are not to give for show, for the praise of men, but quietly and out of compassion.

Yes, we have seen the hands of the Samaritan. They are open hands, giving and ministering hands. His motto was, "What's mine is yours and we'll share it!"

What about your hands? Are your hands clenched? Are they selfish and tight-fisted? Or are they open palms?

There is still so much need in the world today. Hurting hands have done their worst and idle hands have refused to do their work. There is a victim beside every foot path you may care to trod. Prison, divorce, poverty, ignorance, illness, joblessness — as the population increases the number of victims grows. There are now more beaten, stripped, and half-dead people beside life's roads than one can count or carry. The televison shows us. The radio blurts it out. Newspapers tell us the details. Magazines pictorialize it.

Cervantes, the author of *Don Quixote*, said, "Many times I took up my pen to write and many times I put it down not knowing what to say." I have felt the same way while writing this sermon. Human need is so great I have all but been overwhelmed. I have paused at this point, gripped the pen to write, and put the pen down again not knowing what to say. I think the key to responsible living in a world with a bloody victim almost every step of the way down Jericho's road is always to do the most loving, practical thing possible. If you do that, you will always be doing God's will.

As you travel the roads of life, it is important to start where you are. You cannot always be open-handed in India, but you can be open-handed in your own neighborhood. I am thinking of a meter reader who saw a frayed electrical wire in an elderly customer's basement. He fixed it with a little roll of tape he carried with him. I am thinking of a dentist who pulled three teeth from a poor lady's mouth. He wrote her a prescription for pain, then seeing that she could not afford the medicine, reached into his own wallet and handed her the ten dollars. I am thinking of an elderly couple who assisted me when I ran out of gas returning from a revival late at night. They helped a stranger at midnight! Help the victims beside your own driveway and on the way to work.

Yes, start where you are. Do the things within reach and the Lord will lengthen your arm. In Christianity the reward of a job well done is more work! And God will give you an opportunity to reach out from your own neighborhood to other parts of the world. Your own church gives you opportunities to provide money to feed the poor and develop their agricultural programs. The government of the United States can be taught to give more generously and wisely of her resources. Agencies give you a chance to adopt a child orphaned and hungry. Yes, start right where you are. The need is overwhelming. But start! And reach out from there.

### How Many Hands Do You Have?

Now let me ask you a question. How many hands do you have? You've only got two, right? Wrong! Actually, you've got six. We've all got two hands that rob, two that are closed, and another two that are giving. The problem is, how do we get rid to the two that rob, the other two that are selfish, and keep and strengthen the two that are giving?

I think that at least part of the answer is found in this poem called, "Hands" that was written by James D. Smith, an inmate at the U.S. Penitentiary in Leavenworth, Kansas. He writes:

*Hands express many things ...*
*Sorrow, gladness, fear.*
*Hands can push someone away,*
*Or hold them very near.*
*Hands create beautiful things.*
*And some hands can destroy.*
*Hands can spank a naughty child*
*Or mend a broken toy.*
*But there's another use for hands,*
*Which everyone can afford.*
*And that's when you reach out and say,*
*Take my hand, please, Lord.*

Yes, part of the answer comes in giving your hands to God. Christ died for your hands, your fists, and your selfishness. He takes the hurt and stinginess out of them. And he strengthens them to love. He outfits them to serve your brother.

The other part of the answer comes when we give our hands to other people. Joe had been asked to get up at five in the morning and drive a crippled child fifty miles to the hospital. He did not want to do it, but he did not know how to say no. A woman carried the child out to the car and set him next to the driver's seat. All the while she mumbled her thanks through tears. Joe said everything would be all right and quickly drove off. After a mile or so the child asked shyly: "You're God, aren't you?" "I'm afraid not, little fellow," replied Joe. "I thought you were God," said the child. "I heard Mother praying next to my bed asking God to help me get to the hospital, so I could get well and play with the other children. Do you work for God?" "Sometimes, I guess," Joe answered, "but not regularly. I think I'm going to work for him a lot more from now on!"

### Conclusion

And Jesus said, " 'Which of these three, do you think, was a neighbor to the man who fell into the hands of the robbers?' He said, 'The one who showed him mercy.' And Jesus said to him, 'Go and do likewise.' "

262

# A Woman's Place

---

In 1999 I traveled in North Africa. Early one morning I found myself in a village center where a Muslim cleric was holding court on local civic matters.

It seems an Islamic man, angry with his wife, desired to divorce her, for her general failure to satisfy him.

The woman asked him for a chance to speak, and made quite an impassioned plea in Arabic, to which the great crowd of men responded with prolonged laughter.

I asked my Arabic-speaking host, "What are they laughing about?" He told me, "They are laughing because she insists on her rights, but in their religion she doesn't have any."

Indeed, in Islam the man rules supreme, while the woman is little more than a family slave who can be run off with nothing but the clothes on her back.

One forward-thinking Muslim cleric recently mused, "The nations of Islam will never become a great and lasting power because we are like a person paralyzed on one half of our body." What he referred to was Islam's poor treatment of women.

### The World Belittles Women

Sadly, it is not just Muhammadanism that denigrates femininity. The Judeo-Christian faith has much to answer for itself.

For instance, Orthodox Jewish men pray daily thanking God he did not make them women. And if you read the Tenth Commandment in Exodus 20, a woman is reduced to chattel. "You shall not covet your neighbor's house ... wife ... servant ... donkey." In fact, by Jesus' day, the rabbis had a saying: "It's better to burn the Torah than teach it to a woman." So it was that women were kept back from the center of things in the Jerusalem temple. They had their own isolated porch from which they could peer down upon the proceedings.

One can see some of this negative attitude toward women in the text. Jesus is in the village of Bethany visiting the home of Mary, Martha, and Lazarus. They were a wealthy family and opened their home to Christ for rest.

In fact, the very name "Bethany" means in Hebrew *house of rest*. Theirs was a place Christ could sleep late, meditate in their shade-adorned garden, eat a good meal, and bathe at leisure.

So, the text says, "Now as they went on their way, he entered a certain village, where a woman named Martha welcomed him into her home. She had a sister named Mary, who sat at the Lord's feet and listened to what he was saying."

Evidently Martha decided Jesus needed a good meal, so she fussed over him and busied herself in the kitchen. She wasn't so much meeting his needs for food as she was meeting her needs for being the perfect hostess.

But Christ, knowing his time is short, gets up from his nap, I imagine, and finding a crowd of teachable men waiting around, begins to teach more of the scriptures. And Mary slips in quietly to listen.

Now watch what happens! The Bible says, "Martha was distracted by her many tasks; so she came to him and asked, 'Lord, do you not care that my sister has left me to do all the work by myself? Tell her then to help me.' "

Typically we think of Martha's complaint as that of one left alone to wait on all these men while her sister quietly sat out her part. But look closer and you shall see it is not so!

The text says Mary "sat at the Lord's feet and listened" to his teaching. The phrase "sat at the Lord's feet" is a discipleship term. The Apostle Paul testifies that he grew up "seated at the feet of Gamaliel," the Jewish scholar. In those days, you see, a band of male students attached themselves to a scholar and followed him around watching his behavior, listening to his words, questioning him for insights. So, what Martha is really complaining about is, "Look, Jesus, I know my place is here in the kitchen, but there's my sister sitting at your feet, acting like a man! Bid her get up and go to her rightful place."

Here is a woman who has been denied a wider role in temple and society who not only believes it for herself, but is trying to invoke those restrictions on her sister. It is as Tolstoy said of fellow Russian novelist Dostoevsky, "He was sick. And he wanted the whole world to be sick with him."

## Christ Ennobled Women

So, what is Jesus going to do? How will he answer Martha's complaint? Will he brusquely shoo Mary into the kitchen? The great surprise of the text is that Jesus gently rebukes the pot-and-pan-wielding Martha while affirming the spiritually-hungry and studious Mary.

"Martha, Martha, you are anxious and troubled about many things. One thing is needful. Mary has chosen the good portion, which shall not be taken away from her."

Jesus went against the grain of his time and refused to denigrate women. Rather, he ennobled them.

Why? If you look at the original creation story in Genesis 1:27, it says, "So God created man in his own image, in the image of God he created him; male and female he created them" (RSV). Do you see here how God's image is not contained in the masculine image alone? God's image is revealed in both the masculine and feminine genders together.

So, it cannot be that the church, the very body of Christ, can effectively show forth the nature of God and be an exclusive men's club. The church must ennoble women. She must embrace the best of male and female.

But you say, "Did not Jesus teach us in the Lord's Prayer to refer to God as 'Our Father'?" Absolutely! But elsewhere, when Jesus wept over Jerusalem, he said, "I was a hen [not a rooster] and would have gathered you under my wings as a mother does her chicks."

Jesus is the groom. We are his bride. Together we comprise the body. Male and female. Not in competition, but complementing one the other. Completeness in both genders.

The story of Mary and Martha is not an aberration that I have cleverly interpreted. Check it out for yourself. Women were the last to leave Christ's side at the cross, and they were the first at the empty tomb. In fact, it was a woman who first proclaimed the risen Christ! Yet sadly, too true to form, the men thought her to be hysterical, and refused to believe her witness.

What I am striving for you to see with all the might the Spirit inspires within me from the authority of the text is that women count! Why, they comprise over fifty percent of church membership. And with all the things that need doing in and out of the church, how can we expect to succeed if we paralyze half our body, half our labor force, half the image of God by our obdurate behavior?

I challenge you to do some homework! Read Hurley's book, *Man and Woman in Biblical Perspective*. Better still, read the Bible. Read the book of Acts, the record of the early church, and each time a woman is mentioned, mark the place with an orange pen. Then go back and get the big picture by seeing just what a vital part women played in the early church. You'll be surprised at how much orange is there! Why, women were there in the upper room when the fires of Pentecost fell. The woman Lydia was the first convert in Europe. Philip had seven daughters who prophesied. And Priscilla, along with her husband Aquilla, was an important minister in Rome.

### Conclusion

On a certain remote Pacific island before World War II, women followed their men at a humble ten paces behind. After the war they were allowed to walk ten paces ahead. You see, the Japanese had mined the island, so women were used as mine sweepers.

What place do women have in the gospel?

I tell you, much Bible study needs to be done here to find the proper balance in the church. And the time to begin is now, lest any woman be held back by our benighted ungraciousness.

# Sermons On The Gospel Readings

## For Sundays
## After Pentecost
## (Middle Third)

### *The Transforming Power*
### *Of A Changed Perspective*

### R. Robert Cueni

*To Lexington Theological Seminary:*
*a community dedicated to the*
*transforming power of changed perspectives.*

# Foreword

A pastor might not ordinarily think of the middle of Ordinary Time as an exciting season for preaching. Ordinary Time does not have the sense of anticipation that marks the season of Advent nor the gravity of Lent. Ordinary Time does not move toward the satisfaction of fulfillment that we associate with Christmas or the victory and power that emanate from Easter.

However, the sermons in *The Transforming Power of a Changed Perspective* show that preaching through the lectionary in Ordinary Time can be an extraordinary experience. The title sermon reveals the underlying theme of this collection: When we look at the world through the perspective of the reign of God, we are transformed. We become more attuned to God's purposes for us and for all, as well as for God's will for all in the world to live together in love. Our awareness of the divine rule affects not only our own transformation, but empowers us to be agents for the transformation of the world in the direction of God's purposes of love for all.

Robert Cueni's messages sketch the broad outlines of this new perspective. The first sermon uses the Lord's Prayer to alert us to the overarching themes of God's perspective on the world. God seeks to remake this world into an arena in which all persons, circumstances, and events manifest the divine reign. A provocative message titled "It's God's Grace, Not American Ingenuity" uses the parable of the wealthy barn-builder to help us recognize that only God's gracious rule (not our American ingenuity) can satisfy the deepest longings of the human heart for security, and love, and purpose in life.

A sermon on Jesus' statement that divine fire falls from heaven adds to our perspective by helping us consider how God's judgment (represented by the fire) can be redemptive. A challenging message on the bent-over woman concludes "all Jesus did was convince the woman that she could stand up straight under her burden." Similarly, Jesus reminds us that the presence of the divine aegis means that we, too, can "stand up straight."

Making use of an original parable inspired by Jesus' teaching at a dinner party, the author concludes, "Your value as a person does not rely on having your name on the social register. You are the loved child of God." However, coming to the awareness that we are God's love children is only the beginning of transformation into the Christian life. To avoid being "clueless enthusiasts," we need to grow in discipleship so that our perspective comes ever closer to God's.

Along the way, however, we need to avoid becoming "religion police," that is, Christians whose desire to be faithful hardens into rigidity and exclusivism that works against the reign of God. In the very next sermon (on the dishonest manager), Cueni implicitly shows that preachers need also to be wary of "exegetical police" (my term) who would reduce a text to one and only one meaning. In "Jesus' Most Perplexing Parable," Cueni finds not one but three transforming perspectives on the reign of God.

In a sermon that deals courageously with the notions of divine punishment and hell, the writer contends that the rich person (in the parable of the rich person and Lazarus) made his own hell by resisting the transforming perspective of the reign of God, especially as that perspective appeared to him in the form of the opportunity to meet the needs of the impoverished Lazarus. Consequently, as the last sermon teaches, it is important to "monitor what's growing within." We need to use the perspective of the divine rule as a ruler to measure the degree to which we are growing in its directions (or in some others).

I am impressed by the sense of urgency in these sermons. Toward the end of the title sermon, our author implores, "If you want to know the deepest joys, live each day as if it might be your last." I write this Foreword just a few days after September 11, 2001 — the day hijacked airliners were used as missiles to bring down the World Trade Center Twin Towers in New York City and to destroy a part of the Pentagon in Washington, D.C. The suddenness of those events presses the truth of Cueni's claim upon me. I do not know what day may be my last. When the specter of my immediate death flashes before me, I want to know that I have lived toward God's reign with all that I have. These sermons help transform me in that direction.

Ronald J. Allen
Nettie Sweeney and Hugh Th. Miller
Professor of Preaching and New Testament
Christian Theological Seminary,
Indianapolis, Indiana

**Proper 12**
**Pentecost 10**
**Ordinary Time 17**
**Luke 11:1-13**

# Jesus' Lesson On Prayer

Jesus was praying. His followers sat near and watched. Perhaps they were envious that their leader seemed so comfortable in approaching God. It may have been a simple request for a lesson.

Inherent in the disciple's request, "Lord, teach us to pray" is this notion: "Help us to know the proper way to come to God in prayer. Jesus, we are frail human beings. What do we know about the etiquette of prayer? Teach us to pray so that we neither offend God nor embarrass ourselves." Several years ago, the President of the United States appeared on MTV, the television cable channel directed toward adolescents and young adults. Apparently, no one instructed the audience on manners. One of the young people asked the President, the most powerful human being on the face of the earth, about which style underwear he wore. "Lord, teach us to pray. Teach us the proper etiquette in coming to God."

Jesus responded by offering what we know as the "Lord's Prayer." Both Luke and Matthew remember this incident. Matthew records the most familiar version. This one in Luke is the shorter. In fact, it can be recited in twenty seconds. That the apostles mention John the Baptist may mean that John taught his followers a short, specific prayer they said with such frequency that it identified them as a group.[1] Hence the disciples of Jesus request a similar prayer they might consider the "Signature Prayer of the Followers of Jesus Christ." To this day it serves that purpose. This is the universal prayer for Christian worship and personal devotion.

Jesus starts this model prayer with a surprising address to God. He says, *Abba*. The word typically is translated as *"Father"* and that bothers some. Certainly the nature of God cannot be summarized in a purely male image. Let me suggest that Jesus does not use the word *Abba* to describe the nature of God so much as to describe our human *relationship* to God. Rather than as Father, *Abba* is better translated Papa or Daddy. It is an intimate, family form of address. When Jesus starts the Lord's Prayer with "*Abba*," he means we are to come to God in prayer as though we have an intimate, personal relationship with the Creator of the Universe.

"*Hallowed be your name.*" In Hebrew a person's name was more than the appellation by which a person is identified. One's name referred to the whole character of a person. The Psalmist writes, "And those who know your name put their trust in you." That means more than knowing God's name is Yahweh. As William Barclay observes: "It means that those who know the whole character and mind and heart of God will gladly put their trust in him."[2]

To ask that God's character be hallowed or revered is to ask that everything we come to know about God be good. May only good be done in the name of God. May God be given that unique reverence which God's character and nature and personality demand.

When we push this expression a little, we come to realize it speaks not so much about what God is supposed to *do* as it is a prayer about how those who believe in God are supposed to *be*.

We who pray for God's name to be held in reverence are asking that our beliefs about God and our behavior in the name of God are worthy of God. To clarify: Praying "hallowed be your name" is not to ask God to behave in ways that people say nice things about God. "Hallowed be your name" is a prayer that we who claim to believe in God behave in ways that bring honor and not shame to God's name.

In Topeka, Kansas, there is a little church that has received national attention for their ministry of picketing the funerals of people who die of AIDS. The members of that church travel all over this nation in order to walk up and down in front of churches and funeral homes holding signs saying, "God hates fags." The pastor of the church makes no secret of his belief that God has called him to do this. In the name of the One True God, terrorists plant a bomb in a city market and a dozen people who happen to be buying vegetables that morning are killed. In the name of the Prince of Peace, wars have been declared and millions have died. To paraphrase a comment once made by the Methodist reformer, John Wesley: "Some people's ideas of God fit with my ideas of the Devil."

To say "Hallowed be your name," is to pray: "May my life bring honor to God. Because of what I believe about God, may my life be a role model that attracts others to God." That is how we reverence the name of God.

Then Jesus says, *"Your kingdom come."* Jesus has extensive teachings on the kingdom of God. In just the Gospel of Luke the expression is used 38 times. These references are usually parables, metaphors, and analogies, not descriptive prose. Although the Master refers to the "kingdom of God," one never gets the sense it is a place. More accurately, it is an experience or a condition. Consequently, it is more accurate to talk about the "reign of God" rather than the "kingdom."

It is Paul in Romans 14:17 who offers a definition when he writes, "For the kingdom of God is not food and drink but righteousness and peace and joy, in the Holy Spirit." God reigns in this world where peace, joy, and righteousness prevail. As individuals, we experience the reign of God when we do what is right and when we experience the resulting inner peace and joy.

It should be noted that Jesus describes the reign of God as both present possibility and future reality. By faith, this can happen in your life. And it certainly will happen in this world. The kingdom of God will come. God will reign on earth as God reigns in heaven.

Jesus continues, *"Give us each day our daily bread."* This expression gives Bible commentators the most trouble. It demands a complex and nuanced interpretation. At a surface level, it means exactly what it says. "God, please see to it that our material needs are met. Lord, each day we need bread. We need the kind of bread made from wheat flour and baked in an oven. We also need the 'bread' otherwise known as carrying-around money." This is a material request for daily needs.

Scholars believe, however, that Jesus may mean much more than that. The difficulty comes with the word that gets translated as "daily." Luke uses a term here that is not found anywhere else in Greek literature.[3] Depending on the interpretation, it could mean either "bread sufficient for the day" or "the kind of bread one will receive in the kingdom."[4]

Perchance Jesus meant both of these. Precedent exists for each in the Bible. When the Israelites wandered in the wilderness of the Sinai, God provided for them on a day-to-day basis. Each morning, they found sufficient food for the day. By that night, the food supply was exhausted. They had to learn to trust God that the next day the manna would again be available on the floor of the desert.

Saints Origen and Jerome, early leaders of the church, translated this phrase, "Give us what is necessary for daily existence." We might add, "And, Lord, help us understand the difference between what we really need and what we just want."

*"Give us each day our daily bread."* That might also refer to the "spiritual" food we need daily. Jesus did, you will remember, tell us that we do not live by (physical) bread alone. An eleventh-century Irish monk translates the Greek to Latin, *Panem verbum Dei celestem da nobis hodie.* "Give us today for bread the word of God from heaven."

*"And forgive us our sins for we ourselves forgive everyone indebted to us."* Whereas to pray, "Give us each day our daily bread," asks God to supply the spiritual and physical nourishment we need for the present, this phrase speaks to the healing of our past. As human beings we are less than perfect. We do things to disappoint others. Others do things to disappoint us. For that matter, we are frequently a disappointment to ourselves. This disappointment accumulates as the trash of human interactions we know as ill will and guilt. If we do nothing to correct the problem, this trash accumulates until the burden overwhelms us.

For that reason, we give thanks that we have a Heavenly Trash Collector. God takes away not only the burden of our shortcomings, but the hurt that others have unloaded on us. We can be forgiven. We can forgive others.

I understand that diamond cutting is a nerve-wracking occupation. The crystal structure of an uncut diamond has to be studied carefully. Then the stone has to be hit at just the right angle. The cutter's job is stressful because there is only one chance. Strike a large, expensive diamond at the wrong angle and it shatters into tiny, near-worthless fragments.

Thankfully, God did not create us to be like diamonds. It is not "one strike and you're out." Rather than like a diamond, God has given us a life more akin to Silly Putty. Like that children's toy, we can be pulled apart, rolled into tiny pieces, stepped on and flattened, over and over again. By God's grace we can always be pulled back together, reshaped, and made into something more beautiful than ever. We can be forgiven. We can forgive others.

*And do not bring us to a time of trial.* In the more familiar Matthew version, it says, "Lead us not into temptation, but deliver us from evil."

Obviously, this can be misunderstood. We should not think that God puts temptation in our path just to test us. As James 1:13 says, "No one, when tempted, should say, 'I am tempted by God.' " Temptation and trials come with being a human being living in the world. Instead we should think of this part of the prayer as addressing our needs into the future. "God, sustain us through our times of temptation. When the tests come, Lord, may we be made stronger by them, rather than destroyed."

When the Master finished praying, his disciples said, "Jesus, we understand that John the Baptist has a special prayer for his followers. Would you teach us to pray? Would you give us a signature prayer?" Jesus responded, "When you pray, say this ..."

*Father.* O God, you are not distant and uninterested. In fact, you know us so well we can spiritually crawl into your lap and call you Daddy.

*Hallowed be your name.* Grant us the grace, Lord, to behave in such a way that we never bring shame to you. May we who pray in your name live holy lives.

*Your kingdom come.* May we experience righteousness, peace, and joy in the Holy Spirit. As individuals, may we know this reign of God in our lives right now. As human community, may the day come soon when your will will be done on earth as it is in heaven.

*Give us each day our daily bread.* Care for us in the present, Lord, by providing for our spiritual and physical needs each day.

*And forgive us our sins for we ourselves forgive everyone indebted to us.* As you care for our present, so we ask that you take care of our past. Set us free from the guilt of yesterday. Heal our broken relationships. Forgive us, Lord, and make us better forgivers of one another.

*And do not bring us to the time of trial.* God, you forgive our past. You sustain us in the present. Now we ask you to be with us in the future. Keep us from harm's way. Give us grace to resist temptation.

Amen and Amen.

---

1. Fred Craddock, *Interpretation: Luke* (Louisville: John Knox Press, 1990), p. 153.

2. William Barclay, *The Daily Bible Study Series: The Gospel of Luke* (Philadelphia: The Westminster Press, 1975), p. 143.

3. William Barclay, *The Beatitudes and Lord's Prayer for Everyman* (New York: Harper and Row, 1963), p. 217.

4. Dean Chapman, *Lectionary Homiletics*, Volume VI, Number 8, July 1995, p. 41.

Proper 13
Pentecost 11
Ordinary Time 18
Luke 12:13-21

# It's God's Grace,
# Not American Ingenuity

Imagine an enormous open field in the midst of rolling hills. Because the thin grasses have not tasted rain for months, beige, not green, dominates the meadow. A layer of late summer dust hangs heavily over everything. The ground is strewn with rocks. Cicadas buzz in a scraggly, distant tree.

This place serves Jesus as an assembly hall. The Master preaches in a corner of the field, over there, surrounded on two sides by a high stone wall stacked by generations of farmers trying to clear the harsh land of stones that continue to push through the thin soil. Jesus chose this makeshift pulpit well. In the absence of microphone and amplifier, the stone wall becomes a soundboard to project his voice. A very large crowd gathers to hear Jesus.

The Master's preaching style differs from what is common today. Instead of transitioning his thoughts with commentary and reasoned connections, he strings not necessarily related pearls of wisdom along a stream of consciousness. Yet certain themes recur — sin, forgiveness, fearlessness as the necessary attitude for victorious living.[1]

Jesus tells his audience to rely on the Holy Spirit in times of peril, and then he is interrupted. A man in the crowd blurts out, "Teacher, tell my brother to divide the family inheritance with me."

It was common practice to take unsettled disputes to respected rabbis. Jesus must have had that reputation. However, there is a time and place for everything. This man should make an appointment to discuss such a personal matter. Instead he interrupts the Master in mid-thought. This behavior speaks volumes about him.

"Hey, Jesus, I really don't care to hear about the Holy Spirit. I really don't care that there are thousands of other people listening to you. I want you to drop everything and take care of my issue."

We all have encountered people like this. They live in a world bounded on the north, south, east, and west by themselves. A friend tells of hosting the after-performance reception for a noted pianist. For more than an hour, one guest after another approached the pianist to gush over him. He thoroughly enjoyed every over-blown compliment. Finally, the pianist called for the attention of the crowd. "Enough of you saying flattering things about me. Let me tell you how wonderful *I* thought my performance was."

This self-centered character in the crowd jumps to his feet and demands the Master give him undivided attention. "Jesus, stop talking and deal with my issue. I don't care about the needs of the rest of the people here. I am not getting my share of the family inheritance. I want you to do something about it right now!" This spoiled little adult/child then stomps his foot and threatens to hold his breath until he turns blue.

The Bible does not identify this man. The area is not well-populated, however, and we can assume everyone knows him. We don't know his name, but let us call him Eleazar and say that he lives in the village just over the hill. His father died last year and left the shoemaker business and a few gold coins to the older brother. Eleazar is not destitute. He farms a few acres on the outskirts of the village. By the standards of the time, he is comfortable. He is not, however, satisfied. He wants part of that cobbler business and a couple of those gold coins that were left to his brother. The Master knows his story. Eleazar has told it before. Jesus, however, does not want to get sucked into Eleazar's family fight over the inheritance. Few things are more dangerous than an outsider wading into another family's battle over money. Wisely, Jesus sidesteps Eleazar's demand. "Friend, who set me to be judge or arbitrator over you?" Then Eleazar sits down. He is disappointed, but everyone knows he will continue to complain to anyone who will listen.

Now, Jesus must find a way to get back the crowd's attention. They lost interest in the Master's discussion of the Holy Spirit the moment Eleazar brought up the topic of money. It set their minds wandering. "I cannot believe Eleazar is bringing up that inheritance again. I get so tired of hearing him talk about it." "He complains that he is being cheated, but he has more than most of us. I wish I had it as good as Eleazar." "I wonder if my father will leave me any money? That would sure be nice."

Because he knows those thoughts float through his audience's minds, Jesus turns the discussion to how material possessions do not ensure happiness. "Be on guard against all kinds of greed," Jesus says, "for one's life does not consist in the abundance of possessions." Without specifically mentioning him, apparently Jesus thinks the problem with the family inheritance is Eleazar's greed and not his brother's failure to share. Eleazar just cannot get enough.

Remember the scene from the 1970s movie *Jaws*. The marine biologist from Wood's Hole arrives on a New England island resort to help the local sheriff deal with an increase in shark attacks. Locals manage to catch one very large shark. They think this might be the one attacking swimmers. The marine biologist does an autopsy. From the belly of the beast he pulls one large fish after another. Before he is finished, a large pile of fish is removed from the belly. This shark has an enormous appetite. Then the biologist pulls out an electric blender. Then come several chunks and bits and assorted pieces of this and that. He reaches in again to extract an old Louisiana license plate. This shark's appetite knows no limits. It will eat anything!

Eleazar has the same problem. Nothing will satisfy him. He is an eating machine. Of course, he doesn't see it that way. Eleazar claims all he wants is for his brother to divide the inheritance with him. In truth, he is like the man who claimed that all he wanted was the land that adjoins his. When he acquired that, he said that all he wanted was the land that now adjoined his. The more he acquired, the more he wanted.

Getting more of the family inheritance will not satisfy Eleazar. More money will only increase his desire. Eleazar has what has been called "Sea-water Syndrome." The more the thirsty attempt to quench their thirst with salt water, the thirstier they become. By its nature, seawater creates thirst. It does not satisfy thirst. For

Eleazar, trying to satisfy his craving with money equates to trying to satisfy thirst with salt water.

At this point, Jesus launches into a parable. These are the little stories with the surprise endings that the Master regularly told to illustrate life principles. "The land of a rich man produced abundantly. And he thought to himself, 'What should I do, for I have no place to store my crops?' Then he said, 'I will do this: I will pull down my barns and build larger ones, and there I will store all my grain and my goods.' "

Let me pause to draw your attention to a couple things. First, notice that the land produced abundantly even though the technology to increase production scientifically did not exist. Other than the obvious natural fertilizer, chemical additives and soil science were centuries into the future. The rich man just happened to own fertile land. He does not, however, have any trouble taking credit for the abundant harvest. He calls them "my" crops.

Second, notice the interesting way the rich man handles the storage problem. He does not build more barns. He tears down the old barns and builds larger ones. That solution reveals volumes about this fellow. More than increasing storage, he wants to impress the neighbors. "Cost is no object to me. Tear down the old barns." This man obviously has more money than sense. In a cash-strapped economy, he shows no concern for getting the most "bang for the buck." His money decisions are so curious that behind his back the neighbors start referring to him as "the American."

Jesus continues his parable by noting the man has a dream. The day will come, he thinks, when I will have enough. "And I will say to my soul, 'Soul, you have ample goods laid up for many years; relax, eat, drink, be merry.' "

Can you imagine the conversations this man has with his family? "I know I work seven days a week and never get home for meals. When I get those new barns full, however, I will have plenty of time for the family. Kids, just a couple more good years at the farm and we will take that vacation. We will go surfing at Caesaria Maritima on the Mediterranean coast. Yes, my darling wife, I know if I had just added barns instead of building new ones we would have money to send Johnny to college, but better times are coming.

The day will come when those barns will be full and I can say, 'I have enough.' "

That day does come, but it does not bring the total joy he expects. When the barns are full he thinks to himself: I can eat, drink, and be merry. But God says to him, " 'You fool! This very night your life is being demanded of you. And the things you have prepared, whose will they be?' So it is with those who store up treasures for themselves but are not rich toward God."

Contrary to what you might be thinking, death is not punishment for his greediness. God is not fickle or capricious. Death is a normal event in each life. No matter how much wealth you acquire, no matter how successful you become, no matter how many barns you fill, you are going to die. Death always comes one to a customer. This fellow simply learns his appointment with the Grim Reaper comes the same day he tosses the last bushel of wheat into the last grain bin in the last barn.

When God says of him, "You fool!" it refers to the fact that he spent too much of his life building barns and filling them with grain and not nearly enough time building his life and filling it with good things.

The poet from Detroit, Edgar Guest, reminds us of the principle the rich man forgot:

> *Out of this life I shall never take*
> *Things of silver and gold I make*
> *All that I cherish and hoard away*
> *After I leave on earth must stay.*
>
> *Though I have toiled for a painting rare*
> *To hang on my wall, I must leave it there.*
> *Though I call it mine and boast its worth,*
> *I must give it up when I leave the earth.*
>
> *All that I gather and all that I keep*
> *I must leave behind when I fall asleep.*
> *And I wonder often what I shall own*
> *In that other life when I pass alone.*

*What shall they find and what shall they see*
*In the soul that answers the call for me?*
*Shall the great Judge learn when my task is through*
*That my spirit had gathered some riches, too?*

*Or shall at the last it be mine to find*
*That all I had worked for I'd left behind?*

"You fool! You think you filled those barns with grain. You think you did it with hard work and Yankee ingenuity. But you need to know that happened by God's grace. God supplied the fertile ground, the rain, and the sunshine. You cannot take credit for that. God did it for you. If you had only understood this truth, your life would have been so much more satisfying. If you had only trusted God's grace more and not thought you had to rely so heavily on your own strength. If you had only realized how many riches were yours for the enjoying — the beauty of the sunset, the smell of the new-mown hay, the love of your family. Instead, you frittered away your years filling those barns and taking credit for doing what you never could have done without the grace of God. You fool. You fool!"

---

1. William Barclay, *The Daily Bible Series: The Gospel of Luke* (Philadelphia: Westminster Press, 1975), pp. 160-162.

**Proper 14**
**Pentecost 12**
**Ordinary Time 19**
**Luke 12:32-40**

# The Transforming Power
# Of A Changed Perspective

As we wander through the middle of this twelfth chapter of the Gospel of Luke, we notice that Jesus makes some comments that are, at the very minimum, puzzling. He says, "Do not worry about your life, what you will eat, or about your body, what you will wear" (v. 22).

Does Jesus really expect his disciples to stop worrying and to abide by that advice? Jesus' followers were poor people. They had a hard time keeping their families clothed. They did not always know from whence the next meal was coming. Of course, they worried about food and clothing. How could they not?

A few verses later Jesus continues, "Do not be afraid" (v. 32). Just how does a frightened person comply with that command? Let us say the minister is called to the hospital in the middle of the night. A car filled with teenagers has been involved in a traffic accident. The extent of injuries has yet to be determined. Parents from the church wait in the emergency room. Is it realistic to expect them not to be frightened about the news the doctor might bring? Worry so pulsates in their throats that they can hardly catch their breath. "Remember Jesus commands us not to be afraid," falls on deaf ears. Injured loved ones cause us to worry. As human beings we are "hard-wired" for it. How then do we make sense of Jesus telling us not to do what comes naturally?

Let me begin unpacking an explanation by noting that at its heart, Christianity is a radically different way to look at the world. Faith serves as a set of spectacles through which we see the world as God wants us to see it. People of faith think differently because we see differently. Because we see differently, we are supposed to live differently. Seeing the world through God's eyes requires some changes. As Paul puts it in Romans 12:2: "Do not be conformed to this world, but be transformed by the renewing of your mind, so that you may discern what is the will of God — what is good and acceptable and perfect." When Jesus admonishes his followers not to worry and not to be afraid, he is applying that tenet. It is the biblical principle of the transforming power of a changed perspective.

That is not to say fear and worry can or even should be eliminated. In proper proportion and in the right circumstances, fear and worry serve us as gifts of a loving God. Some things produce anxiety in us. Indeed the stock market could crash. The Social Security trust fund could become bankrupt. The nations of the Middle East could set the price of oil at $300 a barrel and force people to use their Sport Utility Vehicles as large flowerpots. These are genuine sources of worry. When Jesus tells his followers not to be afraid and not to worry, he is talking about keeping fear and worry proportional, not eliminating them entirely. We can expect to be frightened. In the right amounts over the right things, that is a wonderful gift of God. However, we should fear the fearsome. Worry, but not about those things over which we have no control. And under no circumstances need we permit ourselves to be paralyzed by anxiety.

The problem, of course, is that these gifts can be misused. *Homo sapiens*, after all, is the only species capable of standing on hind legs and snatching worry out of thin air. That is a misuse of God's good gift. A friend tells of living in married student housing at a major university. The woman in the apartment next door was pregnant with her first child. It is right and proper to be so concerned for an unborn child that one seeks out prenatal care. This neighbor was more than sufficiently concerned. After a regular visit to the obstetrician she came to see my friend and gasped, "The doctor told me today that the baby is forming ears. Oh, Carol! I am concerned. I don't know how to make ears." This woman was a master of raising worry to an art form. That is the species of worry and fear about which Jesus warns us.

286

"Do not worry about your life, what you will eat, or about your body, what you will wear." While wonderful advice, we need to know how to put it into practice. Return to Romans 12:2. We are not to be conformed to this world, but we are to be transformed by the renewal of our minds. We are to seek a faithful perspective on this life. Our lives can be transformed by looking at things the way God wants us to see them.

This twelfth chapter of Luke is one of many places in the Gospel where Jesus paints the world the way God wants us to see it and then invites us to take a peek at the canvas. As might be expected, there is a profound difference between how the world wants us to see life and how God calls us to see it. Our natural inclination is to look only at what concerns us at the present moment. Faithfulness calls us to see things more as God sees them. I know my needs and wants. God knows the needs of all creation. I am very familiar with my little corner of the world. God has intimate knowledge of everything from the tiniest microbe to the most distant collapsing star in the furthest galaxy at the edge of the universe. I have a fairly good memory of my life from about the age of two or three to the present. God has experienced the history of the universe from the time of creation to the present moment. God calls me to try to see more from God's perspective than from the perspective of self.

Jane Parker Huber reminds us that a panoramic view changes the way we think and then the way we live. In her hymn, "When In Awe Of God's Creation," she notes that from outer space, earth is a "mysterious floating marble, strewn with clouds and bathed in grace." From that higher altitude, there are no lines of demarcation that slice us into nations, class, and race. Like a trip into outer space, the Gospel of Jesus Christ lifts us up and permits us to see the world, if not exactly from God's perspective, then at least from higher ground. As the hymn writer claims, the broad horizon of outer space reveals that there are no good reasons to continue hatred. Wars can cease. We can love each other. There can be peace. Seeing the world through the Gospel of Jesus Christ transforms our lives by calling us to larger lives in a larger world. "Do not be conformed to this world, but be transformed by the renewing of your mind, so that you may discern what is the will of God — what is good and acceptable and perfect."

They say that if a newborn shark is kept in a small tank of water it will never achieve its full size potential. No matter how much the shark is fed it will not outgrow its surroundings. In the open ocean a shark that grows to sixteen feet will be full-grown at two feet if kept in a small tank. The shark's environment determines its size. People are the same. If we insist on living in the miniature world of nothing more than personal needs and desires, our growth is stifled. We become consumed by the tyranny of a too-tiny "Me, Myself, and I." When we get entangled in self, we become consumed with worry and fear. Oh, woe is me, what shall I eat? What shall I wear? To paraphrase our Lord, "Quit focusing on yourself. Push the limits of your vision. Haven't you noticed that even crows have enough to eat? God takes care of birds and you are more valued than any bird. Trust God. Don't fret about what you will wear. Take a look at the flowers in that meadow over there. Those lilies never worry and God takes care of them."

With these words the Master offers a perspective which makes it possible for us to live victoriously rather than to be overwhelmed by fear and worry. "Do not be conformed to this world, but be transformed by the renewing of your mind, so that you may discern what is the will of God — what is good and acceptable and perfect."

You might have heard this non-biblical proverb. "The biggest difference between the rich and the poor is that the poor still think if they had enough money they could solve all their problems." I used to think that meant that, unlike the rich, the poor have not learned that one cannot acquire sufficient money to solve every problem. Rich and poor alike will encounter problems.

I have come to realize that is not its meaning. To say, "The greatest difference between the rich and the poor is that the poor still think if they had enough money they could solve all their problems," has little to do with money. It is a proverb about attitude, about perspective. People are not poor simply because they lack money. They are poor because they still think that more money will correct every problem. People are not rich simply because they have a great deal of money. They are rich because of their attitude.

True riches emanate from confident trust in God's loving care. Truly wealthy people may continue to have problems with their children, but they are not consumed by their worry. The truly wealthy may be anxious about a problem, but they are not paralyzed by fear. That which makes a person truly wealthy is not money. It is the power that comes from a transformed perspective.

After telling his followers not to be afraid and not to worry, Jesus goes on to say, "It is the nations of the world that strive for these things," that is for food and clothes (v. 30). As people of faith we are not to content ourselves with the outlook, values, and priorities of this world. (Notice how reminiscent that is of Paul's comment not to be conformed to this world.) After the diagnosis, Jesus offers a prescription. He says that we are to "strive for the kingdom, and these things will be given to you."

Instead of being consumed by worry and fear, work for the reign of God. To state that another way, whenever you find yourself being drained by personal concerns, go out and do something for someone else. What tremendous advice. Nothing escalates anxiety faster than expending all your time and energy thinking about self. Nothing alleviates self-concern more effectively than doing something for others. Be personally empowered by giving of yourself in service to others. Such transforming power comes from that different perspective.

Our Lord finishes off this section of his preaching with a short discussion on when we can expect the end of history and the coming day of judgment. The Bible teaches that God brought the world into existence and that there will be an end of the world. Certainly as individuals, there was a time before we were born and there will be a time after we die. Both our own demise and a coming judgment day for the world are sources of fear and worry. The context of Jesus' remarks in Luke 12 suggests that people were worried about this. The Master informs his audience that it is not known when God will bring about the cataclysmic end of history — and by implication, when individuals can expect the end of their earthly journey. It could happen at any time. It might happen in the middle of this night or at dawn on some day in the distant future. The only thing of which we can be certain is that it will come when least expected. Therefore, we must always be ready. Since we will receive no warning, we need to live every day of our lives as if today just might be the day we will answer to God.

Again that is a very different way to think about things. It is also a very empowering perspective. If you want to know the deepest joys, live each day as it if it might be your last. Live each day as if this just might be the day that ends with you standing before Almighty God being asked to account for your life. Don't put off the really important things until tomorrow. Do not be conformed to the ways of this world. Look at things the way God wants you to see them. That perspective will empower your life. "Do not be conformed to this world, but be transformed by the renewing of your mind, so that you may discern what is the will of God — what is good and acceptable and perfect."

Proper 15
Pentecost 13
Ordinary Time 20
Luke 12:49-56

# Fire Falling From Heaven

Jesus spends much of the twelfth chapter of Luke reassuring and encouraging his followers in the face of possible catastrophic circumstance. "I tell you, my friends, do not fear those who kill the body, and after that can do nothing more" (v. 4). "Therefore, I tell you, do not worry about your life" (v. 22). "Do not be afraid, little flock, for it is your Father's good pleasure to give you the kingdom" (v. 32).

The same chapter ends on a far less positive note. Rather than encouraging reassurance, Jesus says that his ministry will be very divisive. After spending 45 verses trying to quiet the anxiety of his followers, Jesus tells them that he came to bring fire to the earth. He insists that he will not bring peace. Instead, his ministry will divide families and pit individual members of households against one another. The ministry of our Lord is to rain fire from heaven!

I suspect his first century audience understood that imagery more readily than we do. We have only a passing acquaintance with the power of fire. We see flames in the fireplace. We worry about children holding candles on Christmas Eve. We read of an occasional forest fire and hear the siren of a racing fire truck. Our fire departments are so competent that an accidental fire death makes the national news.

Ancient people had a more intimate knowledge of fire. Their only nighttime illumination came from the flames of oil lamps. The smoke of the cooking fire on the kitchen floor constantly irritated and reddened their eyes. Everyone's fingers were callused from working household fires. Their arms and hands bore the scars from burns. Early in childhood they learned that food tasted better cooked, that flames tempered metal tools, and that the kiln's heat hardened pottery. People also knew firsthand the danger of uncontrolled fire. Homes regularly burned to the ground by an overturned lamp or a carelessly maintained kitchen fire. Well into the nineteenth century, devastating fires shaped communities. In fact, fire spurred on the next urban renewal.

This intimate acquaintance with the power and the paradox of fire moved the ancients to think of fire as theophany — that is, fire as a manifestation of God. When Moses was tending the flocks of his father-in-law on Mount Horeb, the Lord God spoke to him out of a burning bush. When the Hebrew people were wandering in the wilderness of the Sinai, the Lord God led them at night with a pillar of fire. On the day of Pentecost, the Holy Spirit, the very presence of God, appeared to the apostles in the upper room as tongues of fire. It did not puzzle his listeners when Jesus said that he was to bring fire on the earth. They believed Jesus to be God's representative, and it was an ancient idea for God's presence to be manifested by fire.

It would also not surprise them that Jesus spoke of God's presence being divisive. The ancients knew both fire and God as being purifying and punishing. They knew how to put metals to the flame to temper and to drive out impurities. The Old and New Testaments use fire as a metaphor to talk about how God punishes, purifies, and strengthens the world. Those folks believed that God worked through fire as well as various fire-like disasters. With a little poetic imagination, even modern folks like us can understand that God works with "fire."

Loren was only fourteen years old when he entered a life of petty crime. By the time he was seventeen he had become one of the regulars in the county juvenile justice system. At eighteen, the judge gave him a choice: enter the army or do hard time in a state penitentiary. He volunteered for the army and was sent to Vietnam. It was at the height of that bloody conflict. He was assigned to a "graves unit" where he worked to identify, tag, and then ship the bodies of young men killed in battle. The judge hoped military service would discipline him. It didn't. When he returned to his hometown, he was even more troubled. In Southeast Asia, he compounded his alcohol problem by taking illegal drugs. With this new addiction, his life of crime took a leap into an abyss. This one-time juvenile delinquent started doing armed robbery.

One night he and a friend held up a liquor store. The clerk managed to notify police and the car chase was on. Loren admits that he considered using the gun he had with him to shoot it out with police. A guardian angel must have whispered the right words in his ear that night. He and the friend decided to surrender.

The judge sentenced Loren to the state prison at Joliet. He had plenty of experience in county jail and the local juvenile detention center. He was tough. He thought he knew how to do hard time. It would not bother him, he thought. Unfortunately, he didn't know Joliet. His years there were experienced as being burned alive at the stake.

Loren paid his debt to society and his first job as a free man was as the church custodian. The congregation frequently used that position as a ministry. Loren quickly proved that he had learned his lesson. His first day on the job he walked up two flights of steps to give a quarter to the church treasurer that he found in the coin return of the soda pop machine. He was indeed an honest man.

Loren was never shy about giving his testimonial. When he came home from Vietnam, he was angry and bitter. He didn't believe in anyone or anything. He knew he was traveling the road to self-destruction and that was fine with him. Loren had chosen the hard way to commit suicide. Then his life was turned around. It was no revival preacher who issued an altar call. There was no gentle voice of God urging him to come to Jesus. It was, however, no less the presence of God — a theophany in fire. As Loren described it, "I was in Joliet only for three weeks when enough terrible things happened to me at the hands of other inmates that I said to myself, 'I will never, ever do anything that will get me into a place like this again.' " His life straightened out. He married and had a family. He established himself as a responsible citizen and then was able to go on and get a much better job than the one at the church. Criminal justice critics will tell you it doesn't happen nearly often enough. But with Loren, the fire that rained down on his life punished him for his foolish choices and then that fire began to purify him and make him a better man.

Those who heard Jesus say, "I came to bring fire to the earth," knew that is what he meant. Fire symbolized the presence of God. They believed God used the "fires" of life to punish and purify.

That backgrounds this passage of scripture. That is not, however, the point Jesus is making. This is not a simple observation about how God can work through devastation to strengthen. In Luke 12:49-56, Jesus claims that the gospel is so radical that the world will experience it as fire raining from heaven. Those who follow his teachings, Jesus warns, will be considered revolutionaries. Jesus tells those of us who strive to follow him even today that when his message sinks into our hearts and minds, it can cause trouble in our families. If we choose to follow the Christ, we can get in trouble at work. This Gospel can have a negative impact on our friendships. If we take our faith seriously, we can plan on losing enemies because God commands we commit ourselves to turning enemies into friends. Adhering to this faith just might get us thrown in jail.

For the most part, this radical edge of the Gospel of Jesus Christ has been lost. Most who now claim Christianity as their religion understand Christ as the Prince of Peace. That means believers can seek personal healing and forgiveness. It means our faith promises contentment and personal security in the here and now and entry to heaven at the moment of death. We refer to nice, kind, gentle people as "Christians."

We seem to have forgotten that the kingdom of God Jesus introduced was quite radical. If you remember, Jesus was crucified. The Romans did not give him an award for keeping Jewish citizens quiet and content. Most of his apostles met violent deaths at the hands of those who were outraged at the revolutionary changes they wanted to make both in society and in the lives of individuals. When Pliny was governor of a province in Asia Minor, he wrote a letter to the Roman emperor telling him that he didn't know what these Christians believed exactly but they were the most willful, obstinate, rebellious, disobedient people he had ever encountered. Therefore he had put some of them to death just on general principles.[1]

Seminary professor Stanley Hauerwas opens one of his classes by reading a letter from a parent to a government official. The parent complains that the family was paying for the very best education for their son. Then the young man got involved with a weird religious sect. The parent pleads with the government to do something about this group that was ruining his son's life.

Dr. Hauerwas ends by explaining that the parent is not complaining about the Moonies, the Hare Krishnas, or some other group. The professor had assembled snippets from different letters written to the Roman government in the third century about a weird religious group called the Church of Jesus Christ.[2]

How that differs from the claims the church makes on people's lives today! Instead of high demands and radical changes, we think Christianity is to make us feel good about ourselves. Rather than an institution inciting revolutionary change, the community today wants the church to be a well-maintained, quiet presence that never threatens property values. Jesus said that he came to rain fire from heaven. But in the last couple thousand years we have managed to get the fire under control by reducing it to candles on the communion table.

Every once in a while, however, someone catches fire for God. Some people catch the vision that there is more to the good life than just acquiring more and more. Some realize that their Christian faith calls them to do something for others, rather than just feeling good about themselves. Sometimes people decide to go to seminary rather than law school. Some decide to pursue a Master of Divinity rather than a Master of Business Administration. Some people feel the heat of God's presence and are moved to extravagant generosity.

Some people catch on fire with the presence of God and do things that disrupt their family life — just as Jesus predicted. Jim was a prominent businessman in town. He belonged to the church, but had never taken it very seriously. Some of his friends were active in a spiritual renewal movement and encouraged him to attend one of the weekend retreats. "You will really enjoy it," they promised.

Reluctantly, Jim went. He didn't really believe the church had anything to offer him. He went and listened carefully. He did not enjoy the weekend at all. In fact, it was a terrible experience for him and for his family. You see, Jim had been embezzling money from the company where he worked.

They talked a great deal about Jesus' teachings at that retreat. For Jim it was as if the Word of God was fire rained down from heaven. The Monday morning after the retreat he walked into the office of the owner of the company and confessed. He spent the next few years in prison. When he returned, he became one of the leaders of that spiritual renewal movement. Jim experienced the teachings of Jesus as disruptive. It was nothing less than a firestorm from heaven. That can happen.

This faith can change your life as well. Be open to that fire God rains down from heaven. Open your heart that God in Christ Jesus will strengthen and purify you. As hymn writer Adelaide Pollard puts it, "Have thine own way, Lord. Thou art the potter. I am the clay. Mold me and make me after thy will, while I am waiting, yielded and still."[3]

---

1. Pliny, *Letters X,* p. 96.

2. *Pulpit Resources*, Volume 23, No. 3, July-September, 1995, p. 34.

3. "Have Thine Own Way, Lord," Adelaide A. Pollard, 1902.

# The Bent-over Woman

As was his custom, Jesus went that Sabbath morning to the synagogue for worship. As he was preaching and teaching, he happened to glance toward the fringe of the crowd where he saw a very crippled woman. She was bent over and was unable to stand up straight. When he inquired, Jesus was told the woman had been that way for eighteen years.

Can you imagine? For nearly two decades this woman spent every waking moment bent double. When she went to the market she did not see the distant green hillsides. She saw only the dirt path in front of her. Instead of the smiling faces of passing children, she saw the tops of dusty sandals. The Gospel writer tells us that the Master was deeply moved by her plight. Jesus called the woman toward him. He laid hands on her and said, "Woman you are set free from your ailment." Immediately the woman stood up straight and she started to praise God.

This irritated one of the leaders of the synagogue. This fellow, we assume a Pharisee, began to criticize Jesus for healing the woman on the Sabbath. "There are six days on which work ought to be done. Healing equates to work and there is no excuse for working on the day set aside for rest and worship." This religious leader believed keeping the law more important than caring for people.

The man's attitude outraged Jesus. The Master responded that the law permits untying and leading a donkey to water on the Sabbath. Certainly the law should care more for the needs of people than animals. The law should make an exception for unleashing this daughter of Abraham who has been kept from drinking from the waters of abundant life for eighteen years.

I assume that Luke, who remembers this story in his biography of Jesus, recorded the event because of this confrontation with the leader of the synagogue. That disagreement offers the most to learn. However, I want us to focus on that bent-over woman. If we don't look closely, we might assume Jesus healed the woman of a physical disease of the spine like osteoporosis or scoliosis. At first hearing, it does seem that when Jesus laid hands on her and told her to stand up straight, the power of God flowed though our Lord's fingers, into her back, and healed a physical defect.

While plausible, that is not what Luke says. The seventeenth century translation known as the King James Version (v. 10) says the woman was "bowed by a spirit of infirmity." That suggests a spiritual problem, not a physical one. The more modern New English Bible translates the Greek by saying, she was "possessed by a spirit that had crippled her." J. B. Phillips cuts to the heart of the issue by saying that for eighteen years the woman had been doubled-over for some *psychological cause.*

Now what might that be? What psychological problem or spiritual crisis could keep a woman bent over for nearly two decades? A minister posed that question to a group of women in the church. They had some interesting observations.

"What bent her over?" One woman answered, "Her children. Eighteen years is the minimum sentence for accepting the responsibility of being a parent." What parent has not found raising children demanding? A friend reports that when his first child was born, he was 6 foot 5 inches tall and had coal black hair. By the time his daughter graduated from college he was 5 foot 5 inches tall and had gray hair. Raising children can wear you down and bend you over.

Another woman in that church group spoke up, "I'll tell you what bent her double. It was her husband. The woman was permanently bowed from bending over picking up after him." Still another woman suggested the woman manifested the results of an unjust society. The burden of being paid only half as much as a man for the same job wore her out.

298

Of course, the woman might have been bent over by some affliction other than one peculiar to women. Jesus encountered the woman at the synagogue. Perhaps this woman had a special reason to go to worship. Churches and synagogues function as trash collection depots. People often come to worship to unload the accumulated burden of guilt. Maybe this woman has been stealing money from the office. It began a few years ago when she started "borrowing" a few dollars to keep her going until payday. She always paid it back. One week she didn't return the money and no one noticed. She took a little more and a little more. Now she owes thousands. She got away with it for years. She is terrified. It is only a matter of time until she is caught. The worry and fear have bent her over.

Maybe she has been having an affair with the man who lives next door. It began innocently enough. A little innocent flirting. Then one thing led to another. Day by day, the weight of the guilt accumulated until now the burden bends her over.

Maybe some other problem weighs heavily on her. A minister friend reports of attending a convention in a distant city. He left the hotel for a very early morning jog around the downtown. As he jogged down one street he passed a long line of the homeless waiting for a local liquor store to open. At 10:30 that night as he walked back to the hotel, he passed some of those same men. They were passed out drunk on the sidewalk, sleeping off the bender they began at 6:30 in the morning when they bought the day's supply in that liquor store. Maybe that woman is bent over from the weight of her drinking problem. Maybe that woman has a husband who sleeps off his benders on the sidewalks of a Galilean village. Addictions bent people over 2,000 years ago, just as it happens today.

Maybe the woman is bent over by some problem over which she has no control. Perhaps she is poor. Abject poverty is a burden capable of bending you double. In Jesus' time the poor were legion. Maybe the burden of poverty bent that woman over. Jesus had compassion for the down and out of his time.

On the other hand, Jesus loved the up and in as well as the down and out. Jesus was a friend to both the rich and the poor. Maybe this woman's problem is not the lack of money. Perhaps she has too much money. Maybe she worries excessively that someone is going to steal from her. Maybe she is worn out buying, cleaning, polishing, insuring, and storing her stuff.

Frankly, we just do not know the *psychological cause* of her bowed back. All we know is that it is severe and she has had it for years. For eighteen years, she has had a very unpleasant perspective on life. She has been walking around looking at passing feet. She cannot see the smile on the faces of strangers passing her. She cannot see the green of the meadow. The woman has what might be called "Post-Locust Plague Syndrome." Prior to insecticides, locusts were a terrible problem. Every few years a cloud of grasshoppers descended and ate every green thing. In a farmer's field, they reduced the crop to bare, brown earth. They ate the grass in the lawn and the thistles in the vacant field next door. Locusts are known to land on the clothesline and eat the green spots out of a tablecloth. Locusts scorch the earth and leave no living plant behind. A plague of locusts emotionally and spiritually devastates a community. That is how that bent-over woman must have felt. Some unnamed burden sucked the strength from her. She no longer can stand up straight.

Jesus has compassion. He calls to her. "Woman, you are set free from your ailment." The woman stands up straight for the first time in eighteen years.

Please take notice, Jesus did *not* say, "I have solved your problem." He did *not* suggest that he cured the ailment. He says only that he set her free from the burden. I want to suggest that all Jesus did was convince the woman that she could stand up straight under her burden. "Woman, you are set free from your ailment. Stand up straight. You can handle it." The woman believed Jesus. His words gave her the confidence she needed and, sure enough, she stood up straight. Jesus changed her life by helping her believe in herself. I know that doesn't seem like much of a miracle. However, let me remind you of this: Enormous change can be wrought by instilling a little self-confidence in another person.

Once upon a time there was a man whose life was being destroyed by his compulsion to tear paper. Paper was never safe when this fellow was around. Whenever he found a paper, he tore it into

300

shreds. No one ever invited him to their house because he tore up their newspaper. If he found mail on the kitchen table, he shredded it. When nothing else was available, he tore wallpaper off the walls and shredded it.

He had no friends. The man was miserable. He attempted many cures. He went to the best physicians in the world. He consulted the finest psychologists. He tried acupuncture and drank herbal tea. Nothing worked.

One day, he heard of a therapist who specialized in his rare paper-shredding compulsion. When he arrived for his appointment, the therapist walked him around the room twice and whispered something in his ear. When he left, he was cured. A year later, he still had not reverted to his paper tearing behavior.

The man's life was transformed. His family was elated. One day his mother asked him what that therapist did to cure him when every other treatment had failed. The man replied that the therapist simply walked him around the room twice and kept whispering over and over again into his ear: "Don't tear paper. Don't tear paper. You can do it. Don't tear paper." The man admitted no one had ever said that to him before. "This guy told me I do not have to tear paper."

Could it be that all Jesus really did was say: "Stand up straight. You can do it"? Could it be that Jesus simply said something to the woman that gave her the confidence she needed? The ensuing conversation with the Pharisee hints that that is exactly what happened. The Lord Jesus launches into a discussion of how just a tiny bit of faith can make a profound difference. He speaks of having the faith of a mustard seed. Mustard seeds are no bigger than sesame seeds, yet one can grow into a plant almost the size of tree. Jesus continues by noting how a tiny bit of yeast can transform the bread dough. A little bit of something can make a profound difference.

There is a non-biblical proverb that holds: "God never gives us more than we can handle." That proverb, of course, is objectively false. There are problems that can crush the life out of us. We can be literally crushed to death. While objectively false, it is subjectively very helpful to believe "God never gives us more than we can handle." If you don't believe you can handle what comes your way, you won't. Without faithful confidence, it takes only a tiny problem to bend you over. If, on the other hand, you believe that God will give you all the strength you need to handle whatever comes your way, it is amazing how you can stand up straight and keep on moving.

You may feel as though you have a bad case of Post-Locust Plague Syndrome. It may seem as though you live in a world where all the green of life has been sucked out. If that is how you experience life, listen to Jesus. "Stand up straight. You are set free from your ailment. God is giving you the strength to get past this." Believe that. It makes a difference.

In the little book of Joel toward the back of the Old Testament is a wonderful promise from God. In Joel 2:27, God says, "I will repay you for the years that the swarming locust has eaten." All that time you have been walking around looking at the dust on top of your shoes, God will repay. Man/woman/boy/girl — stand up straight and walk. You can do it. That is the promise of faith.

Proper 17
Pentecost 15
Ordinary Time 22
Luke 14:1, 7-14

# Divine Dinner Party Decorum

Luke opens the fourteenth chapter by telling us that Jesus "was going to the house of a leader of the Pharisees to eat a meal on the sabbath," and that "they were watching him closely." Notice four important details in this one verse.

First, notice that Jesus is a guest at a dinner party. Important things happen when people gather for dinner. Table talk provides a forum for friends and families to catch up on the events in the lives of one another. At the dinner table, we teach our children manners. At the table we hear the stories that bind us together as immediate family, larger community, even as a nation. We are told what is expected of us. We learn the family secrets that are to be shared with no one outside our circle. Table conversation has a long history laden with religious, social, and psychological meaning.[1] Is it any wonder that as the family of God we gather for worship around the table?

Second, notice that the meal mentioned in Luke 14 takes place at the home of a Pharisee. This was a very important religious group in Jesus' time. Phariseeism began as a religious movement among Jews living outside of Palestine. As sojourners in foreign lands the Hebrew people needed a way to maintain their religious identity. They could not regularly attend worship at the great Temple in Jerusalem. They rubbed elbows daily with those who did not know Yahweh, their God. They had to find a way to keep themselves together as the Chosen People of God. The Pharisee response to the threat of cultural dilution was to say, "We will maintain our Jewish identity by keeping Torah, the Hebrew Law. Even when we live among non-believers, we will keep our religion and ourselves pure. Even when the military powers of this world enslave us, we remain God's people." By faithfulness to the Torah, the observant Jew could say, "I know who I am and the world knows who we are. We are the ones who keep God's Law." At a time when most other cultures were being lost to Roman ways of thinking and doing, the Pharisees offered a method for maintaining Jewish identity.

Third, this dinner party at the house of the Pharisee takes place on the Sabbath. Keeping this holy day for rest and worship was central to Jewish differentiation from the surrounding Roman culture. Jewish law developed 270 different regulations for keeping the Sabbath. These rules governed the minutest details of what one was permitted and not permitted to do from sunset Friday to sunset Saturday. To the Pharisees these rules were essential. Jewish identity as the chosen people of God was bound up in keeping the Sabbath rules.

Fourth, Luke tells us that the Pharisees kept a suspicious eye on Jesus at this dinner party. We should expect that. Jesus was an unknown quantity to the Pharisees. They needed to know "Is he one of us? Is he going to harm or help our efforts to keep our identity pure?" The Pharisees are the ones in charge of this sort of thing. If Jesus did anything to degrade the purity of their religious practice, they had a duty to stop him. They were the religious elite and they took their job very seriously.

"On one occasion when Jesus was going to the house of a leader of the Pharisees to eat a meal on the sabbath, they were watching him closely" (v. 1). Do not think of this dinner party as a casual gathering of old friends.[2] This is one of the social occasions of the year. The party is being held at the home of the "host and hostess with the most-est." This gathering will be featured in next week's *New York Times* society page with pictures showing fortunate attendees holding glasses of champagne. The accompanying article will say things like: "Guests included Isaac Gold, whose father, the late Simon Gold, cornered the market on the precious metal that bears the family name. Sophie Stein, Nobel Prize winner in chemistry, wore a simple dress with a string of pearls purchased from Cartier last spring. Chief Justice of the Supreme Court for

Religious Issues, Rabbi Israel Caiphas, was accompanied by his wife and daughter."

This is the *crème de la crème* of the town. If attendees are not already there, an invitation to this party will slingshot them to the top of the social ladder.

Of course, Jesus does not usually share a foothold on the top rung of that ladder. He has been invited because he has been in the news lately. The Pharisees want to see if he is as good as his reputation. If for no other reason, his name on the guest list shows that the Pharisees are open to new people and new ideas. Most of all, however, the local blue bloods want to check him out. "Is he one of us? Could he be the replacement when Rabbi Caiphas retires? Is Jesus sufficiently prominent that his name needs added to the list of regular guests?" No wonder Luke says that the other guests were "watching him closely."

The dining room is magnificent. The crystal chandelier came from Paris. It has so many baubles three servants needed four days to clean it. The buffet is opulent: beluga caviar, smoked salmon with the heads still attached, sterling silver serving platters, and an orchid centerpiece.

Deciding the seating arrangement has taken hours. In fact, the hostess used a dinner party consultant to be certain that the right people got seated in the right order. In spite of that, Jesus notices that when he thought no one was watching, young Joe Cohen moved his name tag from near the bottom of the table up near the host.

The butler signals "Dinner is served." The rabbi offers a much too long invocation. People find their places and the meal begins. Most of the polite table talk concerns the new director of the symphony, the recently announced leverage buy-out of the local matzo ball factory, and how the neighborhood took a nose dive when the Roman governor bought the house down the street. During dinner's third course, Jesus says in a voice loud enough for everyone to hear. "Folks, I have been talking with my new friend Amos here and he tells me that he has a serious problem with swollen ankles. He's just miserable and so I am going to see if I can heal him."

At that point, the hostess nearly swallows her tongue. She gasps, "Well, I never!"

"Clear off the table so Amos can stretch out," Jesus says. "Careful with the creamed asparagus. Amos, crawl up there and elevate your feet over your head. That is important with swollen ankles." Amos crawls on the table. Rests his head on the bread tray and his wife's face turns as red as her glass of Cabernet. This is definitely not the dignified behavior one expects at a party for Pharisees. Mr. Stein turns to his wife and says, "What will people think when word of this hits the streets?" Jesus makes matters even worse when he leaps into the middle of the dining table. He grabs Amos' swollen ankles and begins to massage them and pray over them.

At this point, Rabbi Caiphas goes ballistic. He begins to lecture Jesus on his inappropriate behavior. "Is it not enough that you behave boorishly? Now you heal on the Sabbath. Romans, Greeks, and assorted other pagans work on the Sabbath, not faithful Jews. You are undermining what it means to be identified as God's chosen people."

Jesus responds to the effect, "Hold on a minute now. Amos' feet hurt. I wanted to give him some relief. The religious law permits rescuing a donkey from a well on the Sabbath. Certainly it should permit the rescue of one of God's children on the Sabbath. You folks are fussing about being decent and following the rules, but should not the needs of people take precedence?"

Then Jesus brings up the issue of the order of seating at the table. He talks about how embarrassing it is to take one of the preferred seats at the table only to have a more important person come along and "bump" you into less prestigious seating. Joe Cohen, the young man Jesus saw switching nametags before the dinner started, drops his eyes and looks like a child caught with a hand in the cookie jar.

Then Jesus launches into a discourse about who should be invited to a dinner party. Don't just invite your relatives, business associates, and rich friends, he tells them. All of those people will turn around and invite you to their next party. Instead of calculated reciprocity, invite the poor, the crippled, the lame, and the blind. "They cannot repay you, for you will be repaid at the resurrection of the righteous" (v. 14).

The Hebrew people of Jesus' time were not unlike people of every generation. They wanted to know, "What gives my life meaning?" The Pharisees in Jesus' time answered that question by saying, "Our lives have meaning because God has a covenant with us. We are the chosen people of God. We stay faithful to God by the careful observance of the Hebrew Law. When we keep the religious law, God is pleased with us and the world knows we are the chosen people of God."

Jesus answered that question in a different way. He took his relationship to God very seriously, but he did not observe all the rules and regulations. Jesus understood that the Jews had a special relationship to God. Just as the scripture taught, they were God's chosen people. However, Jesus expands on that to insist that God has a special relationship with all of creation. We are all in the same family — God's family. We are all the chosen people of God. Our identity, our "worthwhileness" comes from the fact that we are God's children. We keep faith with the family membership, not by observing the law, but by loving one another. For Jesus to be faithful to God, he had to set a higher priority on healing Amos' swollen ankles than he put on keeping the Sabbath or maintaining the dignified ethos of the dinner party. By doing so, he demonstrated his faithfulness to God.

From this you can conclude that you are worthwhile simply because of whose you are. Your value as a person does not rely on having your name on the social register. You are the loved child of God. You cannot improve on that social standing.

To be successful in life, you do not have to sneak your nametag a little higher up the table. Your worth comes from being a loved family member, not from having a better seat at the dinner party. You are a member of the family of God.

A hundred years ago, Ralph Waldo Emerson noted three qualities he deemed marks of true "success": the ability to discern and appreciate beauty, the ability to see the best in others, and a commitment to leaving the world a better place.[3] Notice that Emerson does not say that success comes in having the best seat at the table, acquiring more material possessions, or in belonging to the best clubs. Emerson contends that success comes with appreciating God's world, developing loving relationships with God's people, and with working to improve God's world. Jesus would agree heartily.

In fact, our scripture lesson for today ends with a wonderful suggestion of how to work to make the world a better place. Invite the poor, the crippled, the lame, and the blind to dinner. They are all members of your family. Just think how much richer your table talk will be if you don't just associate with your business associates and closest relatives. Remember around the table such wonderful things happen. Invite everyone to the table. They are all members of the extended family.

---

1. Fred Craddock, *Interpretation: Luke* (Louisville: John Knox Press, 1990), p. 175.

2. I am indebted to Robert Capon, *The Parables of Grace* (Grand Rapids: Eerdmans, 1988), pp. 117-128, for his delightful rendering of the dinner party at the home of the Pharisee. It inspired this interpretation.

3. *Homiletics,* Volume 7, Number 3, July-September, 1995, p. 40.

**Proper 18**
**Pentecost 16**
**Ordinary Time 23**
**Luke 14:25-33**

# Warning To The
# Clueless Enthusiasts

Jesus said, "Whoever comes to me and does not hate his father and mother, wife and children, brothers and sisters, yes, and even life itself, cannot be my disciple" (v. 26).

Let's admit it. Jesus made some strange comments. This scripture for today remembers one of those times. Must we really hate our mother and father in order to be Christian? I thought Christians were to promote family values. Must we really hate our own lives in order to be faithful? Doesn't the Bible promote the abundance of life? Is that not contrary to hating our life? How are we to make sense of this?

Maybe we are not to make sense of it. Perhaps we are simply to obey by doing what we are told. Some claim that regardless of what seems reasonable, every word of the Bible is to be taken literally. This might be one of those times.

Let me suggest that these claims must be taken seriously, but not literally. In this fourteenth chapter of Luke, our Lord tells us something very important, but we might miss the truth if we take his words literally. Let me explain.

Luke says that Jesus is on the way to Jerusalem. A large crowd of supporters accompanies him. The Master knows trouble waits at the end of the journey. His popularity is limited to the north around the Sea of Galilee. The joyous attitude demonstrated by his companions does not extend to Jerusalem. In that great urban center, the Lord has highly motivated enemies, not enthusiastic friends. Those enemies will plot his arrest, trial, and death by crucifixion. Jesus has so informed his closest followers, the apostles, but they have yet to grasp the significance. The entourage of camp followers accompanying Jesus and the twelve are totally clueless. They think this trip to Jerusalem is a circus parade. When, it fact, it is the front end of the Master's funeral procession.

Imagine the scene. A couple hundred people stir a cloud of dust as they head south on the unpaved road. Jesus takes the lead. His apostles come next. James and John, the most ambitious ones, assume positions to his right and left. Occasionally, other apostles push and shove until they walk next to Jesus for a mile or two. Then James and John reassert themselves. Each time the group passes through a village their numbers swell with enthusiastic local fans of the Lord. They know his reputation as a preacher and healer. These folks never intend traveling all the way to Jerusalem. They just want to be part of the parade. They drop out and return home after walking to the next village.

It will make a great story for the grandchildren. "Did I ever tell you about the time I walked with Jesus. Yep, he came right down Main Street. His apostles were with him — James and John, Peter and Andrew. I met them all. When I saw the crowd coming, I jumped up from the breakfast table and walked all the way to Magdala. Didn't get home that night until after midnight. Was your grandmother upset with me! There was not, however, anything to worry about. I had a wonderful time. We laughed and joked. The apostles told us what Jesus had been doing and how we would be blessed if we followed his teachings. I remember the Apostle Peter even gave me his autograph. It was a great day."

Jesus, walking at the head of the parade, overhears the chitchat. The enthusiastic crowd does not grasp the significance of this journey to Jerusalem. In a matter of days, Jesus will be arrested in the Garden of Gesthemene. He will pay the ultimate price for his ministry. There will also be a cost to the followers of the Christ. Stephen, the first deacon in the church, will be stoned to death for teaching of God's love in Christ Jesus. Several of the apostles will be martyred. Paul, who wrote much of the New Testament, will be tormented, ridiculed, arrested, imprisoned, beaten, and finally put to death for being a follower. For the next couple centuries, many

Christians will worship in secret simply to avoid arrest. In the Roman world before the time of Emperor Constantine, being a Christian required more than putting the symbol of a fish on the bumper of your car and attending church a couple times a month. Declaring for Christ opened the possibility of becoming the lunch special for the lions in the Roman arena.

As the crowd walks toward Jerusalem, they have given little thought to the cost of being followers of Jesus. Those folks are enthusiastic about this nice religious procession, but they are clueless about the demands of the faith. Jesus tells them they must give serious thought to their walk with God. He reminds them that no one in his right mind starts to build a tower without calculating how much it is going to cost to complete it. No king decides to go to war without first determining whether or not it is possible to win the war. In that same way, they must count the cost of faith.

That cost, Jesus insists, is very high. "So, therefore, none of you can become my disciple if you do not give up all your possessions" (v. 33). "Whoever does not carry the cross and follow me cannot be my disciple" (v. 27). In fact, following the Christ means your family must be a lesser priority than your faith. You will have to turn your back on your family. (That, incidentally is what it means when it says to "hate" your mother and father.)

In our time declaring for Christ seems to cost little. Go to church on occasion. Learn whether they say the Lord's Prayer with "debts and debtors" or "trespasses and trespassers." Read the Bible every once in a while. If called, tell the Gallup Poll that you believe in God and are a "born again" Christian. Not much to this stuff of being a Christian.

Contrary to the ease with which we can claim we follow the Christ, there is a cost. In fact, if we take this faith seriously, there can be a very high cost. It still might require you to go against the wishes of your father and mother. It might mean picking up the cross. It still might cause you to give up your life. William Willimon, the chaplain of the Methodist Church's Duke University, remembers this happening. A very angry parent phoned him. "I hold you personally responsible for this," he said. "I have spent an enormous amount of money for my daughter to get a B.S. degree in mechanical engineering and now she wants to throw it all away and do mission work for the Presbyterians in Haiti. Can you imagine! A trained engineer digging ditches."

"Now how is that my fault?" the minister responded. "What did I do?"

"I'll tell you what you did," the now shouting father answered. "You ingratiated yourself with her, filled her head with all that religion stuff. She likes you. That's why she is doing this. I hold you personally responsible."

"Now look, buster," the increasingly defensive college chaplain responded. "You had her baptized in the church. You read her Bible stories. You took her to Sunday school. You were the one who paid for her to go skiing with the youth group. It's your fault that she took that stuff so seriously she now wants to go into the ministry."

"I know, I know," the once-angry and now-grieving father lamented. "But we didn't want her to be minister. All we wanted was for her to be a Presbyterian!"[1]

One just never knows when one of the kids might take the Christian faith so seriously she might turn her back on the wishes of the family and become a minister. As an aside, let me say how much the church needs this story repeated. We have a significant shortage of people taking their faith seriously enough to hear God's call to ministry. We need people to turn their backs on the alluring call of the wealth and prestige of this world to serve in ministry. In this next generation, we need people who take early retirements and discover they can't play golf or bridge every day to serve as ministers in small rural congregations. We need people to listen for God's call to ministry in the middle of their lives. If your once-chosen profession is proving to be far less fulfilling than you hoped, perhaps God is calling you into ministry. The Church of Jesus Christ needs ministers. Now doing this might be sacrificial. That, however, is just what Jesus is talking about when he says that to be faithful we have to be willing to turn our back on the wishes of the family; pick up the cross and follow him; give up our life for the Christ.

Let me turn this conversation in a little different direction and talk about another way in which Jesus' warning to count the cost of

312

discipleship is true. Remember that Christianity is at its heart an entirely different way to look at the world. This faith of ours is a holistic worldview. One is not a Christian simply because of occasional church attendance, regular prayer and Bible reading, and the presence of a "Jesus Saves" bumper sticker on the family SUV. Christianity is a comprehensive way to think about the world, to decide right from wrong, and to interpret life's ordinary as well as extraordinary events. Think of faith as a very good set of spectacles through which we see things as God wants us to see them. I am convinced that looking through the corrective lenses of the Christian faith clears up our vision so that we see the landmines and potholes as well as the beauty of God's created order.

Stated most succinctly, this Christian worldview understands not only that there is a God who is Creator and Sustainer of the Cosmos, but also that we are ultimately and personally dependent for our strength on this Ground of our Being. We believe that we come to know this God best in Jesus of Nazareth, the one we claim as Lord and Savior. This understanding of God Incarnate, God made flesh, leads us to realize that all people of the earth are brothers and sisters, children of the same parent God. This Christian way to look at the world determines our core values and influences the way we behave on a daily basis. It is an understanding that helps us feel connected to the very nature of things. It calls us to that strict moral code that values people over things, forgiveness over revenge, and serving others over being served. The faith is a way to look at the world and value justice, mercy, kindness, and love over all else.

This Christian view of a created order in the hands of God moves us to find comfort, meaning, and joy at the awesome mystery of life itself. It makes it possible for us to feel the rush of God's grace-filled hope in the resurrection at the moment of grief when a loved one dies. It empowers us to hope in that most mysterious promise of eternal life as we journey toward our own death.

Growing into this Christian worldview is no simple, easy task. It takes significant time and commitment. That process is complicated, of course, by the fact that there are other competing worldviews. Contrary to the popular notion, ours is not a "Christian culture." Religiously, we are very diverse. More troubling, however, is that the dominant American worldview is not a religious one at all. It is a very secular one.

In one sense, the dominating secular worldview is one which claims to have grown beyond the need to believe in God. We are modern, even post-modern people; we claim we don't need the ancient God of the Israelites, the God who came to live among us as Jesus the Christ. We need trust nothing beyond human enterprise. We have science and laws and government and wealth. These are the only tools we need to confront the problems of living. We need not fear the unknown. As long as we don't do anything illegal, we are free to do whatever we choose. We do not accept any higher moral authority than the whims of self. That which is right is what each person decides is right. Indeed, we have no need for God.

This secular worldview debases our values and stultifies the human spirit. It deludes us into thinking that our technology, knowledge, and wealth can solve all our problems and empower us to the abundance of life. In spite of the allure of its dazzling glitz, this worldview just doesn't bring the joy it promises. In this Age of Disbelief, we desperately need to apprehend the sacred in the midst of the ordinariness of daily life.

It is costly, however, to look through the lens of faith. It is costly to be a follower of Christ. It means giving up the notion that the pursuit of money is the greatest good that leads to the greatest happiness. It means giving up the notion that you personally are absolutely in charge of running the universe. It means learning to ask for forgiveness. It means putting the needs of others first. It means turning the other cheek. It means loving your enemies and doing good to those that hate you. The fact of the matter is that being Christian is costly, very costly. Are you willing to pick up the cross? Are you able to turn toward God even if it doesn't please other people? Are you able to give up your limited life to live?

---

1. Adapted from William Willimon, *Pulpit Resources*, September 10, 1995, p. 45.

**Proper 19**
**Pentecost 17**
**Ordinary Time 24**
**Luke 15:1-10**

# Jesus Encounters
# The Religion Police

Back before the ways of the Taliban became common knowledge, there was a fascinating little article about how they jailed barbers when they didn't do culturally correct haircuts.[1] The newspaper reported that young men in Kabul, Afghanistan, have started wearing their hair the way the actor Leonardo DiCaprio wears his. Long, not only on the sides, but so long in the front that hair can drop over the eyes. They call the style, "the Titanic," named for the blockbuster movie starring DiCaprio about the 1912 sinking of the cruise ship by that name.

The Taliban, the military rulers of Afghanistan, believe this hairstyle offensive to the Islamic religion. They claim long bangs interfere with the ability to keep one's eyes clear when bowing low for prayer. The Afghan government's Ministry of Vice and Virtue has banned that haircut. When bowing to say prayers, one's hair is not supposed to flop down into one's face. That mocks the seriousness of the moment by setting a bad example for other young men of Kabul.

To correct the problem, the Ministry of Vice and Virtue dispatched what the newspaper article called the "Religion Police." These enforcers of good behavior fanned out across the capital city of Kabul and arrested 22 barbers accused of leaving long bangs on teenage boys.

By American standards, a Leonardo DiCaprio haircut hardly illustrates the extremes of American teenage fashion. If the Taliban want to see adolescent rebellion as an art form, they need to check out the orange and blue spike hairdos worn with five pounds of metal body piercings.

Of course, we can discern the underlying principle. The Taliban want to keep their culture pure. To do that, they believe they must control everything they consider contradictory, or inappropriate, or unsavory, or socially disruptive, or in violation of the nature and purpose of pure Islam. By the standards of the religion police, those Kabul barbers had to be stopped. They were undermining Afghanistan's moral and religious purity.

Having religion police in charge of maintaining moral values and religious purity is an ancient idea. In fact, that is the issue at stake in our scripture lesson for today. As Luke 15 opens, we are told that Jesus is preaching to a large crowd. Most in the crowd are, as expected, nice religious people. They long for a closer relationship with God. They are solid citizens. Some in the crowd, however, are rather unsavory characters. Luke lumps them together by referring to "tax collectors and sinners." In ancient Israel, these were the kids with Leonardo DiCaprio haircuts and the barbers who failed to cut their bangs.

As expected, Jesus' audience includes religion police from the Ministry of Vice and Virtue. Specifically, the scribes and Pharisees monitor Jesus' ministry on behalf of the religious establishment at the Temple in Jerusalem. These fellows voice objection to having tax collectors and assorted other sinners in the crowd. They complain about the bad example this sets. "These unsavory characters will affect the youth. Bad apples spoil the whole barrel," they reason. "Get rid of them," insist the first century religion police, the scribes, and Pharisees.

Jesus responds by telling three of the most familiar parables in the Bible. The morning lesson covers two of them: the Lost Sheep and the Lost Coin. Since context determines meaning, let me suggest that we need to listen to these stories as though we are among the scribes and Pharisees. We need to listen as though we believe the religion police do an important job. Listen as though you believe that it is very important to maintain religious purity.

As with all the parables of our Lord, these stories contain some genuine surprises. Jesus begins by asking, "Which one of you, having a hundred sheep and losing one of them, does not leave the ninety-nine in the wilderness and go after the one that is lost until he finds it?" (v. 4). When he finds the sheep, he rejoices.

Lest you miss the obvious, in the story, the shepherd represents God. The sheep that wanders represents sinners and tax collectors. The 99 sheep with the good sense to stay close represent all the good religious people in the audience. The message is simple: All the shepherd's sheep are equally important and all God's children are equally important.

This parable is also found in the Gospel of Matthew 18:10-14. There are, however, a couple of very significant differences. In Matthew, the shepherd leaves his flock in the relative safety of the side of the mountain. In Luke, the sheep are left alone in the danger of the wilderness. In Matthew, it says "if" the shepherd finds the lost sheep, he rejoices. Luke says, the shepherd keeps looking for the lost sheep "until" he finds it. Although the message is essentially the same, Luke's version describes God's love as being even more radical and persistent.

To paraphrase the message in Luke: "You are tending sheep in a very dangerous place — the wilderness. Ninety-nine of your sheep have the good sense not to wander. One, however, wanders off where it could lose its life to snake bite, lion attack, poisonous weed, or falling off a cliff. As a loving shepherd, would you not leave the 99 to those same dangers of the wilderness in order to find that wandering sheep? Certainly you would continue to expose the 99 to danger until you found that one. Certainly you would never give up on it."

What goes through the mind of the people in Jesus' audience who have more than a thimble of common sense? "Well, no, Jesus. I don't think I would do that. I would not risk 99 sheep for the sake of one. That just doesn't make sense."

Yet Jesus insists that God will do that. God's love is reckless. By most worldly standards, God's love is even foolish. For God is so concerned about these tax collectors and sinners that God will never give up on them. That is the difference between God and us members of the religion police. God believes each child is so valuable that God is willing to risk 99 for the sake of one. God will keep searching *until* that lost one is found.

Jesus follows with a nice inclusive gesture. After the story about the male shepherd, he tells a parable about a housewife who has misplaced one of ten silver coins she owns. Each of those coins represents about ten days' wages and would have taken months to save. They are valuable. This woman is understandably concerned for her loss and she responds appropriately. She tears the house apart looking for the coin. She eventually finds it and is so excited that she throws a party for all her friends, family, and neighbors. Jesus says that woman's joy over finding the coin is like God's joy when one of those sinners repents (v. 10).

Consternation must have swept across Jesus' audience. "Why would that woman throw a party for a lost coin? The party costs must have been equal to the coin's value."

Yet, that is the point Jesus makes. Even as that single coin was important to the woman, so one person is of ultimate importance to God. God's grace is radical. God's love is reckless. God can really surprise religion police like you and me.

A few years ago, one of the major Protestant denominations had a serious debate over whether or not there can be salvation outside of faith in Jesus Christ. A minister I know took a conservative position on the question. "Only those who accept Christ are saved. All others are outside of God's redemptive grace."

Then that minister's father died. The minister had to admit that his father was not a Christian. He did not accept Christ as Savior. His father was not even a particularly moral person. In fact, by almost any standard, his father was an unrepentant scoundrel. He was never faithful to any woman to whom he was married. He drank to excess. He consistently cheated on his taxes and in his business. He barely stayed ahead of law enforcement. He even cheated his own children out of their inheritance.

At his father's death, the minister realized that in spite of everything, he had never given up on his father. The minister still loved his father. In the midst of all his failing, the man still had redemptive qualities. In a moment of insight, the minister realized that God must continue to love the minister's father. In fact, if God didn't love his father, then the minister's love would be greater than God's. The minister had never given up on his father and neither had God. That is the message, after all, of the parable of the lost sheep. God's risky love and radical grace is downright amazing.

One of the most divisive issues in our society today revolves around the place of gay and lesbian persons. Every mainline denomination argues about it. Almost everyone has a story to tell about how the issue has touched his or her family. Nearly everyone has a strong opinion one way or the other. Homosexuality is simply one of those issues about which it is almost impossible to have a calm discussion.

A minister I know has always been on the negative side of the issue. He has been fond of saying, "God created a couple named Adam and Eve, not Adam and Steve." Then the minister changed churches. His new church is in the heart of a major East Coast city and has an active gay and lesbian group in it. After he made the move, he discovered that the chairperson of his board of directors was gay.

This minister made a 180-degree turn. He no longer makes angry pronunciations. Instead he speaks with amazement at what wonderful people these are. He talks about how all God's children are loved and how God doesn't abandon any of them. The grace of God is far more risky, radical, and even reckless than those of us in the religion police like to admit.

As a young woman, Carroll was full of promise. She graduated near the top of her high school class. She went to college, received Bachelor's and Master's degrees. She even started work on a Ph.D. before, in her late twenties, the dark cloud of mental illness descended over her life. For the next thirty years Carroll struggled. She could not hold a job for more than a couple weeks. Her personal hygiene seldom rose above the marginal. Her aimless wanderings through the city streets, endless hours spent reading at the public library, and the sight of her sponging handouts in the local shopping area made her a well-known sight in town.

Many with Carroll's illness end up homeless, living under a bridge. Had it not been for people of her church, Carroll might have met that fate. The church folks encouraged her, supported her, transported her, fed her, and befriended her. It was not easy. When her illness was at its worst, she would call church people and ask they give her $10,000. Her minister became infuriated each time she sat in the front pew, waited until the sermon started, then stood up and slowly put on hat, gloves, and coat before marching down the center aisle — totally disrupting the worship service. She regularly called members of the congregation in the middle of the night to ask for a ride home. Almost everyone who knew her thought at least on occasion, "I wish that they would just put her in a mental hospital and throw the key away."

It would have been very easy to give up on a person like Carroll. The religion police demanded it. She was not a good example for the young. She was never going to get any better. She was never going to make a positive contribution. The folks at church, however, did not do that.

Carroll died recently. At her funeral, a large crowd gathered. Hardly anyone was a member of her biological family. She had not been capable of a relationship of reciprocity for decades. Consequently, she really didn't have friends — at least in the sense of friends to whom she gave as much as she received. The people at her funeral were the ones who had given of themselves to her care and in return were given still another opportunity to give to her care. Among that group, there was a theological consensus. God loved Carroll in the same way the shepherd loved that one sheep that wandered away from the flock. God never gave up on her and we should not give up on her.

Part of the acceptance of Carroll, however, might have been the realization that "but for the Grace of God, there go I." Any of us could be become the one the religion police want to exclude. Thanks be to God whose radical grace and reckless love never give up on us.

---

1. Kansas City *Star,* January 26, 2001, p. A14.

**Proper 20**
**Pentecost 18**
**Ordinary Time 25**
**Luke 16:1-13**

# Jesus' Most Perplexing Parable

In the scripture lesson for today Jesus tells a perplexing parable about a thoroughly dishonest employee who was praised for his dishonesty. In this story Jesus not only seems comfortable suggesting that it is acceptable to compromise with moral failings, but our Lord appears to commend his disciples to "go and do likewise." For centuries, preachers, commentators, and scholars have struggled to make sense of this outrageous tale.

Let me give some context. The fifteenth chapter of Luke opens by telling us that Jesus is preaching to a large crowd. Scribes and Pharisees object that our Lord spends too much time with the "sinners and tax collectors." As the religious authorities of the time, they have responsibility for monitoring the orthodoxy of Jesus' teaching and then reporting back to the Temple authorities. The religion police are upset that the Master is so welcoming of the morally objectionable that he actually eats with sinners. Jesus responds by telling the parables of the Lost Sheep and the Lost Coin. The fifteenth chapter of Luke concludes when Jesus tells the Parable of the Prodigal Son to the scribes and Pharisees. That story continues the theme of God's risky love and radical grace by describing how a loving father welcomes back a wayward child who has just frittered away his inheritance on fast living.

Luke 16 opens by indicating Jesus turned his attention away from those who were trying to undermine his ministry, the scribes and Pharisees, toward those who support him, his disciples. Remember that these folks have just overheard the story about the kid welcomed home after having wasted the family's money. His father gave him a party and did not even tell him, "I told you so."

Let me extrapolate on the ideas as well as paraphrase the story Jesus tells immediately after the Parable of the Prodigal Son: Once upon time there was an incredibly wealthy landowner who heard that the manager of his properties was incompetent or corrupt or both. The rich man called the manager into his office and fired him on the spot. "Clean out your office. Turn in the account books and get out!"

This manager might have been lazy and incompetent. He might have been dishonest. He was not, however, stupid. He thought to himself. "Without this job I am in big trouble. I cannot dig ditches for a living. Shovel handles give me blisters. I am too embarrassed to sit in the intersection holding a sign 'Homeless. Will work for food, but prefer a handout.' Before the word gets out that I have been fired, I had better make some friends among the boss' customers. If I do it right, I can worm my way into the good graces of those rich folks. With luck, so many people will owe me favors that I will not have to work another day in my life. I had better hurry, however. When it gets out that I have been fired, my plan will not work. This scheme is possible only if people believe I am being generous on behalf of the boss."

This conniving scoundrel immediately rushes down to Ruben Levine's Olive Oil factory and offers a deal. "Ruben, you are the Olive Oil King of Galilee, but you are behind on your payments to my boss. You know how much I have always valued our friendship. Well I am going to help you out. You owe my boss 800 gallons of olive oil. I pleaded your case with him and he has agreed to reduce that debt to 400 gallons if paid today." Ruben is thrilled by the opportunity to settle his account.

Immediately the scheming manager heads off to Sam Shapiro's grain farm. "Sam, no one in this valley raises as much wheat as you do. I know you can afford to pay your debt to my boss, but after I told him what a valued person you are, he gave me permission to offer you a deal. Today and today only, you can have a twenty percent discount." The wheat farmer jumps at the opportunity.

Like Ruben Levine, the Olive Oil King of Galilee, Sam Shapiro, the wheat farmer, owes this conniving property manager a big favor. Each of those fellows has also come to think very highly of the generosity of the rich landowner.

The deceitful manager is pleased with himself. He records these deals in his account books. He may have fallen out of favor with the richest man in town, but he has built a bridge to the future. Two other very important people in town, Sam Shapiro and Ruben Levine, owe him big.

He expects the rich landowner to throw a fit when he finds out that he has been giving deep discounts. Imagine his surprise, as well as the surprise in Jesus' audience, when the dishonest manager drops off the account books and the boss praises him. "Your plan was absolutely ingenious," the landowner says. "You have greatly enhanced both our reputations by using my money! In doing that you have put me in an untenable position. Sam and Ruben think that you convinced me to give them the discounts. If I tell Sam and Ruben that you were not authorized to do that, I look bad, not you. Rather than angry, I am just amazed at how clever you have been."

Jesus follows the parable with some curious comments. He says to his audience, "I tell you, make friends for yourselves by means of dishonest wealth so that when it is gone, they may welcome you into the eternal homes" (v. 9). Jesus concludes this discussion with the familiar "No slave can serve two masters. You cannot serve God and wealth" (v. 13).

My guess is that very few of you here this morning have ever heard a sermon on that parable. It ranks as one of the least known in the Bible. It doesn't take any particular insight to understand why. The story praises a scoundrel. That message does not seem in keeping with the other teachings of Jesus. Julian the Apostate went so far as to cite this parable as evidence of the inferiority of the Christian faith and its founder.[1]

I hope this does not upset you too much, but there is no particular agreement on what this parable means. Different scholars interpret it differently. In fact, every commentary I consulted put a slightly different spin on the story's meaning. I suggest it has always been that way. I don't think the people in Jesus' first century audience had the same interpretation. At dinner tables across Galilee that night when this story about the dishonest manager came up, different people gave different interpretations. That is a very normal thing to happen. Different people understand things differently because they are in different places in their lives.

On any given Sunday morning, the minister preaches only one sermon to the congregation. However, every parishioner hears a slightly different message. "Pastor when you said, 'Thus and so about this or that,' it was so meaningful to me. I seemed like you were preaching just to me." The minister thinks, "I did not say anything like that. That is what they heard because that is what they needed to hear." God can use the words of a sermon to bring the message that God wants.

Certainly that happened when Jesus told the Parable of the Dishonest Manager. Different people in Jesus' audience got different messages. Let me offer just three possibilities. All of these can be heard in the parable.

First, some people in Jesus' audience went home that night with the message, "Hey, its only money. Don't make such a big deal out of it."

Remember the context. Jesus had finished telling the Parable of the Prodigal Son. That is the story about the willful child who demanded his share of the family inheritance, then ran off to a distant country, and wasted the money. He goes home and his father welcomes him.

Some people in Jesus' audience had inflated notions of the importance of money. Consequently, these folks were aghast at the way the Prodigal Son treated his inheritance. To them, wasting money on fast living is the sacrilegious equivalent of mistreating holy objects. They think of money as a minor deity in their worldly pantheon.

The message that the Christian faith offers over and over again is that there is nothing sacred about money. In fact, rather than a holy icon, money is just a tool. Money is to be used to accomplish worthwhile things. It is not to be put on the altar and bowed down

324

to. Money is just a resource and it is the most renewable resource on the planet. These folks heard Jesus' admonition on not being able to serve both God and money very clearly. To these folks, Jesus taught a lesson on the place of money.

On the other hand, others in the crowd listened to the parable and their minds gravitated toward the rich landowner. The behavior of the property manager cost him big bucks. Yet the landowner does not get upset. In fact, he is only appreciative that his reputation has been enhanced. To those whose minds fasten on the wealthy landowner, the message is that relationships and reputations are more valuable than gallons of olive oil, bushels of wheat, or stacks of money.

Wise people know to use their fortunes to improve their reputations. One morning in 1888, Alfred Nobel, one of the world's leading industrialists, opened a French newspaper and was shocked to see his own obituary. It was a mistake, of course. It was Alfred's brother who had died. However, Alfred Nobel had an opportunity to read about how other people saw him. The obituary simply called him "The Dynamite King." He had made a fortune in manufacturing and selling explosives, but it rankled him to be thought of that way.

Alfred Nobel decided to use his wealth to change that reputation. He immediately arranged his estate to establish the Nobel Prize, to be given each year to the person or persons who do the most for the cause of world peace. In the past century, it has long been forgotten that the name Nobel once meant "The Dynamite King." Today the name stands synonymous with promoting world peace.[2]

Let me make a third and final observation. Some people listened to Jesus offering praise for that less-than-perfect manager and heard it as encouragement for their less-than-perfect lives. "If that rascal manager could do something worthy of praise, perhaps there is hope for me." Ordinary people can identify with the imperfections of others. That is why stories of rogues and tricksters were very popular in Jewish folklore.[3] It is also why the great heroes of the Bible are always shown to be frail human beings. Jacob, the patriarch, deceived his father, cheated his brother, and scammed his father-in-law out of most of his flock. Great King David lusted after the neighbor lady, committed adultery, and when he got her pregnant, plotted to have her husband killed. The apostle that Jesus chose to head the church, Peter, denied he even knew the Lord on the night of Jesus' arrest.

Ordinary people like us love stories about imperfect people doing something good. As imperfect people ourselves it gives us a little hope. I will admit that that is not a central theme of the parable of the dishonest manager, but it is what many people hear because that is exactly what we need to hear.

Lesson one from the parable: It is only money. It is a renewable resource, not a holy object. Don't worship your money. Use it as a tool for doing good.

Lesson two: Friendship and a good reputation count for more than money. In fact, wise people will use money to do good and thus to improve their reputation.

Lesson three: Even less-than-perfect people like you and me stand a chance with God. Thanks be to God for that.

---

1. *Lectionary Homiletics*, Volume VI, Number 10, September 1995, p. 31.

2. John T. Carroll and James R. Carroll, *Preaching the Hard Sayings of Jesus* (Peabody, Massachusetts: Hendrickson Publishers, 1996), pp. 116-117.

3. *The New Interpreter's Bible: Luke and John*, Volume IX (Nashville: Abingdon Press, 1995), p. 310.

**Proper 21**
**Pentecost 19**
**Ordinary Time 26**
**Luke 16:19-31**

# That Rich Man
# Made His Own Hell

---

The lesson for today continues the discussion on the proper use of material possessions by describing what happens when a person tries to "serve both God and wealth" (Luke 16:13). Today's Parable of the Rich Man and Lazarus leaves us repulsed by the gory details, puzzled by the literal description of eternal life, and hopeful that the Lord didn't really mean all those terrible things about the punishment due us "Haves" for our treatment of the "Have Nots."

Let me wander through this tale with you. It concerns an incredibly wealthy, yet unnamed man and a desperately poor beggar named Lazarus. Surprisingly, the two are neighbors — at least neighbors of a sort. Lazarus begs at the checkpoint where the armed guard lets visitors in and out of the rich man's gated community. The rich man regularly steps over the beggar on his way in and out of his home.

In spite of the physical proximity, the two dwell in parallel universes — the widely separated worlds of Sumptuous Luxury and Grinding Poverty. Consequently, the rich man knows the beggar only in a tangential way. He has an intellectual knowledge *of* Lazarus, but not an emotional caring *for* him. The rich man doesn't know if Lazarus has a wife and kids. He doesn't know if Lazarus' mother worries about her boy. They don't socialize with one another. The rich man knows *about* Lazarus. He just doesn't connect *with* him as a fellow human being.

The rich man doesn't have time for such things. He is after all, a Captain of Industry. He has to run as fast as he can just to keep up with his business. To satisfy the demands of his family, he has to run twice as fast as he can. Pursuing personal goals occupies his waking hours and dreaming of his future fills his sleeping hours. He does not have time to fret about the plight of Lazarus. The rich man physically excludes Lazarus with a fence around his house and emotionally excludes him with a fence around his heart.

In moments of candor, the rich man will tell you he really does not care for poor people. They are lazy. They want the government to support them. They are prone to crime. Jesus says that Lazarus has open sores from an unnamed illness — probably some ancient equivalent of AIDS. The rich man will tell you, "That is a terrible but avoidable plague that responsible folks like us avoid. Quite frankly, 'People Like That' differ from 'People Like Us.'" Of this the rich man is certain: The life of Lazarus may be hell on earth, but it is a hell of his own making.

Most of the people in Jesus' audience resonate with the thinking of the rich man. Common belief in the ancient world assumed anyone as poor, sick, and miserable as Lazarus had to have done something to warrant God's punishment. Folks might not have known what Lazarus did wrong, but it must have been terrible.

Jesus continues the story by telling us that eventually both men die. Funny how that works. No matter how good the medical care, no matter how healthy the diet, no matter how much exercise, no matter how rich or how poor, death still comes one to a customer. When informing his audience of the death of both Lazarus and the rich man, however, Jesus' puts an unexpected twist on the story. The Master says that after death, the rich man is punished and the poor man is blessed. Jesus' audience is shocked.

Let me give some background. Not everyone in the first century necessarily believed in an afterlife. Those who did, however, assumed that the blessings and punishments in this life were extended into the next. Therefore, the suffering of Lazarus and the blessing of the rich man should have continued after death.

Gasps ripple through the audience when Jesus says that Lazarus dies and goes to be with Father Abraham and the rich man dies and goes to a place of punishment. This reverses expectations. Jesus is teaching that the blessed shall suffer and the suffering shall be blessed. The rich shall be poor and the poor shall be rich. The last shall be first and the first shall be last. The Master goes on to suggest that Lazarus is blessed in the afterlife because he has already known enough hell in his earthy life. The rich man, on the other hand, deserves to be punished for being callused to the plight of that poor man.

Let me pause for a moment to remind you that this is a parable. We should listen to it as though it is a story. The Master is not distributing a "User's Travel Guide to Heaven and Hell." Consequently, this passage of scripture should be taken seriously, but not literally. Scholars tell us that the afterlife described here is of Hades, not of heaven and hell at all. Hades was believed to be a place where all the dead, both righteous and wicked, go to await the final judgment. By the first century, this much older concept had evolved to where it was assumed that Hades was divided into regions according to the moral states of the dead.[1] That notion fits Jesus' telling in the parable.

The rich man is miserable in the afterlife. He is tormented by thirst. From his assigned seating in steerage at the bottom of Hades he has some sort of window through which he can see others awaiting judgment. How surprised is the rich man when he peers through this window to see Lazarus resting in the bosom of Abraham.

(Please note, the beggar is with Abraham, not with God. Abraham is the great patriarch of the people of Israel. The people in Jesus' audience assumed that if Abraham was going to welcome any Jew, it should have been the rich man who did so well in life that his house is in a gated community. Wealth, it was assumed, was the reward for goodness.)

The rich man cries out for relief. He asks that Abraham dispatch Lazarus to bring him some relief. "Father Abraham, have mercy on me, and send Lazarus to dip the tip of his finger in water and cool my tongue; for I am in agony in these flames" (v. 24). This self-consumed man still thinks it's all about him and his wants. He still thinks that the poor man's job is to serve him — "Father Abraham, send Lazarus."

Abraham denies his request. The rich man finally realizes that he should have been more compassionate to the beggar. He admits he was so wrapped up in himself that he didn't even notice Lazarus outside the gate with his sign: "Homeless. Will work for food." The rich man realizes that it is too late for him. He turns his worry toward the rest of his family. He begs Abraham to send a message to his brothers back at the gated community. Let them know that he is being punished in Hades because he did not demonstrate sufficient compassion for the less fortunate.

The rich man even has a plan for how Abraham can impress them with that message. The patriarch should raise Lazarus from the dead and assign him to tell his family. The resurrected beggar walking into the gated community where he was never permitted in life would so impress the rich man's family that they would understand the punishment for not having compassion.

The rich man just doesn't get it. He still thinks it's all about him and his need. He even still thinks that it is the responsibility of Lazarus to serve him and his family. "My five brothers will be very impressed by a dead beggar walking into our family compound. Resurrected beggars don't usually get past the gate house!"

Again, Father Abraham denies his request. The patriarch tells the rich man that if his brothers will not be guided by the words of Moses and the prophets, they will not be convinced by a beggar raised from the dead.

Rich man, you lived behind a high wall, a deep moat, and a locked gate. You even put a fence around your heart to keep out the needs of others. The teaching of the law and the prophets requires the faithful to "love God and love neighbor as self." Love requires more than not harming others. Love must reach out actively. Love demands more than indifference. The requirements of love cannot be satisfied simply by not harming others. Love requires that you help. Rich man, you created a chasm of indifference between you and others, a chasm that cannot be spanned. No one did this to you. You did it to yourself. You created your own hell. You made choices and now you suffer the consequences of those choices.

That, my friends, is the uncomfortable, but important lesson that dwells at the heart of this story and that speaks to this present age. We are responsible for our decisions and those decisions have consequences.

330

Frankly, we don't like that. It runs contrary to what we want to believe about our faith. We live in an age that delights in understanding God in Jesus Christ as the All Compassionate One. We believe God forgives and lets us start all over again. In fact, we believe so much in the God of compassion that we sometimes forget we also serve a God of judgment. This parable debunks our notion that God never holds anything against us, as long as whatever we do, we do with a good heart, with good intentions. The rich man in the parable tried to live behind a wall of indifference. He didn't do any real harm to Lazarus. He just didn't really get involved and try to help him. He didn't mean to do anything wrong, but he created his own hell.

I read regularly in the newspaper the plight of refugees in far off places. I cannot always even pronounce the names of the countries. Too bad those folks must live in tents. Too bad they gather drinking water from muddy streams. Too bad they must watch their children die of starvation. Too bad warring factions maim and kill the innocents. It is a cruel world out there, but so long as the United States doesn't have a strategic interest, I don't think we should get involved.

I heard recently another of those ghastly reports on the spread of AIDS in Africa. They say that hundreds of thousands of children have already been orphaned and that there is nothing to stop hundreds of thousands more from becoming orphans. This modern day Black Death threatens to destroy the family-based culture that has operated on that continent for 10,000 years. It is a shame, but it is not my problem.

I'm sure it doesn't happen often, but there does seem to be evidence that some of the products we buy in our stores are made by young children in the sweatshops of Asia. I feel bad about ten year olds working twelve-hour days stitching soccer balls, sewing dresses, or making shoes, but what can I do? It is just not my problem.

A scientist studying global warming reports that at the current rate of melting, the ice pack on Mount Kilamanjaro will be gone in fifteen to twenty years. That is just more of that environmental alarmist stuff. For the sake of future generations they want us to conserve fuel and protect endangered species, and not to drill for oil on the frozen tundra and deplete the ozone layer. If we do that, it will cost us money. It will be inconvenient. Not to do it might be problematic for our children and grandchildren, but that is their problem and not mine.

The message from the parable of the rich man and Lazarus is that our actions have consequences. It is not necessary for us to be actively engaged in doing something harmful toward others. There is a high price to pay just for our indifference toward others. In fact, our indifference causes God great distress.

### Indifference

*When Jesus came to Golgotha they hanged Him on a
    tree,*
*They drave great nails through hands and feet, and made
    a Calvary;*
*They crowned Him with a crown of thorns, red were
    His wounds and deep,*
*For those were crude and cruel days, the human flesh
    was cheap.*

*When Jesus came to Birmingham, they simply passed
    Him by*
*They never hurt a hair of Him, they only let Him die;*
*For men had grown more tender, and they would not
    give Him pain,*
*They only just passed down the street, and left Him in
    the rain.*

*Still Jesus cried, "Forgive them, for they know not what
    they do,"*
*And still it rained the winter rain that drenched Him
    through and through;*
*The crowds went home and left the streets without a
    soul to see,*
*And Jesus crouched against a wall and cried for
    Calvary.*[2]
— G. A. Studdert-Kennedy, 1883-1929

We are accountable for our actions. Our decisions have consequences. Our indifference disappoints God as much as our worst moral failings. That is the message of the scripture today. If you ask, "Where is a word of hope in this passage?" I can only say, "Let us not wait around for the resurrected beggar named Lazarus to be seen walking the neighborhood. Begin today to live as God calls us to live."

---

1. *The New Interpreter's Bible: Luke and John,* Volume IX (Nashville: Abingdon Press, 1995), p. 317.

2. G. A. Studdert-Kennedy, "Indifference," in *The Masterpieces of Religious Verse,* edited by James Dalton Morrison (New York: Harper and Brothers Publishers, 1948), p. 195.

**Proper 22**
**Pentecost 20**
**Ordinary Time 27**
**Luke 17:5-10**

# Monitor What's Growing Within

As the seventeenth chapter of Luke opens, Jesus turns his attention away from his enemies, the scribes and Pharisees, back to his supporters, the disciples. With an economy of words, only ten verses, the Master offers four teachings — one on tempting others, one on forgiving others, one on the need to act on your faith, and a fourth on how doing this is no big deal. Just keep on doing it.

Let's see how Jesus weaves these four teachings into a tight, narrative tapestry.[1] (In our examination of the text for today, we will also include Luke 17:1-4.) Jesus begins by warning the faithfully mature to be careful not to tempt the less mature. This demand brings us to the interface between the freedom that we have by faith in Christ Jesus and our responsibility to help others. In ancient Israel, religious law governed every detail of daily life. There were rules and regulations on everything from what to eat to how to prepare the food to how to wash the dishes. There were rules on public behavior as well as rules governing the most intimate aspects of relationships. Hebrew law specified over 250 regulations just on what was permitted and not permitted in order to "Remember the Sabbath and keep it holy." Paul emphasized that because of what God has done in Jesus Christ, people of faith are set free from following all those rules and regulations. Our relationship to God, Paul writes, is established by having faith, not by keeping rules.

Of course, freedom is never free. It brings its own set of problems and responsibilities. The Corinthian Christians once asked Paul if it was acceptable for them to eat the meat from animals sacrificed to pagan idols in the various temples around town. Sacrificed animals, after all, were the source of the best cuts available at the butcher shops. Christians didn't believe in those pagan gods. What harm could there be in having a rack of lamb or a nice sirloin from a goat sacrificed at the Temple of Apollo?

Paul responded to that inquiry by noting that for the spiritually mature, there was no problem. But some of the folks in the Corin-thian Church were new to the faith. Just a few weeks ago they worshiped those pagan gods. They might not yet be strong in their faith. Therefore, the mature Christians should be careful not to flaunt their freedom in any way that tested the faith of the new Christians.

In Luke 17:1-2, Jesus makes this same point. He reminds his most mature followers that they have an obligation to the less mature. "It would be better for you if a millstone were hung around your neck and you were thrown into the sea than for you to cause one of these little ones to stumble." That which is perfectly acceptable for parents can be destructive for children. And that which is not a problem for those who are strong in the faith could destroy the faith of a new Christian.

Lesson one from verses 1 and 2: Out of love, plan to be a role model for others. Lesson number two comes in verses 3 and 4. Out of love, stand ready to set straight anyone who steps out of line. Then, if they ask to be forgiven, forgive them. In fact, as people of faith we have an obligation to forgive and forgive and forgive and forgive.

Obviously, these two lessons place enormous demands on Jesus' disciples. It is incredibly difficult to be a role model for others. It is even more difficult to forgive repetitively — simply because that other person asks to be forgiven. Luke tells us that in unison, the apostles said, "Increase our faith" (v. 5). To paraphrase, "Jesus if you expect us to do that, we will need to be substantially stronger in what we believe. We are not perfect. We are bound to do things that cause others to stumble. As for this continual forgiving stuff, we are not certain we are up to that. We might forgive once or twice, but the third time can't we just throw the offender out of our group? We just don't have sufficient strength to do what you ask. Lord, increase our faith."

Jesus responds with the third thread in this teaching tapestry. "If you had faith the size of a mustard seed," the Lord said to them, "you could say to this mulberry tree, 'Be uprooted and planted in the sea,' and it would obey you" (v. 6). To understand this verse, scholars wind us through the nuances of Greek clauses. Let me cut to the bottom line. Jesus means, "You already have faith sufficient for what I am asking. All it takes is faith no bigger than a mustard seed. If you act on that tiny faith that grows within you, you can tell that mulberry tree over there to pull itself out by the roots and jump into the ocean and it will."

Obviously, this is figurative hyperbole. Don't take it literally. Faith is not a magician's trick by which we are empowered to do spectacular landscaping. "Tulip bulbs, plant yourselves. Mulberry tree, show me your roots. Then dance over to the lake and jump in." The point that Jesus makes is that there grows within each of us a tiny capacity for faith sufficient for the task. Elsewhere Jesus emphasizes the wonder of the mustard seed. It is half the size of a grain of rice, yet it grows into a bush so large birds come and build nests in it. The implication is obvious. If we will act on the seed of faith growing within us, we will be amazed at our capacity to get good things done.

Please note that our Lord uses this notion of "having faith" in a very specific way. To Jesus, having faith is not adhering to a certain set of beliefs or doctrines. To Jesus, to have faith is to have a spiritual force in your life that calls forth and shapes everything about you.

Let me put that in a different way. Having faith *in God* differs from believing *there is a God*. A theologian once explained the difference this way. He said, "When I say I believe in my wife, I don't mean that I believe I *have* a wife. I *know* that is true. When I say I *believe in my* wife I mean I have faith that my wife will be my wife. I can trust her to be my wife. When I say I have faith *in God,* I mean that I trust God to be God. God will be the Person God is as God." When Jesus comments that we have the faith to tell a tree to move, he means that if we trust God to be God, we have all the faith we need.[2] And that capacity for believing grows within us — even though it might be as tiny as a mustard seed. We need to be aware of our capacity to trust God to be God. We need to monitor it. We need to act on the faith that grows within.

Unfortunately, more than faith grows within us. Lesser-valued things also grow within. As Jesus notes earlier in this passage of scripture, we also have the capacity for setting a bad example. Like a mustard seed, our ability to set a bad example can grow until we are nothing but a stumbling block for others. We have the capacity to forgive one another over and over again, but we also have the capacity to hurt one another over and over again. Frankly, if we are not monitoring, growing, and acting on the seed of faith within, we are likely to grow and to act on our capacity to sin.

Harry Emerson Fosdick, perhaps the greatest preacher of the first half of the twentieth century, once commented that he was listening to a couple of old friends. They were pontificating on the world's problems over lunch. Neither of these men had ever developed the gift of faith within themselves. As he listened, Dr. Fosdick realized that without faith these two lived in terribly small, self-centered worlds.[3] Indeed, without cultivating the possibilities of faith we get wrapped into our own self-interests. When the outer edge of our world stops at our own ego, we live in a tiny world. As the ancient Zen proverb puts it, "Self is the sound of one hand clapping." The not so old American proverb holds, "Those who live only for self, deep down they are really shallow." At a time before political leaders consulted focus groups, President Woodrow Wilson observed that the rise to spiritual maturity requires serving others and not just serving self. We all need to monitor and control the seed of self-centeredness that grows within.

There is also within each of us the seed of anger. If carefully tended and grown, that seed can grow into violence. In human beings this capacity for anger is both universal and enormous. Several years ago, two young men named Terry and Timothy became offended at the way the United States government handled the Branch Davidians in Waco, Texas. They talked constantly about their anger. They nursed their displeasure until it became a bubbling cauldron of rage. They began to hate their government and plotted to strike out against it. Timothy McVeigh and Terry Nichols did not monitor and control the anger within them. They made a bomb and left it in front of the federal building in Oklahoma City.

Mary Lee Sooter and her husband pastored the Eagle Heights Baptist Church. This congregation had some tough rules on following the faith — no dancing, no card playing, no movies. But Mary Lee was not judgmental. She was known for her sweetness. The Sooters had a daughter named Jenny. When Jennie became 24 years old she announced to the family that it was time for her to leave the nest. She got a job, rented an apartment, and even decided to join a church that was closer to where she was living.

Jenny's mother, usually bubbly and encouraging, became very distraught over her daughter's decision to leave home. Mary Lee didn't believe her daughter was ready for independence. She was immature, naive about the ways of the world. Mary Lee asked her daughter to remain with her parents. When the young woman insisted on moving out, her mother shot her to death and then committed suicide.[4]

When children are small, parents act in what we believe is their best interest. In fact, the smaller the child, the more control we must assume over their lives. But as children grow, healthy parenting requires we give up control over their lives so that they can learn to be responsible for themselves. Mary Lee Sooter could not bring herself to give up control over her daughter's life. She was not confident of the Proverb, "Bring up a child in the way she should go and she will not depart from it." She did not trust God to be God and for God to be faithful. Multitudes want to have control over their lives and the lives of those around them. The only thing unusual about Mary Lee is the extreme to which she went when she began to lose control.

That is part of the lesson Jesus teaches in Luke 17. The potentially destructive desires of ego, control, gluttony, covetousness, pride, lust, sloth, anger, and envy exist within us. But the seed of faith is also there. We need to monitor what is growing within. If the mustard seed of faith is not germinating and growing, then there is a good chance that one of these other seeds can take over.

The first three lessons in Luke 17 make significant demands on Jesus' followers. We are to be role models for doing good and not do anything that causes others to stumble. We are to forgive others over and over again. We are to act on the seed of faith within us, and we are to make certain that seed is nourished while we keep in check the growth of the weed seeds that can also grow within us.

These lessons, coming one on top of the other, must have left them breathless. "Wow, this is tough stuff." Jesus, sensing that his listeners were overwhelmed by the demands, launches into a parable about how slaves do not make a big deal out of the service to which they are called. They just do it. That same is true for us. Don't complain about it. Don't magnify the difficulty of it. Just do it. Be a role model for others. Forgive others, over and over again. Monitor the anger, selfishness, envy, greed, and everything else troublesome that might be within you. Keep those troublesome things to a minimum. But whatever you do, carefully nurture the faith that is within you and act on it. Don't make a big deal out of it. Just do it. For you will be amazed at how much can be accomplished by faith. It is God's love that simply will not let you go.

---

1. Fred Craddock, *Interpretation: Luke* (Louisville: John Knox Press, 1990), pp. 198-201.

2. *Lectionary Homiletics*, Volume III, Number 2, October 1992, p. 6.

3. Quoted in *Pulpit Resources*, Volume 14, Number 4, October 1986, p. 4.

4. "Faith Eases Pain For Congregation," Kansas City *Star*, Metropolitan Section, March 5, 2001, p. B1.

# Sermons On The Gospel Readings

## For Sundays
## After Pentecost
## (Last Third)

*Music From Another Room*

## Stephen M. Crotts

*To Bryan Patrick Crotts,*
*My son,*
*Newly minted in divinity school,*
*Soon to be ordained,*
*A lifetime of preaching ahead!*
*What songs shall you sing!*
*What music shall you play!*
*What souls shall you touch!*
*All in God's grace in Jesus!*

# Introduction

It was one of those hotel ballroom conferences. I was finishing my sermon to the crowd. But in the next room, another conference was cranking up with a soloist's rousing rendition of "The Star-Spangled Banner."

Hard job, this preaching.

Lots of competition.

Distracting noise is a portion of today's world.

"Muzak" is piped in for the elevator ride to the top floor. The adjacent car at the stoplight pulses rhythm from a cranked stereo system. A neighboring teen's boom box carries across the fence line to one's own porch.

The television blares. A lone walker whistles. Politicians' inane sloganistic jingles lodge like a bad headache in our brains.

Words. Noise. Music.

Why would anyone want to add to today's din? Because God has spoken in Jesus Christ. Because the Bible is a reliable account of his message. Because Jesus himself bid his disciples to go into all the world telling the Good News of God's mercy to all who trust Christ.

Yes, we are a noisy people. Full of opinions. But we can grow quiet listening as Christ speaks.

The other day I heard the faint strains of a lovely violin concerto. I strained to listen. I cut the television off, opened the door, and sat on the back steps to listen, enthralled, while my elderly neighbor rehearsed a song for her church orchestra.

Indeed! It was music from another room. But it became mine as a gift when I made myself available.

These several texts are like that. They are not hit parade songs, commercial advertisements, television sitcoms, or political opinions.

343

They are not of this world, but are the Word of God, harmony to our weary ears. They are music from another room! From God's own heaven itself! And the tune is healing to all who listen.

Stephen M. Crotts
Innisfree
Burlington, NC

**Proper 23**
**Pentecost 21**
**Ordinary Time 28**
**Luke 17:11-19**

# Thanksgiving When You
# Don't Feel Like It

Have you ever had this experience? You walk into a dark room to do something, flick on the light switch, and nothing happens. I suspect a lot of our Thanksgivings are like that. Thursday late in November rolls around and suddenly it's Thanksgiving! So everybody gives thanks! But quite often the gratitude is just not there. Like the light switch, we reach for it at the appropriate time and it won't work. It's burned out.

In the text, ten lepers, disastrously afflicted with leprosy and quarantined from their families, are healed by Jesus. As the joyous reality settles over them, they each begin to move toward home. One suddenly stops, thinks of Jesus the healer, and returns to give thanks. The other nine, however, never even bother to look back. The works of God, rather than the God of works, is what interests them.

And Jesus, seeing the tenth leper kneeling before him in thanksgiving, voices the lament, "Were not ten cleansed? Where are the other nine?"

What if it happens to you this year? What if during this season of appreciation you're just not in the mood? What if Thursday finds you grumpy? What if your complaints outnumber your blessings? What if all your prayers seem unanswered and bitterness swells your heart?

Well, that's what this sermon is about. You might say it's a sermon on how to have Thanksgiving when you're just not in the mood.

## Discipline

As a first help, might I hazard a word that's fallen from favor in our society of late? The word is discipline. Our forefathers were acquainted with this word. They lived by doing what was right. They lived by doing what was necessary, even if they didn't feel like doing it.

Today, however, we live by our feelings. Never mind that something is right or that something needs doing. Our question is: "Do I feel like doing it?" Twenty-first century man likes to boast about himself as "Man Come of Age." But I tell you that living life on a feeling level is not a step into maturity; it's a dip into childishness!

You parents know how children can be. "But, Daddy, I don't feel like eating breakfast this morning." "Mommy, I don't feel like visiting Grandma!" And we adults won't take feelings for a reason and force children along anyway!

Yet in ourselves we live by our feelings and allow ourselves to get away with it. If we don't feel like going to church, we just don't go to church. If we don't feel like doing a job we promised to do, then we just don't do it. And so it is that we allow our moods, our whims, our feelings to conquer right and necessary tasks!

A solution the Bible offers to this sorry state of affairs is discipline. Hebrews 12:11 says, "Now discipline always seems painful rather than pleasant at the time; but later it yields the peaceful fruit of righteousness to those who have been trained by it." You joggers know what the Bible is talking about here, don't you? Many days you just don't feel like running. Usually that's when one needs to run the most! So you get up, get dressed, and get started. And at first it is agony! But slowly something marvelous happens. You get into gear. Things begin to flow! And suddenly you're having one of your best days. The same discipline can work for thanksgiving, too. For when we bring this same sort of discipline into our faith, then we can have thanksgiving even when we don't feel like it.

## Fellowship

There is yet another exercise that can help us give thanks when we're not in the mood. And that exercise is fellowship. Hebrews 10:25 says, "... not neglecting to meet together, as is the habit of

346

some, but encouraging one another, and all the more as you see the Day approaching."

Let me put it this way. Has the battery on your car ever run down? When it does we usually get the jumper cables and hook up with a battery on another car. And soon both cars are running with both batteries fully charged! People can be contagious like that as well. Put your child in the church nursery with chicken pox — and magic! Suddenly all the kids have it!

Seriously, on a higher plane, you know how it is. We come to church grumpy, depressed, just not feeling like it. But it's right to worship. It is a necessity. So, we, with discipline, override our feelings and go in and join the group. A hymn is sung. Prayers are uttered. The choir ministers to us. And oddly, we find ourselves glad to be at worship!

Those of you who've discovered the discipline of regular worship know exactly what I'm talking about today. You came in not feeling like it. And now you do! The fact is, people are contagious! If you just don't feel like worshiping, then get with some people who do, and they'll rub off on you.

This, dear people, is the genius of Christ's church idea. It's a community, a support group. When we're down in the dumps, there are always enough saints *up* that they can draw us *up* along with them.

### Inventory

So what do you do when it's time for thanksgiving and you're not in the mood? The scriptures challenge us to discipline and fellowship. And now, here is a third exercise. I call it inventory. The psalmist in Psalm 103:2 exclaims: "Bless the Lord, O my soul, and forget not all his benefits." Yes, forget not God's benefits, his bounty to you! Take stock!

Let me be personal with you for a moment. I've been a bit depressed for the past two months. The past year has seemed to me to be a bit unproductive. And I've allowed myself to become somewhat down in the dumps and grumps. Fact is, this sermon was born out of a sense of personal need this week. You see, I'm preaching

347

to myself this morning because I fear it will suddenly be Thanksgiving and I won't feel like it myself!

At any rate, about two weeks ago I took an inventory of my year with Jesus Christ. I got out my prayer list and began to look for causes to give thanks. There I found abundance! Three growing, healthy children. A loving, patient wife. Two good friends who've stood by me in thick and thin this year. A three-week trip to Africa, Asia, and Europe. Some of the best snow skiing I've ever experienced last winter. A chance to attend a Reformation Conference in Dallas and get to know some of our denomination's most able men. My mother's renewed health. My brother's good marriage. A chance to drive and enjoy a restored 1950 Chevy. A book of mine honored by a magazine as Book of the Year. Getting to rake leaves with my family. Having a front row seat to witness baptisms, marriages healed, divorcees starting over and making a go of it in Christ; watching the jobless become gainfully employed, the sick and bitter find release in forgiveness; students discovering Christ and the Word; a group of elders struggling and growing and triumphing together; racial barriers falling; people becoming disciples; the birth of a mission vision; a chance to study music and history thoroughly; and a church opening like a flower before Christ the Son.

Well, that was about one-tenth of my personal inventory. And as I was in the midst of it, I began to be ashamed of myself. The words of Friar Laurence as he chides the lovesick and pouting Romeo in Shakespeare's play *Romeo and Juliet* came to me. "A pack of blessings light upon thy back; happiness courts thee in her best array; but, like a misbehaved and sullen wench, thou poutest upon thy fortune and thy love. Take heed, take heed, for such die miserable."

We're all guilty of forgetting the Lord's benefits to us, aren't we? We toss aside a thousand blessings just to focus on one woe. And even when we make a conscious effort at inventory, we still underestimate our stock in Christ. But, nonetheless, look back. That's what gratitude is, isn't it? It's love looking back at the past.

Coming through customs last May after a long overseas trip, a big Texan in front of me was asked by the customs agent, "Do you have anything to declare?" And he said, "I declare I'm glad to be back in the United States!" Seriously, look into your past. Do you have anything to declare to God in gratitude? An inventory can help you get started.

## Conclusion: An Attitude Of Gratitude

In closing, let's suppose! Suppose that I were to give each of you a bowl of sand and tell you that there were particles of iron in it. You might look for them with your eyes and find a few. You might even search for them with your clumsy fingers and discover a few more. But if you'd take a magnet and sweep it through the bowl of sand, it would draw to itself all of the iron, even the all but invisible particles of metal.

And so it is with life. The ungrateful heart, like your finger in the sand, discovers so few blessings, but let the thankful heart sweep through the year and as the magnet finds the iron, so the grateful heart will find in every day some gift of God.

*Time* magazine recently made the statement: "Never have so many had it so good and felt so badly about it." It seems people are dipping into their bowls of life and only finding sand. Yes, the magnet of gratitude is gone, lost from the grasp of many a man. And so we go through life finding precious little to be thankful about, but let us remember, "It is a good thing to give thanks unto the Lord." As God's people in Christ, let's remember that and do it today, and every day, even when we don't feel like it.

**Proper 24**
**Pentecost 22**
**Ordinary Time 29**
**Luke 18:1-8**

# Praying Through

No doubt you have heard about the postal service's "Dead Letter Department." That's the place where mail goes when it is not clearly addressed or has insufficient postage and the sender's identity cannot be determined. There the letter is opened and its contents examined for clues to the sender's identity. If the return address cannot be determined the letter is destroyed. It never reaches its destination, and any requests made by the writer remain unanswered. How about you? Do you feel like your prayers end up in some kind of dead letter department? Do you feel like your prayers never reach God? If you do, then this text is for you! Here in Jesus Christ's own words we are told how to address our prayers to God so that they will be received and answered. The parable of a cold-hearted judge and a pesky widow tells how.

**Ask, And It Will Be Given You**
First of all, Christ told us to ask in prayer. He said, "Ask, and it will be given you" (Matthew 7:7). And he gave another example of this in the parable of a widow who went to the judge asking for justice in a civil matter.

As one studies the New Testament accounts of Christ's life, it becomes obvious that the Lord was not afraid to ask things of God. He asked for wine at a wedding party. He asked for more bread and fish to feed a crowd. He asked God to heal the blind, the lame, the mute, and the possessed. Jesus asked much of God. He did not feel like he was imposing. And here in the text, Jesus is telling us to do the same. He is assuring us that we can ask much from God. I

351

know that in my own life I have often been reluctant to ask God for my needs. I used to think perhaps God was too busy to be troubled over my affairs. I didn't want to bother him. After all, I could not be very important to him. But slowly I have begun to realize that I am a child of God. I am not some orphan. I am not a disinherited son. I am the child of the King of the universe. And my Father has told me, "Ask, and it will be given you."

Once in graduate school my wife and I were running very short of money. Inflation had taken a big bite out of our income. We had a new baby. Rent was going up. Gasoline had soared. And our electricity bill had more that doubled. For several weeks I worried and schemed and grew irritable. I could see no way out of our financial plight. During those weeks I am ashamed to say that I never once prayed about things. I guess I sort of figured seminary students were supposed to be poor. My wife watched me quietly as I turned into a tyrant through worry. Finally she simply said, "Stephen, why don't we pray about it?" Well, I agreed, and together we told God all about it and asked for his help. Things began to happen!

That very afternoon the landlady stopped me while I was emptying the trash. She said, "Stephen, for some time now I've been wanting to ask you to be the groundskeeper for this apartment complex. You can do the work between your studies. It'll be good exercise for you. And we'll pay you $2.50 an hour." I quickly accepted and right away we had an extra $25 a week for income. And I was also getting some much needed exercise.

The next day Kathryn and I found an anonymous letter in our mailbox. In it was a check for over $200. Someone had sent it just to help us out.

Well, I can assure you that our family was praising the Lord! He had indeed answered our prayers! But then it suddenly dawned on us. The !etter was postmarked two days before we had prayed for help and the landlady had been thinking of offering me that job long before I had decided to pray. We began to doubt. Perhaps this new financial help was not an answer to prayer after all. Maybe it was all just a coincidence. But then it hit me. I remembered a promise of God from Isaiah 65:24. There the Lord says, "Before they call I will answer, while they are yet speaking I will hear." What the Lord had done was to go ahead and prepare the answer to our prayers, then he had also promoted our asking!

Now, asking prayer works just this way. The Good Lord has something he wants done. He prepares all the resources that will be needed. Then he begins to prompt us mentally so we will ask him to allow us to do the job. Thus our prayers become a simple asking for what God already is eager to do.

As you live the Christian life you will undoubtedly find God prompting you to ask him for things. It may be talent, wisdom, health, money, help, or a hundred other things. But whatever, do not be afraid to ask God for that which you feel prompted. You won't bother him. He cares about you. You won't impoverish him. The Lord owns the cattle on a thousand hills. "Ask," Jesus said. "Ask, and it shall be given you."

### Seek, And You Will Find

Christ not only told us to ask in prayer. He also told us to seek. Jesus said, "Seek, and you will find" (Matthew 7:7 RSV). The widow does this in the parable. She "kept coming to him" with her plea.

It is true that Christ did a lot of asking in prayer. He asked for bread, wine, healing, and a host of other things. But Christ also prayed prayers of seeking. In the Garden of Gethsemane the Lord searched for God's will. He said, "Lord, I ask in prayer that this cup pass from me. Let me not go to the cross, suffer, and die. I ask for some other way!" But then Jesus began to seek in prayer. He said, "But Lord, if this is not your will, if I must die, then your will be done." Here we find an example of Christ searching in prayer. He is looking for God's will. He is trying to find out what the mind of God is so he can obey it.

Jesus told us to pray like this when he said, "Whatever you ask in my name, I will do it" (John 14:13 RSV). Now the key to this verse is the phrase, "in my name." Jesus did not say, "Whatever you ask, I will do it." He said, "Whatever you ask *in my name*, I will do it." The Greek word used here for "in my name" means more than just a label. If you called on someone's name in the

Greek world, you were calling on his actual presence. So Jesus was saying, "Whatever you ask in my presence, I will do it."

As Christians we believe in the presence of Christ. We believe Jesus is with us by the power of the Holy Spirit. In fact, we believe that Jesus is so present with us that we can actually take on the mind of Christ. The New Testament scriptures tell us that we should have in us the actual mind of Jesus Christ (Philippians 2:5).

Now right here is a great secret of prayer. When we pray, we should ask in the mind of Christ. Jesus said, "Whatever you ask in my name or in my presence or rather, in my mind, I will do it." Thus prayer is not overcoming God's reluctance. It is taking hold of his willingness. It is not presenting your arguments in order to make God change his mind. Prayer is searching for the mind of Christ and then praying in it.

When confronted with a need, it is not good to go right out and pray about it by telling God what you want. You may not know the mind of Christ in the matter. You may ask in the flesh and not in the spirit. So first ask the Lord to reveal to you his mind. Say, "Lord, here is a need. Teach me your mind. Teach me how to pray about this."

Do you see how prayer is not getting God to see it your way, but getting you to see it God's way? Let's suppose that you are in a rowboat fifteen feet from the shore. You throw an anchor ashore and pull yourself to the dock. Now, what have you done? Did you pull the land to you or did you pull yourself to the land? Of course! The land did not budge. You did. You moved to the shore. Seeking prayer works like this as well. You throw out an anchor to God. You seek in prayer, in scripture, in fellowship, in obedience, and you pull yourself to God's mind and ask in it.

Saint Paul knew how to seek in prayer. He said, "God, I am sick. I have this thorn in my flesh." Three times Paul went to God and asked to be healed. And there in God's presence Paul began to know the mind of Christ. He quit asking to be healed. He started asking for strength to bear the affliction for the glory of God (2 Corinthians 12).

In your own prayer life you too will want to learn seeking prayer. You will want to learn to pray in Christ's name, in his presence and

354

mind, and not in your name and in your mind. When you are facing a need, take that problem directly to God. And do not limit God by telling him what to do about it. Just envision the problem in both your hands. Then envision God. Think of his presence. Meditate on his marvelous light, his love, and his power. Then lift the problem right up into God's presence and leave it there.

A little boy knelt down to say his bedtime prayers. His parents heard him reciting the alphabet in very reverent tones. When asked what he was doing, he replied, "I'm saying my prayers, but I cannot think of the exact words tonight. So, I'm just saying all the letters. God knows what I need, and he'll put all the words together for me."

Now, that is not far from a proper way to pray! In seeking prayer we are looking for Christ's mind. We are not sure quite how to word our prayer. So we ask God to take our words and fit them into the correct prayer. We ask him to edit our prayers by cutting out the unnecessary, making corrections, and adding the necessities. We ask God to take our minds and make them his. We ask the Holy Spirit to pray through us. And when we seek in prayer like that, Jesus assures us in the text, we shall find.

### Knock, And It Shall Be Opened!

Moving along from asking and seeking prayers, we come to knocking prayer. Jesus said, "Knock, and the door will be opened for you" (Matthew 7:7). The widow in the parable did this with the judge. She "kept coming." The judge said she was "bothering me."

Here, we need to know that there is more involved in answering prayer than your will and God's will. There are other such forces as hard hearts and God's decision to give people a free will. You might be praying that God will save your son. But your son's heart may be stoney toward God. You want him saved. And there is nothing God would like better than to save him, but here is a barrier. God has given your son a free will. He will not violate it by forcing himself on anyone. And your son's cold, cold heart has chosen to leave God out.

There is also the barrier of the satanic. The Bible says, "For our struggle is not against enemies of flesh and blood, but against the rulers, against the authorities, against the cosmic powers of this present darkness, against the spiritual forces of evil in the heavenly places" (Ephesians 6:12). An example of how satanic forces can hinder answers to prayer is found in Daniel 10. There the prophet prayed for more than twenty days without an answer. Finally an angel visited him and explained the reason for the delay. He said, "O Daniel, man greatly beloved ... from the first day that you set your mind to understand ... your words have been heard, and I have come because of your words. The prince ... withstood me twenty-one days; but Michael ... came to help me ... so I ... came." Here we are taught that satanic powers hindered an answer to prayer. And here we must come to scripture with a sense of wonder. There is much about this world that we do not know. Our finite minds are so frail. Things like Satan, evil, and spiritual warfare boggle our minds. We cannot understand them completely. But God has revealed some of this in scripture and we can accept it by faith. And by faith, scripture teaches that satanic barriers can hinder prayer.

The book of Job is perhaps the best place in scripture to study knocking prayer. There, righteous Job is devastated. He loses his children, his friends, his property, and his health. Satan has horribly afflicted him. His wife urges him to curse God and die. But instead, Job begins a knocking prayer. "Oh, that I knew where I might find him, that I might come even to his dwelling! I would lay my case before him and fill my mouth with arguments. I would learn what he would answer me" (Job 23:3-5).

Thus Job begins to knock in prayer. He blindly gropes for God. He patiently and sometimes impatiently yearns for deliverance. Again and again Job reaches for God in prayer. Though his body is wasting away, though all seems lost, though he cannot understand, Job has faith in God. His heart is filled with hope and he says: "For I know that my Redeemer lives, and that at last he will stand upon the earth; and after my skin has been thus destroyed, then in my flesh I shall see God ..." (Job 19:25-26).

Thus with hope, faith, and persistence Job continues to knock in prayer. Finally God comes to him. Though the Lord does not explain the affliction, he does heal Job. He restores his fortune and gives him more children than ever before. As Jesus promised, it will be opened to those that knock. And Job triumphantly says to God, "I know that you can do all things, and that no purpose of yours can be thwarted ... I had heard of you by the hearing of the ear, but now my eye sees you" (Job 42:2, 5).

Perhaps Jesus was thinking of Job when he told the parable of the friend at midnight. "Which of you who has a friend will go to him at midnight and say to him, 'Friend, lend me three loaves; for a friend of mine has arrived on a journey, and I have nothing to set before him'; and he will answer from within, 'Do not bother me; the door is now shut, and my children are with me in bed; I cannot get up and give you anything'? I tell you, though he will not get up and give him anything because he is his friend, yet because of his importunity he will rise and give him whatever he needs" (Luke 11:5-8 RSV). Here Jesus teaches us the value of persistent prayer. When confronted with closed doors, hard hearts, and satanic barriers it becomes necessary to knock in prayer. Now a knock does not mean one rap on the door. A knock is a loud and repeated rapping sound. And so must our knocking prayers be repetitious.

The question might arise in your mind as to why we must occasionally pray repetitiously. Do we do so to beg God into helping us? Do we do so in order to force him into changing his mind? No! Repetitious prayer is better seen as unleashing spiritual power. Have you ever tried to open a rusty water valve? It is frozen stiff with corrosion. You strain and strain at it but little progress is made. So you rest awhile then try again. With all your might you grip the handle and twist. It budges a bit. You rest again then return for another try. Slight progress is made and a trickle of water begins to flow. After yet another rest you have at it again. More progress. And so you persist until the valve is wide open and the water full on. Repetitious prayer works like this as well. To persist in prayer is to open more and more the spiritual channels through which the power of God can flow. Closed doors, hard hearts, and satanic obstacles give way to the relentless pressure applied by both God and the kneeling Christian.

The Bible gives us numerous accounts of knocking prayer. Moses, during a battle, lifted up his hands and prayed continuously until the sun went down and victory was won (Exodus 17:8-16).

Daniel engaged in earnest supplication for 21 days (Daniel 10). And in Acts we are told that the church prayed all evening for Peter's release from prison (Acts 12). Even now many people are praying and knocking on God's door for many things. Some of them have been praying for months, years, even lifetimes! Missionary societies have been praying for years that China will reopen for the church. Saints are praying persistently for a real revival to wake up the western church. Mothers are praying for erring children, and women are knocking for their husbands. In each case, things all but appear hopeless. Hearts seem too cold. Barriers seem too large. But the power will begin to trickle! Who knows if even one more twist will not open things up all the way!

**Conclusion**

What the world needs is more Christians who, like the widow, come to God presistently asking, knocking, and seeking his will for their lives in and for the world.

**Proper 25**
**Pentecost 23**
**Ordinary Time 30**
**Luke 18:9-14**

# Worship Wars!

We pastors call it The Worship Wars. One can see the frowning battlements in the faces seated in pews, hear the rumble of its artillery in negative comments, and feel the white heat of its lethal shrapnel in board meetings.

"It's boring!"

"Why, those songs are so old, every time I sing them I get a backache!"

"Worship is becoming a nightclub act! What will we do next?"

"Choruses are 7-11 worship. Seven words repeated eleven times!"

Any pastor, any active church member alive today is in the trenches of this warfare.

Thankfully, the scriptures can be our guide through the mine-fields of this battleground. And today's text, a parable of Jesus, is a good place to begin.

Jesus told the story of two men who went into the temple to pray. Each had a totally different experience. So, let's interview them, each in turn.

### Worshiper Number One

"So, Mr. Pharisee, I understand you are a devoutly religious man. Is that true?"

"You've got that right!"

"Well, you went to church today. What happened in there? In the text Jesus said you stood by yourself and prayed, 'God, I thank you that I am not like other people: thieves, rogues, adulterers, or even like this tax collector. I fast twice a week; I give a tenth of my income.' "

"Well, sir, three things happened for me in worship. First, I had *one eye on myself*. You see, I have exquisite taste. Just as I like to drive the best of cars, wear stylish clothes, and eat fine foods, so I like to shop around for a church that meets my standards. Worship should please me, stir my feelings, reinforce who I am."

"But, sir, is worship all about you? Or is it about God?"

"Don't interrupt! As I was saying, in worship three things happened for me today. I saw myself, my tastes fulfilled, my virtues, my wants. And the second thing I saw was my neighbor. It's important to spot the spiritual lowlifes. One cannot judge too carefully. Why, I've actually come to enjoy measuring and rating people."

"But you sound like a man with little Jack Horner religion! You know the nursery rhyme? Little Jack Horner sat in a corner eating his curds and whey. He stuck in his thumb, pulled out a plum, and said, 'What a good boy am I!' "

"So, what's wrong with that sort of religion?"

"It's just that you judge others by their flaws, yourself by your virtues, and always get such a marvelous comparison."

"Somebody has to be the watchdog around here to see that the big hair in the choir isn't adulterating or the preacher isn't being overpaid and that my taste in music is upheld."

"Well, you certainly have strong opinions, sir."

"And they are right, too, I assure you!"

"So, you have one eye on your neighbor, one on yourself. What is the third thing that happened in worship for you?"

"I keep one on myself, one eye on my neighbor, and third, I keep no eye on God."

"Thank you, Mr. Pharisee. Your values and attitudes as well as your zeal in enforcing them, are most clear, and duly noted."

### Worshiper Number Two

Now, we turn to the second worshiper in the temple. Jesus said he was a tax collector, said he went into the same temple to pray. He did not stand up front, but stood far off, and he would not even lift up his eyes to heaven, but beat his breast, saying, "God, be merciful to me, a sinner!"

Let's move closer now and see if we can interview him.

"Sir, sir! Oh, Mr. Tax Collector! I understand you've been to church."

"That's right."

"Could you tell us what happened in there?"

"Oh, that's easy! I saw God. We were singing the hymn, 'Immortal, invisible, God only wise. In light inaccessible, hid from our eyes.' I tell you, I can get lost in extolling the marvelous perfections of Almighty God! Yes, and what's more, I saw God in the scriptures and in the sermon. Seems I learn something new every time I come into his presence."

"Can you tell us about how you saw yourself in church?"

"You bet! It's like this. Last year I was washing my white car when it snowed overnight. Now, snow will tell you what white really is. My car looked yellow by comparison. Same with God. You glimpse him in worship, and suddenly you see yourself in comparison, and you don't look so good. That's why I got real humble real fast. And it just seemed natural to ask for his mercy in Christ."

"But what about other people?"

"Listen, I've had more trouble with myself than with any other person on earth!"

"Where did you learn your ways of worship, I might ask?"

"Oh, I learned them in scripture. Look at Isaiah 6, the story of the prophet's encounter with God in the temple. Read it carefully and see what happened. He saw God high and lifted up. He saw his own sin — especially his ugly tongue. He saw his redemption so lovingly and fearfully provided by God, and he saw what God had for him to do."

"But what about your tastes? Your desires? Your personal preferences?"

"Listen, I don't go to church asking, 'Do I like it?' I go asking, 'Does God like it?' You see, worship is not all about me. It's all about God."

## Conclusion

Well, ladies and gentlemen, there you have it. Two men. The same church service. Two totally different approaches to worship.

Mr. Pharisee about whom Jesus said "... trusted in himself that he was righteous and regarded others with contempt," so cleverly told us he came to church with one eye on himself, one eye on his neighbor, and no eye on God. And I might point out that Jesus said even though this man went to church, he was not a part of the community for he was "standing by himself." And Jesus said pointedly that he was never forgiven by God, for "all who exalt themselves will be humbled." I guess you might say he was so self-conscious he lost his God-consciousness.

The second gentleman, however, the tax collector, "went down to his home justified." It seems that even though he was not satisfied with himself, God was.

So, from the text, which of these two men do you relate to in worship? You went to church today. What happened?

# The Process Of Love

In William Shakespeare's play, *A Midsummer Night's Dream*, the actors roam the stage looking for a scarce potion that can make humans fall in love. What with our church splits, divorce rate, homicides, racism, and terrorist wars, such an elixir, such a love potion, could come in handy in our own day.

Jesus Christ told us in the Great Commandment to love our neighbor (Mark 12:28 ff). Then he stuck around to show us how it's done. What we have in the Gospels is not just words of love, but the deeds themselves all demonstrated in Christ's treatment of people. We call this "relational theology." And nowhere are the four principles of how Jesus modeled this love better found than in the story of Zacchaeus.

**Data Collection**

Notice how love begins with the gathering of information about an individual. Jesus strode into town and spied Zacchaeus "short of stature," "trying to see who Jesus was," peeking in and out through the milling crowd, and finally running "ahead" to climb a sycamore tree to see him. Christ also took the time to comprehend the facts that Zacchaeus was a tax collector and rich.

Fact is, one cannot love someone he does not know. Love is relational. And without some level of knowledge, love does not exist.

Jesus had intrinsic knowledge. He could look at the woman at the well and tell of her failed romances. He told Nathaniel just looking at him that he was a Hebrew in whom there was no guile. And, indeed, sometimes God gifts us with such discernment.

363

Haven't you ever looked deeply in another's face and seen broken commandments, great suffering, or bitterness?

Mostly, however, we get to know people by taking the time to ask questions and listen. "Who are you?" "What brings you here?" "What are you thinking?"

Many years ago, I'd been to a Christian camp in upstate New York. Five days of two-a-day meetings had exhausted me. So when I got on the plane in Albany, I planned to sleep. But the elderly woman beside me wanted to talk. "Are you flying to Baltimore?" "Yes," I said wearily, "there I'll change for North Carolina." Then I shut my eyes and slumped in my seat, all body language meant to say politely, "Leave me alone. I'll go to sleep now."

Still the woman rattled on. "Oh, I do hope it is not raining in Baltimore!"

I thought to myself, "Lady, who cares?"

On and on, she talked. So finally I sat up and politely inquired, "Why are you flying to Baltimore and so concerned with the weather?" That's when she told me her husband was dead, his casket was in the jet's storage, and his graveside funeral would be in Baltimore. So she was hoping for good weather.

I asked God to give me strength to listen to her for an hour. And she told me how they met, about his career in sales, how their only son died in a war, and of his last years in an awful bout with cancer.

The plane landed and I walked her to a taxi that would take her to a funeral home. As I shut the door, she was saying to the driver, "Do you think it will rain today?" And I caught myself praying, "Please, God! Let him listen to her."

## Affirmation

After Jesus gathered information about Zacchaeus as a rich, lonely, unpopular taxman with enough spiritual hunger to cause him to climb a tree to see what was going on, Jesus moved to the second step in expressing love. He affirmed the man.

Once a person opens up to you, gives you a glimpse of himself, he can be insecure. "Does he like me?" "Will he make fun of me?" "Will he think I'm okay?" And unless you give him or her some sign of approval, of respect, the relationship can go no farther.

That's why Jesus parading through Jericho looks up and sees this lonely, quizzical face peering at him through the tree branches, and blurts out for all to hear, "Zacchaeus, hurry and come down, for I must stay at your house today."

Can you imagine being lonely, going to a basketball game alone, and come half-time, Michael Jordan leaves the court, walks up to the nosebleed section where you are seated, shakes your hand, calls you by name, and asks if he could have supper with you following the game? It's something like that with Zacchaeus and Jesus.

I can just see that little fellow shinny quickly down from the tree, square his shoulders, and walk like a Bantam rooster with Jesus to his house. "I *am* somebody!" he was thinking. "Jesus needs me. *Me!* Do you see?"

God has wonderfully gifted each of us with what we need to affirm other people. We can smile at them, shake hands, pay a compliment, say, "I like you!" give a gift, hug, catch their eye, or even spend time with them.

Out in public stores I see parents sometimes shred their little children's self-esteem when they jerk their tiny arms and hiss for all to hear, "You're bad! I'm sorry I had you. Just wait until I get you home. I'm going to beat you good!" Can you imagine one's self-image after growing up for eighteen years in that home?

Contrast that with the seven-year-old kid who finally swings at a pitch in a little league game, gets a hit to the outfield, and stands at home plate jumping up and down celebrating. The crowd is yelling, "Run! You gotta run!" The kid looks confused, suddenly turns, and runs out to tackle the pitcher. The bleachers are in stunned silence. But a father proudly stands up and affirms as he claps, "That's my boy! That's my son! Isn't he some athlete? He can hit! He can tackle!"

Affirmation builds trust. It says, "You are safe with me!"

### Problem Solving

Now Jesus takes the third step in love. He begins to deal with Zacchaeus' problems. And we've all got them. He was short, probably never chosen to be on a playground team as a kid. He'd been hurt. So now he was a tax collector with a big government stick.

365

And he could hit back. Besides that, he was rich. He could prove he was somebody now. But when he went home alone at night, his life was all rather hollow.

Do you remember from your childhood the fairy tale about a wicked witch who turned the handsome young prince into a green, slimy, warty bullfrog sitting on a lily pad? "You'll never be restored until a lovely princess comes along and kisses you on the lips!" she cackled. Well, what chance is there that will happen? Yet one day a beautiful princess comes along the garden path, sees the ugly frog prince, but looks again, this time deeper. She sees beyond all the ugly to the real need, and she kisses him. Slowly all the ugly falls away until the young handsome prince is restored.

That's what Jesus does to us. That's what he did for Zacchaeus. The text doesn't give the details. But, somehow over supper Jesus probed the man's lonely tortured soul. They spoke of greed and revenge, of loneliness, and of love, of real purpose in life, of joy and peace. And somehow Zacchaeus turned from his darkness to the Light. He repented. He trusted. He took the hand Jesus extended to him.

## Goal Setting

Now Jesus takes the final step of love. He's gathered data on the man, affirmed him, and sat at table to deal with the man's problems. Now he will set goals. He told the woman caught in the act of adultery, "Go and sin no more." He told Legion after his exorcism, "Go home to your friends and tell them there how much the Lord has done for you." He told the paralytic, "Sin nor more that nothing worse befall you."

Zacchaeus set his own goal. He stood and proclaimed, "Look, half of my possessions, Lord, will I give to the poor; and if I have defrauded anyone of anything, I will pay it back four times as much."

Goal setting is like a doctor's prescription. It is medicine, charting out a new course with God for improvement, change, growth. A worthy goal can be to get debt-free, to quit drinking, to join a small group Bible study, to memorize scripture related to your personal struggle, or to let go of money you've been hoarding so it can work for Jesus.

366

Jesus had a rich young ruler come running up to him, inquiring, "What must I do to be saved?" And Jesus gathered data on the man — rich, young, ruler. He affirmed him. The Bible says he looked on him and loved him. Then he dealt with the problem — "He trusted in riches." And he set the goal: "Go sell all you have and give it to the poor and come follow me, and you shall have treasure in heaven." But the Bible says the lad's face fell. And he went away sorrowfully, for he did love his money. And Jesus let him walk away. He would not water it down.

So, you see, in loving people, not even Jesus could go every step, all the way, with every person.

## Four Bases

It may help one to understand these four steps in the process of love as the four bases of a baseball game. First base: data gathering. Second base: affirmation. Third base: dealing with problems. And home plate: goal setting.

No one gets a hit and scores by running straight to third base. You'd be out! The bases must be taken in turn. Likewise, in loving people, we mustn't head for third base. "You smoke too much!" "You're fat!" "You talk too much!" We must take time to get to know people. Build trust by affirming them. Only then have we earned our right to be heard, to meddle in their hurts.

## Conclusion

I delight in the *Peanuts* comic strips, especially Lucy who is in love with piano-playing Schroeder. In one strip, Schroeder is playing a concerto while Lucy looks at him doe-eyed, asking, "Do you know what love is?" Schroeder stops the music and says, "Love is a strong bond or attachment toward another, a decision to act in their best interest." Then he resumes his concert. Lucy looks at the audience and laments, "Gee, on paper Schroeder is just great!"

And our challenge in Jesus Christ is to take what Christ has taught on paper and live out these four bases, the process of love, with our spouses, our children, neighbors, nation-states, the boss at work, and the newcomer at church.

We, in Christ, can each be God's love!

# O Perfect Love! (Where Are You?)

The Bible teaches history began in a garden at *a wedding* between Adam and Eve. Jesus launched his public ministry at *a wedding* in Cana where he worked his first miracle turning water into wine. Afterwards, Christ began to call himself the *groom*, and the church his *bride*. And scripture teaches history will end one day, according to Revelation 19, at the *marriage* supper of the Lamb.

So, written large in scripture is the meaning of life. God is our lover who pursues us desiring a covenant relationship akin to *marriage*.

If one takes his date to a fancy French café, what is the little meal before the big meal called? The *hors d'oeuvre*. In an Italian restaurant it is called the *antipasto*. In an American restaurant it is the *appetizer*. Whatever one calls it, its purpose is to whet your appetite for the big meal that follows. And Almighty God has given us the gift of *marriage* as the little relationship that reflects the greater relationship between Christ and his church. *Marriage* is but a foretaste of glory divine!

When the Bible talks about love, it often uses the Greek word *agape*. This love is more than a feeling, more than a friendship. It is a love of the human will. Indeed! It is a choice to act in the other person's best interest.

This sort of love is required in any marriage relationship. Sure, love sometimes feels good. And it can often become a friendship. But over the long haul, marriage requires *agape* love, a choice to act in the other person's best interest.

A symbol of this love is embodied in the wedding reception custom of cutting the wedding cake. The man slices a piece of the cake, bread with icing, basic nurture with sweetness, and he offers it to his wife, who receives it. It is like saying, "I will nurture you and we shall have bread and married love, the sweetness of life." And by taking it, the bride says, "And I will receive it from you."

Then the love is returned. For the wife takes cake and offers it to her husband. "And I will receive from you." So it is that the newly married couple starts married life with a powerful symbol of what it means to love and be loved by God and by one another.

In the text, Jesus reminds us, "Those who belong to this age marry and are given in marriage, but those who are considered worthy of a place in that age and in the resurrection from the dead may neither marry nor are given in marriage." That's because we, in heaven, become the bride of Christ.

Now, be perfectly clear as to what the Bible is saying here. Earthly marriage is but a foretaste. It is a lesser relationship that one day must give way to the greater relationship. It is a trial run that will give way to the real thing, life eternal with Christ our groom, and a love that nurtures us to wholeness.

With this in mind, what Paul wrote in Ephesians 5:25 is very motivating! He urged husbands: "Love your wives as Christ loved the church."

**Communication**

Certainly one way that Christ loved and continues to love the church is by communication. Jesus came in the flesh. He spent time with us. He speaks to us in scripture and listens to us in prayer. O perfect love, where are you? One place is in communication.

A cartoon in a sports magazine showed a picture of a man with his hand on a television knob. He was saying to his wife, "Martha, do you have anything to say before the baseball season starts?" Why is it that married couples stop talking? Sometimes the man works too long and hard. Troubles start in a marriage when a man is so busy earning his salt that he forgets his sugar. Then there is a wife who's never home. She's out shopping, carpooling the kids, or attending some club meeting. And before you know it, each mate has changed. They've gone off in separate directions. Their values have changed. Their goals are different. And they are waking up each morning next to a stranger!

Listen to this: What blood is to the body, communication is to love. Stop talking and love dies. An ice age sets in! You become strangers.

A lady wrote the following letter to her pastor. "Dear pastor, you've heard of the sphinx? Well, I married him. My husband never talks to me. He just comes home, slumps in a chair, doesn't move or make a sound until bedtime, unless he wants his drink refilled or a snack." Is that your marriage? What can you do to get the life-blood flowing again? Take some walks together. Join a couples' club and eat out, go to the movies, and dance. Read some of the same books or take up the same hobby, perhaps something like fishing or bicycling. Put your kids to bed earlier. Get a pair of rocking chairs and sit down beside one another and watch the sun go down. Spend time with your mate like Christ spent time with his church. Communicate!

## Courting

O perfect love, where are you? It's in the way Jesus loved the church. It's in communication. And it is also in courtship. God wrote love letters to the church. They are printed in the Bible. God wooed us with the prophets, with gifts, and he came and knocked on our door and introduced himself personally in Bethlehem so long ago.

Why is it that once we get married we stop courting and romancing? When we were wooing our wives we opened the door for her. That sweet delicate thing didn't have the strength to do that for herself. Then we got married and stopped. It's as if after she wed us she got strength to do a lot of things for herself. And what about you wives and your hair? Do you still fix it up for him special like you used to do for a date? I've been in most of your homes and I've seen the Emily Post book on etiquette on your shelves. If I told you that you didn't have any manners, you'd get mad. Yet one Sunday not too long ago I stood out front of the church and watched you leaving and very few of you fellows escorted your wives to the door. Very few of you women even held hands with your man! O perfect love, where are you? In romancing! And many marriages would be happier if the man tried as hard to keep his wife as he did to win her, and vice versa!

Did you hear about the fellow who was driving home from work listening to the radio preacher suggest that his listeners surprise their mates? "How long has it been since you took your wife a gift? How long has it been since you made her feel special?" he asked. "Tonight when you arrive home, instead of growling, 'When will supper be ready?' why not surprise her with a gift?" The fellow thought to himself that that sounded like a good idea, so he stopped and bought some candy and a bouquet of flowers. He also bought himself a dashing new hat. When he got home, instead of going in the back door, he rang the front doorbell. His wife, in hair curlers, opened the door and saw him standing there wearing a radiant smile and a new hat, with candy in one hand and flowers in the other. She said, "Listen, buster, the baby has colic, the washing machine has broken down, and your son and another boy got into a fight at school and were expelled. And now you make my day by coming home drunk!" It's been a long time, men. It's been so long since we've courted our wives that they've forgotten the meaning of the word.

Why not take one night a week and have a date with your wife? Call her up from the office and ask her out. Hold the door open for her. Make it a habit. And some day for no reason at all, bring her a gift. Say, "Honey, I saw this in the store window and it was lovely. It made me think of you! So I bought it for you!"

### Complimenting

Passing on from communication and courting, let's ask the question again. O perfect love, where are you? In complimenting. Do you see how Jesus affirmed the church? He looked at Peter, a big, burly, swaggering, cursing, impulsive hothead, a man he knew would thrice deny him, and the Lord complimented him. Of all things! Jesus said, "Peter, you are a rock, and I'll build my church on you!"

Men, ladies, how's the complimenting going in your marriage? Are comments like these frequent in your home? "What! Leftovers *again*!" "Don't you ever clean up?" "Nobody can cook like my wife, but they come pretty close in the Army." "Who does your hair? Nobody!" "Why can't you bring home more money?" Listen, all those put-downs will get you nowhere. What you want to do is build up a person's ego, not tear it down. Make a person feel worthy and they will be worthy. Treat your wife like a queen and you'll get to be the king. But if you treat her like a slave, guess who gets to be the other slave?

A father-in-law gave his new son-in-law a gift on his wedding day. He said, "Son, right here is all you'll ever need." The boy opened it and found a watch. Across the crystal were the words, "Have you complimented your wife today?" Have you, men? Have you, ladies? Is affirmation becoming habitual in your relationship?

**Commitment**

O perfect love, where are you? It's in the way Jesus loved his church. It's in communication and courting and complimenting. But according to the Bible, it's also in commitment. Jesus gave it all for his love of the church. He endured criticism, loneliness, blood, sweat, and tears. He didn't even stop short of death. He was totally committed! Your marriage, for it to work and last, must be this way, too. There's no magic in marriage, just hard work and commitment.

A tomcat and a tabby were courting on the back fence when the tomcat leaned over to her and said, "I'd die for you, beautiful thing!" The tabby gazed at him longingly and asked, "How many times?" You might not have nine lives to offer, but you've got one! And that's what it takes for wedlock to work. A young couple came to me not long ago to make arrangements for a wedding. I was delighted that they both asked to read their wedding vows in advance. But after they heard them I was disappointed when they wanted to change them. She wanted to leave out the phrase, "As long as you both shall live," and substitute in its place, "As long as you both shall love." I very firmly declined. I told them that I performed no trial weddings, and that marriage required a lifetime commitment "for better or worse, for richer or poorer, in sickness and in health, until death do us part."

Americans today have lost the meaning of the word commitment. They're little committed to their education, the church, their jobs, the country, even their mate. The only thing a lot of people today are committed to is themselves! We seem to go into everything with a parachute on. "If it doesn't work out, if I don't like it, or if it gets boring or hard, all I have to do is bail out." Listen, Christian marriage is for life! It has no parachute! It's a lifetime commitment! The Bible says, "Therefore a man leaves his mother and father and cleaves unto his wife and the two become one flesh. What God has joined together, let no man put asunder."

## Cancellation

O perfect love, where are you? In communication, courting, complimenting, and commitment. It's in Christ's example of love for the church. Perfect love is also in cancellation. It's in forgiveness. Men rough-handled Christ. They whipped him, denied him, and betrayed him. They crucified him. And Jesus said, "Father, forgive them for they know not what they do."

Marriage requires that kind of canceling forgiveness, too. If love is blind, marriage can be a real eye-opener. Arguments will come. Feelings will be hurt. Rights will be violated. Mistakes will be made. Sins will be committed. Forgiveness is important if marriage is going to work.

Two men were discussing their wives. One said that every time he and his spouse got into an argument, she became historical. "You mean hysterical, don't you?" his friend inquired. "No, historical. She keeps bringing up the past!" Many marital relationships end like that. Each mate keeps score on the other. It's a running battle on who owes whom the most. And finally a breaking point comes. And not only is the marriage broken up, the two people are pretty busted up, too.

Here is where our Christian faith can be helpful. The Lord's Prayer teaches us to pray, "Forgive us our debts as we forgive our debtors." Jesus told us to forgive 70 times 7. There's a couple who make it a practice of letting the other person know when they feel

374

slighted. They talk it out, argue it out, and then the offender asks, "Will you forgive me? I'm sorry." The injured party looks the other in the eye and says, "Yes, I will forgive you." Then they pray the Lord's Prayer together. This kind of routine cancellation keeps the slate clean. It keeps grudges and conflict and turmoil from festering and building up steam to explode like Mount St. Helens. It's like cleaning house twice a week instead of once a year. It makes the job easier and makes the home livable.

How's the cancellation doing in your marriage? Do you forgive freely and regularly? Do you keep things clean between the two of you? One man says, "Yes, but my wife cheated on me. I know it. She committed adultery." Forgive her! And ask God to help you forget it and start over. You can go shopping in the city and forget where you parked your car. You can even forget deep, wounding sins of the past. Get some counseling and find out about the healing of the memories. The Lord has a way of minimizing the emotional impact of painful sins. He has a way of helping you with cancellation.

**Conclusion: The Right Person**

O perfect love, where are you? It's in the way Christ loved the church. That's the way we're supposed to love our mates. That's the way of a man with a maiden.

In an *Andy Capp* cartoon strip, Andy and his wife Flo are arguing. They're getting all worked up when, suddenly, harsh words start flying. They come to blows and fight out into the street. Suddenly Andy stands up, kisses his wife, and says, "I was wrong, Flo. I forgive you." And as they walk off to the soccer match together, Andy says with a wink, "Marriage is not so much finding the right person as it is being the right person." What sort of person are you? Are you the kind of person who will grow to love your mate like Christ loved the church?

**Proper 28**
**Pentecost 26**
**Ordinary Time 33**
**Luke 21:5-19**

# What The Church Should Be
# Doing Until The Second Coming

In folklore and literature there are many famous deadlines. You recall how "Oil Can Harry" grabbed the fair maiden and said, "If you don't give me the deed to your ranch by sundown, I'll tie you on the railroad tracks!" Then there is the Mafia's Godfather contract. "Either your signature or your brains will be on the contract tomorrow." And who could forget lovely Cinderella and her deadline, the stroke of midnight! In our text for today Jesus is talking about another famous deadline, his second coming. And in this rather lengthy text Jesus is talking about what his disciples should be doing until that fateful return.

### Look Up!

First off, Jesus told his disciples to look up! He said, "When these things begin to take place, look up and raise your heads, because your redemption is drawing near" (Luke 21:28 RSV). What were some of "these things" Jesus said were evidence that his coming was soon?

Our Lord predicted earthquakes. In one year China, Russia, Japan, California, Mexico, and Iran, had earthquakes.

Jesus also said there would be famines. Russia's crops have been disappointing in recent years. They are buying wheat from American farmers. Did you know that at least half of the world population is underfed or malnourished? Over 22,000 people starve to death each day.

Christ also mentioned that there would be wars and rumors of war before his return. In the twentieth century there were over 3,000 wars. In fact, more people were killed in war in the twentieth century than in all other centuries combined. And just look at the wars and rumors of war still at hand: the Mideast, South Africa, Iran, Iraq, Ireland, Yugoslavia, Korea, and of course, terrorism.

The Lord also mentioned pestilence. At first thought of pestilence one thinks of locusts and swarms of pesky insects. Actually the Greek word for pestilence means, "Trouble with the soil or little troublesome things in the air." It makes one think of pollution, doesn't it? And we've got plenty of that in the air, in the soil, and in our water.

If you are like most people you have a tendency to say, "Now, now. Don't get all excited! We've always had wars and pollution, quakes and famine." Yes, that is true. But the Bible qualifies how man's problems will come upon him in the end. The word is travail (1 Thessalonians 5:3, Romans 8:18-24, Mark 13:14). The Bible predicts that man's difficulties will come like birth pains, like a woman in travail. The pain comes with greater and greater intensity and the pains come closer and closer together. Isn't this just what we are seeing happen to us with war — closer and closer together, each one intensifying? And isn't the same true of quakes, famines, and pestilence?

Christ also predicted that many would come in his name. "I am he!" they will say (v. 8). Did you know that Korean cult leader Sun Yung Moon claimed to be Christ? Thousands followed him! The radical Muslim group that took over the Grand Mosque in Mecca claimed that their leader was the Messiah also. And again, thousands followed him. The Lord also predicted that before his return there would be terrors and great signs from heaven, persecution, men fainting with fear, the fall of Jerusalem, the dispersion of the Jews, and their eventual return to form a New Israel. Jerusalem fell in A.D. 70. From that time until 1948 the Jews were scattered. Now they have their own nation again. Prophecy, history written before it happens, is being fulfilled right before our very eyes!

"When these things begin to take place," Jesus said, "Look up and raise your heads, because your redemption is drawing near." Isn't this just the word so many need to hear today? Many Christians are walking around with their chins on their chests. "The world's going to the dogs!" "I quit! The liberals have got it all!" Cynical, bitter, defeated, critical — many Christians look at the world and look down. But Jesus said, "Look up!" Remember Peter walking on the water with Jesus? As long as Peter looked up and at Christ, he was sustained. But when he took his eyes off Jesus and focused on the sea and its waves, he began to sink. That's just the point Christ is making here in the text. When quakes, war, fear, famine, and pollution are all around you, don't look at all these evils and sink into despair. Look up! Look at Jesus and be sustained. Your redemption draws near! Jesus is coming! Have hope!

### Speak Up!

What should the church be doing until the second coming? Look up! And Christ says we should speak up! The Lord predicted, "You will be brought before kings and governors for my name's sake. This will be a time for you to bear testimony" (vv. 12-13). In other words, the church until the second coming should always be expectantly, optimistically looking for Christ's return. And we can speak up telling the gospel to the world. Recently a pneumonia vaccine was developed that can prevent an infection that kills thousands of people each year. The news has been filled with happy reports of this saving drug. It's good news and people are telling it everywhere! The gospel should get us even more excited! Christ can cure more than pneumonia. He can forgive sin, overcome death, build character, establish justice, and instill love. Isn't that exciting? Why be ashamed to talk about him? As Christians we can tell the world that man is fallen and sinfully broken like "Humpty Dumpty." We're broken in our relationship with God, neighbor, self, and creation. Education can't save us. Neither can politics, welfare, medicine, or science. But what all the kings' horses and men could never do for Humpty, God can and is doing for people in Christ! He is right now restoring us to right relationships with God, man, self, and creation. He can make us whole again!

I preach about 200 times a year, and quite often people ask me what I preach about. Well, actually, when I stand before a crowd I know that there are two basic kinds of people out there. There are those not in Christ and there are those in Christ. To those not in

Christ I say, "Get in quick!" I tell them about the cross, repentance, and faith. The message to those in Christ is this: "Enjoy all that it means to be in Christ!" It's simple, isn't it? And don't you think you can share that with your friends and loved ones? "Speak up!" That's God's Word to you at this time! Tell the world that there is a God. Tell them that he loves justice, mercy, compassion, righteousness, and faith. Tell them that he died on a cross to forgive their sins. Tell them he knows all about them and he still loves them. Tell them he wants to adopt them as his child, to bring them into his family, the church, where they can be fed and cared for. Tell them they can work with God to make the world some better. Tell them Christ is going to return again to judge the world and restore it. Yes, tell them! But tell them it all begins for them with repentance and faith.

If there is someone here today who does not know Christ as his Savior, I'd like to take this chance to say, "God loves you! He wants to adopt you as his child. Why not turn to him by faith in Jesus and allow the Lord to put you in shape to love God, men, yourself, and creation? God is so good! And God wants to be good to you!"

### Conclusion: I Shall Return!

During World War II General Douglas MacArthur left the Philippine Islands. The Japanese were approaching in overwhelming numbers and MacArthur left to muster his forces. Leaving a small and outnumbered army behind, MacArthur promised, "I shall return!" That word was to give hope to those who remained behind in the difficult years of enemy occupation. Christ has given that same promise to his church. In Acts 1 Jesus is asked when he will return to establish his authority. He tells them, "It is not for you to know ... But you shall receive power when the Holy Spirit has come upon you and you shall be my witness." After saying this, Christ ascended. The disciples sat there dumbfounded and gazing into heaven. To shake them from their stupor two angels came and said, "Why do you stand there looking into heaven? This Jesus, who was taken up from you into heaven, will come in the same way you saw him go into heaven."

This is to say that we shouldn't sit around gazing into heaven, occupying a lot of time trying to blueprint the future. The second coming is not an excuse to flee the world. It's an incentive to stay and heal it, to make the world better until Christ returns to make it the best! And that's what the church should be doing until the second coming! Look up! Don't be afraid! Be faithful! And speak up! The Lord is coming!

# How To Break A
# Bad Habit For Good!

After helping his child with homework, a man said to his wife, "I wish we still had those kinds of problems — the sort where you can find the answers in the back of the book."

Where *do* we go to look up the answers to our problems? Lust? Profanity? Temper? Poor eating habits? Talking too much? Where is the book with the answers in the back?

Frankly, I've always been suspicious of those self-help books with flashy titles like "Ten Steps to Successful Child Rearing" or "Five Months to a New You" or "How to Succeed in Business Without Really Trying." I've tried such steps and *still* failed!

So, when it comes to how to break a bad habit, I want to be very careful not to promise too much, not to make you think there is a quick fix for all your problems.

Jesus promises Christians, "I will not leave you desolate; I will come to you" (John 14:18 RSV). And the way he comes to us is by the indwelling presence of the Holy Spirit whom we receive by faith. Christ called the Holy Spirit "the Helper." In the Greek the word is *parakletos* meaning reinforcer, one called alongside to help. And at least one of the ways he helps is by ridding our lives of sin. The actual process is called "sanctification," a kind of divine inner-maid service that moves in to help us clean up our inner life.

I wish I could tell you sanctification of every sin is as easy as squirting a muddy car with a high pressure water hose. The dirt just dissolves and quickly falls away! And, indeed, I've known times when deliverance from some besetting sins was effortless,

383

instantaneous, and permanent! Heroin addicts immediately cleansed and such.

But it's just not so in every case. Sanctification is more often than not a process. It's three steps forward and two steps backwards. It is a lifelong pilgrimage beset with tears, frustrations, hard work, faith, and ultimate joy. As Paul put it, "We ... are being changed from one degree of glory to another; for this comes from the Lord who is the Spirit" (2 Corinthians 3:18 RSV). Note Paul's phrase — "changed ... from one degree ... to another." That's what we may expect. A process. By degrees.

Though salvation is an event, sanctification is a process. And the Holy Spirit is here to help us with that process.

In the text we're reminded of God's faithfulness to his own. "Then Jesus said, 'If you continue in my word, you are truly my disciples; and you will know the truth, and the truth will make you free.' They answered him, 'We are descendants of Abraham and have never been slaves to anyone. What do you mean by saying, "You will be made free"?' Jesus answered them, 'Very truly, I tell you, everyone who commits sin is a slave to sin. The slave does not have a permanent place in the household; the son has a place there forever. So if the Son makes you free, you will be free indeed' " (vv. 31-36). Let's turn now to scripture and see how his words happen in our lives.

### Worship About It

First, take your habit to the Lord in worship. Thank God for the situation you find yourself in. Thank God for the chance to see his power at work in your life. Then claim your victory ahead of time by faith. Hebrews 11:13 talks of God's people who saw salvation from afar and believed in it by faith. Affirm God's deliverance in your life even if it is afar off!

### Accept The Responsibility

Next, accept the responsibility for your behavior. None of this blaming your parents for rearing you so strictly or society for making you grow up on the wrong side of the tracks or even fate for your birth, saying, "That's just the way I am."

A well-known college president recently said that a B.A. degree should be reinterpreted as a Bachelor of Alibis degree because students today are so adept at making excuses for their poor study habits and subsequent mediocrity. Don't you be one of them!

Remember Adam and Eve in the Garden? They sinned and God came calling them to accountability. But both the man and the woman tried to push their problems off on someone else. They passed the buck. They rationalized. Never did they accept responsibility for their behavior. And this is our problem in beginning to deal forcefully with the sinful habits in our lives. We don't want to own up to it. We refuse to say, "I'm doing this. It is wrong! And I am responsible."

**Confess It**

Third, attack your habit by confessing it to God in prayer.

And here is where we must be totally honest. Often we pray, "Oh, God! I did it again. Please forgive me! Help me to stop!" But what we should really be praying is this: "Dear God, my mind is full of lust. I realize you do not like this. But I do! I'm in bondage to it. I know I should stop. But deep down I don't want to yet. I like it. Father God, somehow you're going to have to do surgery on my wants and cut this craving out of me!"

During World War I, ace fighter pilots flew in aircraft made of wood frames held together with wire and canvas. And often a pilot flying patrol duty would hear a gnawing sound from the back of his plane. A rat had gotten aboard his airplane while it was on the ground, and it was now gnawing on the wood! And if it chewed through a control cable, the pilot would lose control and crash. So, quickly the pilot would execute a procedure known as "taking the rat up." That meant the pilot flew just as high as his plane would go, and there in the thin atmosphere the rat would perish, thus saving the aircraft and pilot. Confessional prayer works something like that. When we take our sins up into God's presence and blush over them before him, they somehow cannot exist in his holiness.

Go ahead and try it! Take your sin to God's throne. Hold it in complete honesty before God's face. And I tell you, if you pray like that often enough, you'll either quit the sin or you'll quit the prayer!

## Visualize The Consequences

A fourth principle in dealing with the force of sinful habits is to visualize the consequences of continuing the sin. What happens to people who do not gain control of their tongues? Do gossips please God? Does making negativistic comments all the time make friends? Does becoming a neurotic talker appeal to you? Think of the embarrassment, the evil, the hurt, the friendlessness, the waste, the robbery of God's glory!

Yes, visualize the consequences. Know what you're running from!

I know of a Boy Scout who went camping with his troop in the Great Smokey Mountains. During the night one of the older boys yelled, "There's a bear in the camp! Run for it!" Everybody scrambled for safety, except my young friend. He got up slowly and began to walk toward the truck, thinking it was all a hoax the explorers were pulling. But when he turned to look in the direction of the campfire and saw a real brown bear standing on his hind legs crushing a food cooler between his paws, he found the incentive to run faster!

Yes, know what you're running from! There's incentive in it! Visualize the awful consequences of sin — the separation from God, from people, from self. Learn to fear it, to hate it as God does, and to flee it just as speedily as Joseph fled Potiphar's seductive wife in Egypt.

## God's Timing

Fifth, ask God to give you a sense of his timing.

Quite often we push our unimportant sins to the forefront while holding our really favorite sins in the background. We confess like one of my sons who met me at the door saying, "Dad, I spilled glue on the porch today." Later I found out he also got into some paint and smeared it on the side of the car. Our confessions to God are often a smokescreen, a diversionary tactic designed to keep God busy with minor habits of ours so he won't have to go meddling in the real favorites of ours!

But look at it this way. God, who loves us, has a timetable for our maturity. And God does not go after all our sins at once. That would utterly overwhelm us! Rather, one sin at a time, little by little, he sanctifies us. First to go was Apostle Peter's self-assurance. It was replaced with faith. Next went his swaggering profanity. Next went his cowardice. Then went his racial prejudice. And it's that way with us. Don't give your timetable to God! Accept his. Pray, "Okay, God! What's first? Do you want to do this all at once or over a period of time? You're the doctor!"

A man who tried to quit smoking on his own strength and timetable failed and failed again for over seven years. But when he got the flu last year, he lost all taste for cigarettes. And after his recovery he never went back. That's how God can work in his own time and way!

### Meditation

A sixth principle for the great riddance of evil habits is Christian meditation. In Psalm 119:11 the psalmist admits he lays up God's Word in his heart so that he won't sin against God! Aye! Here's a real key!

Most of us try to break a habit by focusing on the habit. For instance, we have poor eating habits and are consequentially 35 pounds overweight. So we go on a diet. "I will not eat. No chocolate pie. No strawberry jam. No fried chicken or Pepsi or sweet rolls or yum! No homemade peach ice cream!" And the trouble with this plan of attack is that we humans tend to do what we think about! So, when we diet by focusing on what foods we won't eat, we break down and eat those very foods!

Look at it this way. Think of the number 8. Now, don't think of eight. Don't let it into your mind. Crowd it out! Stop it! Stop it! Stop it! You can't, can you? But now divide 100 by five and subtract two and multiply the answer by 3.6. And do you see how you forget number 8 in the process? That's how Christian meditation works.

Another illustration! How do we get the air out of a jar? We could create an elaborate vacuum system and suck it out.

Or we could simply displace the air by filling the jar with water. Meditation works like that, too. We displace our cravings for food, our focus on sweets, and our insatiable desire for drink, with

God's thoughts about our body being God's temple, our god not being the belly, and the fruit of the Spirit being self-control. And in time we become like our thinking. Sinful habits are simply displaced, crowded out of our lives as godly thoughts come in.

### Prayer And Fellowship

Just after the earthly ministry of Jesus Christ, the Roman philosopher Seneca said, "O that a hand would come down from heaven and deliver me from my besetting sin." And that's just what we have in Christ, our Lord. The hand of flesh, of self-reliance, of human resolve is weak. But the arm of God is stronger than any of our habits. God is able and ready and willing when we are! And God can tear down strongholds in our lives (2 Corinthians 10:4).

Now, to pass on! A seventh principle in habit-breaking is fellowship and prayer. In Luke 22:31 (RSV), Jesus told Peter, "Simon, Simon, behold, Satan demanded to have you, that he might sift you like wheat, but I have prayed for you that your faith may not fail." And in the company of Christ's spirit and God's people, Peter did not fail!

Now, Satan would like to sift you and me, too. He'd like to sift out our faith, our habits of worship and love and patience and such, and leave only our bad habits. But what saved Peter from that will save us, too! Christ-faith, fellowship, and prayer!

Indeed, nothing of Satan can sift a man like alcohol. It can sift his job, his family, his character, and his usefulness right out and leave only a groveling, spineless inebriate. But Alcoholics Anonymous knows what fellowship, prayer, and faith in Jesus can do! And they have the best cure record of any detoxification work in the world.

Whatever your habit, enlist the help of friends. Ask for their prayer support. Spend time with them. Pray with them. The burdens we share are divided. Yet the joys of victory we share are multiplied!

### Act By Act Courage

Habits are formed act by act. You've seen that delightful children's sermon where a piece of thread is wrapped around a child's hands. It can easily be broken. But after the thread has been wrapped around a dozen times or more, it cannot be broken. One is bound! Our habits are like that. The same sinful act done over and over again binds us fast! But just as a habit is formed act by act, so it can be undone act by act by act. Most habits cannot be thrown out the upstairs window. They must be coaxed down the stairs and out the door one step at a time.

So, begin to undo your habit one act of resistance at a time.

Take joy in every act of resistance.

When you give in, don't quit! You can lose quite a few battles and still win the war.

And remember, saying, "Yes," to God is just as habit forming as saying, "Yes," to Satan. Say, "Yes," to Jesus often enough and the momentum of good habits will be just as strong in your life as the force of evil habit once was.

### Read And Study

Another principle is to read and study. Take careful notice of the fact that the Bible and history are full of people who in God's grace broke all sorts of habits. The book of Acts tells of Paul's habit of legalism and how he broke it. Peter rid himself in Christ of both profanity and bigotry. James and John conquered the habit of temper. And there are further testimonies of history that witness to broken habits of alcoholism, homosexuality, lust, lying, materialism, over-eating, and the like.

Read! Study! See how others did it in Christ! And profit!

### Commitment Reminders

Remember the nursery rhyme, "Pussycat, pussycat, where have you been?" "I've been to London to visit the queen!" "Pussycat, pussycat, what did you there?" "I frightened a little mouse under her chair!"

Often we set out to achieve some worthy goal but find ourselves distracted along the way. So, we forget our aim and succumb to our habit again. God realizes our short attention span and has given us guidance on how to sustain our mental and spiritual focus for prolonged periods of time. Proverbs 6:20 and following tell us to "tie it around our neck" so we won't forget. Commitment reminders — that's what we're talking about here! If you overeat, needlepoint it and hang it on your dining room wall, "Lord, what do you want me to eat?" If you talk too much, put a note on your car dashboard, "Shut Mouth!"

But perhaps the best commitment reminder is the Lord's Supper. There Jesus says to his disciples, all of us so prone to forget what we're up to, "Do this in remembrance of me." And the amazing thing about the Lord's Supper throughout scripture and history is that God has encouraged and refreshed and strengthened his people there. So come often and eat, drink, and remember!

### Conclusion: Not "Try" But "Trust"

Really now, it is so easy to break some things, isn't it? Your watch, your arm, a favorite glass flower vase — why they have all broken for us with ease of careless trifle!

But habits are just not so broken! They are like rubber balls. The harder we throw them down, the higher they bounce!

Example: New Year's resolution number one: "I will stop smoking a pack of cigarettes a day." Result: Now we smoke two packs.

Example number two: January 1: "I will lose 30 pounds." Result? June 6: "I gained sixteen pounds."

Ah, but listen, dear one! "God is faithful and he will not allow you to be tempted above that which you are able. He will with the temptation offer a way of escape."

In Canada, alongside the St. John's River, lumberjacks fell huge trees, roll them into the water, and float them downstream to a sawmill. Sometimes the logs tangle together and wedge against both banks, forming a logjam. The timber men go onto the jamb with saws and try to cut it apart. Failing, they often resort to dynamite. If that doesn't work, they simply wait for rain and the rise of the water level which sweeps the river clean.

I can relate to Isaiah 64:5 (RSV), "In our sins we have been a long time, and shall we be saved?" Oh, the habits I've tried to saw out of my life! My God, not even my best personal dynamite works! And sometimes I want to give up! It's just too hard! Can't you relate?

And then the Holy Spirit comes and reminds me, "Yes, there's great pain in changing. But it's nothing compared to the pain of staying the way you are. I'm here to help. Put your hand in mine. I'll sweep all this logjam away! Trust me. Act with me. One log at a time...."

# Final Touch!

When Sean O'Malley died in Ireland and was dutifully laid out in his casket for viewing at his wake, Elizabeth Winfield came by to pay her respects. She said to Fiona, Sean's widow, "He looks good. And I detect a slight smile on his face, don't I?"

"Yes, well, you know Sean was always a bit daft. I suspect he is just slow to realize what's happened to him."

Ah, yes! Death ... as poet A. E. Houseman put it, "The road all runners come." And before death happens to you and you and you ... and me, let's see if we cannot be quick to figure out from scripture what is going to happen to us.

Malachi 3:17b indicates those who have life with God are God's "special possession"; whereas Jesus says our Christian pilgrimage begins with poverty and ends in the kingdom of heaven (Luke 6:20). Entwined, these two truths of God share quite a comfort.

### Found

First consider how a jewel became a jewel. There was a time when it was nothing more than an ugly rock buried in some hill. There it was discovered, value was seen in it, so it was taken to the workshop.

Years ago two South African boys were playing soccer with a fist-sized stone. A geologist watched their play, and eventually asked to see their stone ball. He offered them money to purchase a real soccer ball in exchange for their rock. They readily accepted. And he took the stone to his workshop. There he washed it, cut and polished it, and today it is the third largest diamond in the world.

We, too, were once diamonds in the rough — sinners, lost, encrusted with wrong, ugly to God and others, kicked about by the devil himself. Aye, this is where we all began.

When Jesus said, "Blessed are you who are poor," he was saying, "Blessed are those who realize their total spiritual poverty before the Lord." Indeed, we were helpless as a rock. Ah! But Jesus cast his loving eye upon us. And in his trained look of grace, he saw value in us. He saw through the dirt of sin, the rough edges of evil habits, to the uncultivated beauty deep down within. And he bought us. Paul wrote in Romans 5:8 (RSV), "But God shows his love for us in that while we were yet sinners Christ died for us." The good Lord didn't wait for us to be perfect. He did not demand we fix ourselves. He took a chance on us. He bought us "poor," like a stonecutter buys a jewel in the rough.

### Cut And Polished

Ah, but now the rough stone is in the master's workshop. There crude rocks are washed and the process of cutting and polishing is begun. Slowly the ugly falls away and the real beauty of the gemstone emerges.

In Christ we, too, go through a process of cutting and polishing. For after Christ purchases us, he takes us to his workshop and begins to shape us. He accepts us poor, but makes us rich. He claims us as we are, but his great love will not leave us as we are. Right now each of us is being handcrafted into a precision-cut jewel.

If our purchase price is the cross, called justification, then the cleaning and shaping of our lives are a process called sanctification. And it is carried out in the church where we are shaped by the teaching of scripture, by caring friends, and by suffering.

Indeed, pain is a gift that nobody wants. Yet it is a valid portion of life in a fallen world. Acts 14:22 warns, "Through many tribulations we must enter the kingdom of God." Just as no diamond in the rough is spared the process of cutting and polishing, so no Christian is spared sanctification and the accompanying pain.

What separates us from non-Christians is not that we suffer but how we suffer. Non-Christians suffer without hope. They are often driven to despair and alcohol. But in Jesus, we have hope. We know God can bring the beauty out of our hurts. The Apostle Paul, himself a man familiar with hurts, wrote in Romans 5:3-4 (RSV), "More than that, we rejoice in our sufferings, knowing that suffering produces endurance, and endurance produces character, and character produces hope." Job, in the crucible of his own agonies, confirmed the same thing. He wrote, "When he has tried me, I shall come forth as gold" (Job 23:10 RSV).

I suppose that every burden of suffering appears to us as an oppressing and overwhelming weight. But do not forget that these weights are only stones, such as are attached to deep-sea divers, that they might descend to the sea floor and fish up pearls. And when they have gathered great riches, the stones are released, and the divers are drawn up with their riches.

C. H. Spurgeon once said, "Many men owe the grandeur of their lives to their tremendous difficulties." Sir Walter Scott learned from lameness. George Washington, the patient statesman, learned from the snows of Valley Forge. Lincoln, the liberator, learned from his early poverty. Disraeli, the crusader for fair play, learned from the prejudices against him. Theodore Roosevelt, the disciplinarian, learned from his asthma; Edison, the inventor, from his deafness; Chrysler, the creative genius, from the hot grease pit of a locomotive roundhouse. Robert Louis Stevenson, the poet, learned from tuberculosis; Helen Keller, the inspiring example, from her blindness; and Jane Needham, the author of *Looking Up*, learned from her iron lung. Pain doesn't have to tear us down. It can build us up. It is the process whereby God cuts and shapes us into jewel-like brilliance. Peter put it so well in 1 Peter 1:6-7 (RSV): "In this you rejoice, though now for a little while you may have to suffer various trials, so that the genuineness of your faith, more precious than gold ... is tested by fire, may redound to praise."

### Mounted

Now comes the good part! Jesus said the poor will one day know "the kingdom of heaven." And Malachi says God will one day look at us and shout, "Mine! Those who revere the Lord shall be ... my special possession on the day when I act...."

Comfort yourselves with this, O beloved of God! When an artist finishes a masterpiece, he frames it. When a sculptor completes a carving, he places it on a pedestal. And when a jeweler finishes a stone, he mounts it. This is our hope in Jesus Christ! When God finishes with us down here, he takes us up there. As Isaiah 62:3 confirms, "You shall be a crown of beauty in the hand of the Lord, and a royal diadem in the hand of your God." Listen again to God's own promise from Revelation 21:3-4 (RSV). "Behold, the dwelling place of God is with men. He will dwell with them, and they shall be his people, and God himself will be with them; he will wipe away every tear from their eyes, and death shall be no more, neither shall there be mourning nor crying nor pain any more, for the former things have passed away."

Did you ever wonder why Jesus said from the cross, "It is finished!"? The purchase price for you and for me was paid in full. His own sufferings were over. His life work was complete before God. And his soul, a precious gemstone, was going home, a prize to God. And that day will come for each of us as well. God will shout, "Mine!" And He will take us to himself in paradise. We shall be as cut rubies, sapphires, emeralds, and topaz. Works of the highest art. Prized by God! And we shall be satisfied!

**Conclusion**

In Eric Marshall's book, *Children's Letters to God*, a child writes, "Dear God, what is it like to die? Nobody will tell me. I just want to know. I don't want to do it. Your friend, Mike."

Yes, like Sean O'Malley, all laid out in his casket smiling, we, too, can be a little slow to realize what's happening to us! But no more! Justified, sanctified, and one day glorified — that's the way of life in Christ. But it all starts when we kneel in poverty at the foot of the cross. Will you join me there now?

**Christ The King**
**Luke 23:33-43**

# The Crowd That Watched God Die

Have you ever noticed how people are attracted to the scene of tragedy? There was a time in our country, when there was going to be a hanging, that people gathered with picnic baskets and children to watch a criminal die. Once a tornado cut a path of destruction through a town in North Georgia. When Sunday afternoon came, there was a huge traffic jam of curious tourists. And even here we are not so different. When there is a traffic accident we slow down to look, and we even return later to examine the wrecked vehicle. The people of Jesus' day were no different. In today's text we are told that they had all gathered atop Golgotha to witness Rome's grizzliest handiwork. The attraction that had drawn them from their jobs, their homes, was a crucifixion. Three men criminally convicted and condemned were tied and nailed to rough wooden crosses. The blood spurted and oozed, the groans of the dying permeated the air, and all the while, the text says, "The people stood by, watching." They had been drawn to the execution as if it held some magnetic power. Jesus. Jesus of Nazareth was dying. He was the man in the middle. He was the preacher, the miracle worker, the prophet. He was the Son of God, the Savior. And he was dying before the eyes of the crowd.

### The Indifferent

There were many characters watching atop the mount that day. There were many attitudes there just as there are many attitudes here this morning. First of all, there were the indifferent. They were soldiers mostly. Caesar's orders had made them come, otherwise they'd have been sleeping in the barracks or gaming in the taverns. They resented being told what to do. Especially did they dislike crucifixion duty. It wasn't a pleasant sight to watch nails driven into human flesh. Even the most battle-hardened soldier was horrified by it. And it took so long for a man to die. The hours crept by like an arthritic turtle. So the men, indifferent to the death of Jesus, began to gamble for the few belongings of the convicts. It was their way of passing the awful time away.

The soldiers are also here with us today. The church has in its membership indifferent souls. They come to church out of duty and are thoroughly bored. They would rather sleep late or be off playing at some game. And quite often the indifferent ones are the youth of the community. They wouldn't set foot inside a church but their parents make them come. Like the soldiers they are under orders of Caesar. And they gamble their time away at the foot of the cross.

Stop and think about this for a moment. Calvary! The Son of God dying! The horrible power of sin broken! How could anyone turn his back and gamble at a time like this? How could anyone be indifferent?

Perhaps it was ignorance. Perhaps it was blindness. The Son of God was dying for their sins and they were indifferent. They simply gambled. And Jesus said, "Father, forgive them for they know not what they do." On the East Coast, there is an old drawbridge. Over it pass cars and trains and under it pass great ships. Years ago an old man and his son operated the bridge. The boy used to play along the spans of the bridge while his father stood dutifully at his post. One day while the bridge was open to let a ship pass, the father got a signal that a train was fast approaching. Quickly he began to lower the bridge into place. But suddenly he noticed that his son had slipped and fallen into the joint of the bridge. The man had to make a quick decision. To allow the bridge to fall into place would crush his only son to death. To stop the bridge and rescue his son would mean a train wreck and the loss of many lives. The father, his heart aching, sacrificed the one for the many. His son died as the bridge connected and the train sped by. Imagine the grief of the father as he watched the faces of the people in the coaches as the train passed. Some were eating and joking, smoking cigars in the dining cars. Others were reading magazines. They were indifferent! His son had died for them! And they could not care less. How like that crowd on the train were the soldiers. How like their indifference is our indifference today. We come to church yawning and indifferent. The Son of God died for us and we don't take it seriously. We are blind and ignorant.

### The Hateful

Yes, the crowd stood by watching. God was dying on the cross for the sins of the world. And some were indifferent. But they were not the only ones there that day. There were others. There were the self-righteous. They were the Pharisees. And they didn't need Jesus. They had their own religion. And full of jealous hate, they had gathered atop Golgotha to watch him die. The self-righteous were all there that day. Dressed in their long robes, with their arms folded, they smiled approvingly. Some of them had received gifts from his hands, food and wine. Some had received healing from his touch, leprosy gone, sight restored. Christ had been good to them, but now they cursed him; they taunted him; they hurled his sayings back at him. *Mr. Carpenter, you have nails in your hands ... You cannot build the temple up there! ... He saved others; let him save himself!* The Pharisees, the self-righteous, the pious — they were all there that day. And they didn't need Jesus. They believed they were good enough without him.

Yet Christ called them *whitewashed tombs*. He said that for all outward appearances they were like the clean, polished marble of a tomb. Yet on the inside they were rotten and full of dead men's bones. It is true of us today, is it not? Outwardly we can appear moral and upright. When we pass, people say, "Ah, look at him. He's the backbone of the town, a righteous man indeed!" Yet inside we are full of lust and deceit. We are rotten with prejudice and malice. The Bible says, "Let any one who thinks he stands take heed lest he fall" (1 Corinthians 10:12 RSV). This is not bad advice today. Let us examine ourselves to see if we are sinners. Let us not parade around in arrogant self-righteousness. Let us not pretend to be more moral than we are. Rather, let us examine ourselves before God. It may be that, like the Pharisees, we need Jesus more than we think. Have you seen the television commercial where the store clerk says confidently, "Impossible! I couldn't have perspiration problems." Then he takes off his jacket, sniffs, and admits, "My coat told me I need a new deodorant." Perhaps you are like a Pharisee. Take off your self-righteous mantle and look inside. Do you judge others for the same things from which you excuse yourself? Are you a critical person? Are you insecure in how good you are in comparison to others? Do you feel like you don't need Jesus very badly? If so, look inside. The thoughts and attitudes you find there may tell you something. You may find yourself saying, "Whew! My sins told me I'm not as good as I thought. I need Jesus Christ now more than ever!"

**The Sorrowful**

Yes, there was a crowd watching God die that day. And in that crowd was almost every attitude. There were the indifferent and there were the self-righteous. And there were also the sorrowing, those who could not understand. John the Beloved was there. So were Salome and Mary, the mother of Jesus. They were there watching, the faithful, those who could not understand. They heard the heavy hammer blows as the nails were driven into place. They saw the cross as it was lifted into position and fell with a thud into its hole. And they turned their heads away and sobbed uncontrollably. God, why! Why? What had Jesus ever done? He taught the blind to see and the lame to walk. He fed the hungry and made the grieving to sing. God, why?

Have you ever walked in on the middle of a movie? You did not see the beginning. And the ending is still a mystery to you. All that you know is what you see going on directly before you. And the cast is a jumble of unknown characters. The plot is confusing. The same is true of our human predicament. We have walked in on the middle of a grand drama of sin and salvation, death and deliverance, pain and progress. But we only see what is before us. We missed the beginning of the drama. The ending is still a mystery to us. Like Mary the mother of Jesus, we stand at the foot of the cross and witness the awful carnage of innocent suffering. The question that keeps choking in our throats is: "God, why?" Why does my loved one suffer so? Why is my career ended when my dreams are for bigger and better things? God, why? Why the pollution, the earthquake, the famine? Why cancer and car wrecks? *God, why?*

Like the faithful disciples who stood by watching and grieving, we need to get the whole picture. We need to see the beginning of the drama, a world created by God and called good. We need to see man's rebellion and disobedience after the example of Satan. And we need to see man so broken that God had to come himself to heal us. We need to stand at the foot of the cross and look up to Jesus and remember at what a high price our salvation is bought. But we must not stop here. We must see Good Friday, but we must also see Easter. We must view the cross, but also see the crown! The tomb goes with the resurrection. As the rainbow follows the storm, so the ascension follows the crucifixion. Get the big picture! Listen to the whole story! There's a new world coming! Man will not only look into the open, freshly-dug grave. He will look out from the empty open tomb at Paradise!

Yes, on Calvary, as they watched the Son of God die, there were those who did not understand. The Bible predicted the crucifixion. Jesus told them plainly time and time again that he must go to Jerusalem, suffer, and die. They should have expected it. God had previewed the coming events for them. Yet when it all happened, they were just as surprised as if he'd never told them. And now their grief was excessive. They could not comprehend it all. *God, why?*

### The Faithful

The indifferent, the self-righteous, those who could not understand; they were all there that day. They watched as the Son of God died. But there was at least one other person watching atop Golgotha that day. He was a common thief. He was dying on a cross just like Christ, except that he deserved to die. He was a sinner. But unlike the rest of the onlookers, this thief was the one who understood what God was doing at Calvary.

"Jesus," he called painfully, "remember me when you come into your kingdom." And Jesus, with great effort, lifted himself and turned to look upon the face of the thief. His words formed slowly, yet firmly, "Truly, I tell you, today you will be with me in Paradise."

The thief recognized what God was saying from Calvary. The cross was not an X-mark placed across life, a divine judgment on a human error. The cross was a divine plus-mark for all men. God was saying, "I count you worthy of this!" You will recall the old song, "Tie A Yellow Ribbon 'Round the Old Oak Tree." It is a ballad about a prisoner who had been released from jail. Not sure that his wife still loved him and wanted him home, he wrote to her and said, "Tie a yellow ribbon around the old oak tree and I'll know I'm welcome home when I see it. If it is not there, I'll keep going." Well, you recall what happened. The ex-convict was on a bus when he passed the house. And what did he see but a hundred yellow ribbons tied around the tree. The thief recognized something of the same in the cross. God had tied a scarlet ribbon around an old cross tree. And he was saying to the world, "You can come home now!"

This is what the thief saw that the others missed. The cross was an open door home. God was loving the world so much that he was sacrificing his only begotten Son so that whoever believed in him might have everlasting life.

## Conclusion

Yes, the crowd stood by watching. Some were indifferent. Some were self-righteous. And some did not understand. But there was at least one who saw what was going on and he believed. And did you know that every attitude expressed atop Mount Calvary is still expressed in our world today? You and I are represented by at least one of those characters from Golgotha's crowd. Are you indifferent? Are you self-righteous? Do you feel like you don't need Jesus? Do you not understand the world in which we live? Is *God, why?* your constant thought? Or are you like the thief? Have you lived a life of sin and hurt? Broken every law? But do you now see the error of your ways? Will you pray, "Jesus, Lord, remember me when you come into your kingdom"?

Surely we were all there atop Calvary. Surely we can find ourselves in the crowd. The soldiers, Mary, the Pharisees, the dying thief — if we are honest we will see something of ourselves in each of the characters at the cross. The truth of the matter is that we are the crowd atop Golgotha. I am sometimes indifferent like the soldiers. I have been self-righteous as any Pharisee. I have again and again cried out, "God, why?" But like the thief I have also been penitent. "Jesus, Lord, remember me...." Yes, I was there at Calvary. Were you?

God saw man at his worst on Calvary. But there we see God at his best, a most divine and loving Savior. The cross is the key that unlocks an imprisoned world. It was the best sermon God ever preached to man and all it said was: "You can come home now. The door to Paradise is wide open. The cross was for you and you and you. So why don't you come on home?"

# Let's Talk Turkey

Let's talk turkey! And since that old bird isn't saying much these days, let's allow the Bible to speak to Thanksgiving.

In our text a group of people hustle around the Sea of Galilee to see Jesus. They are curious, wanting to learn more. In short, they're trying to figure out where Jesus belongs in their lives. Is he just another rabbi? Or is he God? What do his miracles mean? Is he a means to get more of the material things of life? Who is this man?

Since it is Thanksgiving Sunday, let's consider: If you go down to the hardware store, you will find that stepladders come in several sizes — short, medium, tall, and tallest. Thanksgiving celebrations come in a number of sizes as well.

## Self-satisfied Thanks

Much of our thanksgiving is a self-satisfied kind of thanksgiving. We think of the Pharisee who went into the temple to pray. "God," he said, "I thank you that I am not like other people." This is the lowest form of thanksgiving. It represents a kind of selfish and conceited form of gratitude. This form of gratitude never reaches God. He wasn't talking to God. He was praying with himself.

Certainly this form of thanksgiving will be widespread this year. People will sit at their tables and say, "I'm glad I'm not poor, ignorant, and jobless. I'm thankful I'm not sick, hungry, and a sinner. I thank God I'm not forced to live under some oppressive dictatorial government. Yes, I'm glad I'm a fine, rich citizen of the

405

most powerful United States." People might not say it so clearly, but that's what they'll mean.

Archie Bunker of television's *All In The Family* was celebrating Thanksgiving once. His daughter Gloria was going to have a baby, and as you know, Michael, her husband, was Polish. Archie was elated until Michael pointed out that Archie's grandson was going to be half Polish. "No more dumb Polock jokes, hey, Archie?" Michael ribbed. Archie was crestfallen. Immediately he and Michael got into an argument over race. Archie was saying how superior he was to Spics, Whops, Chicanos, and Blacks. "I'm grateful to be Angel-Saxon," he said. Michael retorted, "Sure, Arch, you really had a lot to do with where and what you were born, didn't you?" "Sure, I did," Archie said seriously. "You don't think God would want to waste me on no off-breed, do you? I'm thankful, Meathead! Thankful!" This is the kind of conceited, self-satisfied thanksgiving that we're talking about. It's like the nursery rhyme character, Little Jack Horner. He sat in his corner eating his Christmas pie. When he stuck in his thumb and pulled out a plum he didn't thank God. He congratulated himself. "What a good boy am I," he said.

Sadly, in the text some of the seekers pursuing Jesus resorted to this sort of thanksgiving. "Our fathers," they preened, "ate the manna in the wilderness." "We are Jews," they were saying. "We come from good stock."

**Simple Courtesy**

A second form of thanksgiving represents a higher expression of gratitude. You remember the story! Ten men with incurable leprosy, ten men with no place to go, ten men condemned to live lives as social outcasts. And Jesus came by and healed them (Luke 17:11-19). Immediately the ten cleansed lepers sprinted for the city. "I'm going home," one said. "To my former job," another thought. It was a time of glad feelings. Yet one leper came to himself in his headlong dash back to the city. We are told, "Then one of them, when he saw that he was healed, turned back, praising God with a loud voice. He prostrated himself at Jesus' feet and thanked him." Simple courtesy would demand this sort of thanksgiving, yet only one out of ten was courteous. Nine men felt "lucky." Only one felt grateful. And it was just this grateful man who not only was healed, but who got to know the healer as well. This story points out quite clearly how discourteous we all can be. A man can get so caught up in his blessings he forgets to thank the Blesser. Our fortunes, our healings, our plans can sweep us away. They can make us feel lucky and we forget gratitude to God. French author, Colette, once attended a film which was the story of her life. Afterwards an acquaintance said to her, "It looked as if you were a very happy child." Colette replied, "Yes, it is too bad that I didn't realize it at the time." Isn't this just the way of us? We sit in the lap of luxury and don't know it.

Gratitude is love looking at the past. It is making known to God and to other people how they benefited us. One family I know has Thanksgiving meals not once but several times a year. They'll call you up and say, "Come to a Thanksgiving meal this Tuesday night." They might not have turkey, but hamburgers instead, yet I tell you it is a banquet of gratitude. Anytime one of the family members is thankful for something he says, "Let's have a Thanksgiving!" And all the family joins in. Last year this family had seven such thanksgivings. One for a new house, others for medical reports, a promotion, a college degree, a new grandson, a report card, and so on. What about you? Does simple courtesy drive you to say thanks often enough?

Some of the crowd of seekers in the text can be seen fumbling through this level of thanksgiving. Jesus had fed them. They'd eaten their fill. So now they followed him around the lake hoping for another blessing. But the Master chides them, "Is it me you seek, or the blessing?"

### Thanks For Being You!

Yes, you can give thanks in a self-satisfied way. You can even give thanks for your own personal material blessings. But there is a third and still higher form of gratitude. The psalmist said, "Let them thank the Lord for his steadfast love, for his wonderful works to humankind" (Psalm 107:8). This sort of gratitude is not for personal blessings, nor is it for material gifts. Instead, the psalmist is giving thanks for who God is. He is giving thanks not for the gifts, but for the Giver. He is thanking God for who God is and how God acted.

Some of this is what Christ is getting at in our text when he says God fed our fathers manna in the wilderness. And now God has fed us to the full. So Jesus can say, "I am the bread of life." In short, Jesus is saying, "I'm not just a blessing. I am the Blesser!"

Stop and think for a moment. Where would you be without God? You probably would never have been born. Even if you were, you would be unsaved. There'd be no church. No pastor would ever have come here to preach. You'd have no Bible, no life after death, no answered prayers, and no hope. Have you ever given thanks for who God is? Have you ever thanked him for being loving? Have you thanked God for his creativity, for Christmas and Easter and Ascension and Pentecost? Have you thanked God for walking in the cool of the evening to search for us when we were fallen? This kind of gratitude is rare, for we mortals are more interested in the blessings than in the Blesser. If you take a trip for a few days and return home, your children will meet you at the door. In merriment the kids will cry, "Daddy! Daddy! What did you bring me?" They're not thankful Daddy is home. They want to know what's in it for them. The gift and not the giver enthralls them most. This Thanksgiving why not crawl up into your heavenly Father's lap and say, "Dear Father, I am indeed thankful for all your gifts to me. But what I am most grateful for is you. Thanks for being who you are!"

### Thanks And Giving

Yes, stepladders come in numerous sizes. And so do Thanksgivings. A fourth form of thanksgiving is the highest form of all. Saint Paul in 1 Corinthians 11:23-24 tells us of Christ's thanksgiving, saying, "The Lord Jesus on the night when he was betrayed took a loaf of bread, and when he had given thanks, he broke it, and said, 'This is my body that is for you.'" That's beautiful, isn't it? To think that the Lord was so in tune with God's mind that he saw meaning in a cup of sorrow and death! And he thanked God for it.

Think of it!

Jesus was born in Bethlehem, which in Hebrew means house of bread! He was laid in a manger, a feed trough for cattle! And he grew up to call himself "the bread of life." And a little later at the Last Supper, Jesus would say, "This is my body, given for you." And he was thankful he could do it for you and you and you ... and me.

Saint Paul was this kind of a thanksgiving person as well. In Acts 16 a vision is given Paul. "Come over to Macedonia and help us," the man in the vision cried. Confident that this was a call of the Lord to preach the gospel in Macedonia, Paul and Silas left at once for their new mission field. But what a reception awaited them! The record of Acts tells us that a "multitude rose up together against them," and when they had been beaten with many stripes, they were "thrust ... into the inner prison." Now the question: What did Paul and Silas do while in jail? Did they curse? Did they moan in self-pity? No. Acts 16 tells us that around about midnight they sang hymns of praise!

Christian ministry is still a risky business today. People haven't changed much in their response to the gospel. When a man accepts Christ and a call to minister, he takes his own body and says, "This is given for you." Calls of God to serve people still lead to beatings and jail. A close friend of mine in the preaching ministry wrote me a letter in the past year. His church was eating him alive and he was asking for my prayers. Some were grumbling that his salary was too high, that he was using too much electricity and they were paying the bill, and that he was meddling in their affairs by preaching on adultery, justice, and race. But you know what most impressed me about his letter? With all the pain he was bearing, there was a current of praise and gratitude throughout his letter. Here he was giving his life and also giving thanks about it.

I remind you that the first Thanksgiving held here in America did not come from ideal circumstances either. Back in 1621, after a morning worship service, Elder Brewster suggested that beginning Tuesday and continuing through Saturday there would be a Festival of Thanksgiving. Such an announcement must have caught people by surprise because it had been a ghastly winter. Exactly half of the colonists had died the first winter. You will remember that they made their graves flat so that the Indians, in case they were hostile, would not know how many of their number had died. When Martin Rinkart wrote the hymn, "Now Thank We All Our God," it was not because everything was pleasant. He had just lived through a terrible plague. From our point of view the pilgrims, Rinkart, Paul, and Jesus had little for which to give thanks. Chances are, however, that their gratitude was much more genuine than ours. Affluence has rendered us flabby and self-satisfied. And as a result, we are much more prone to complain about what we lack than give thanks for what we have.

Jesus, knowing his own crucifixion was coming, broke bread and gave thanks. That's thanksgiving in the highest form! Jesus shows us about *thanksgiving*. Thankful that his body would be broken, thankful for the atonement of the cross, thankful his blood would bring a new covenant, Jesus gave thanks and gave his life.

Is there any real thanksgiving in you today? You've been quite willing to *take* and give thanks. Will you be willing to come and *give* and offer thanks as well? Will you only sit and gorge yourself this Thursday and offer a smattering of *thanksgetting* prayers? Or will you find some way to do as Jesus and *thanksgive* your life?

What size will your Thanksgiving celebration be this year?

# Lectionary Preaching After Pentecost

The following index will aid the user of this book in matching the correct Sunday with the appropriate text during Pentecost. All texts in this book are from the series for the Gospel Readings, Revised Common Lectionary. (Note that the ELCA division of Lutheranism is now following the Revised Common Lectionary.) The Lutheran designations indicate days comparable to Sundays on which Revised Common Lectionary Propers or Ordinary Time designations are used.

**(Fixed dates do not pertain to Lutheran Lectionary)**

| **Fixed Date Lectionaries**<br>*Revised Common (including ELCA)*<br>*and Roman Catholic* | **Lutheran Lectionary**<br>*Lutheran* |
|---|---|
| The Day of Pentecost | The Day of Pentecost |
| The Holy Trinity | The Holy Trinity |
| May 29-June 4 — Proper 4, Ordinary Time 9 | Pentecost 2 |
| June 5-11 — Proper 5, Ordinary Time 10 | Pentecost 3 |
| June 12-18 — Proper 6, Ordinary Time 11 | Pentecost 4 |
| June 19-25 — Proper 7, Ordinary Time 12 | Pentecost 5 |
| June 26-July 2 — Proper 8, Ordinary Time 13 | Pentecost 6 |
| July 3-9 — Proper 9, Ordinary Time 14 | Pentecost 7 |
| July 10-16 — Proper 10, Ordinary Time 15 | Pentecost 8 |
| July 17-23 — Proper 11, Ordinary Time 16 | Pentecost 9 |
| July 24-30 — Proper 12, Ordinary Time 17 | Pentecost 10 |
| July 31-Aug. 6 — Proper 13, Ordinary Time 18 | Pentecost 11 |
| Aug. 7-13 — Proper 14, Ordinary Time 19 | Pentecost 12 |
| Aug. 14-20 — Proper 15, Ordinary Time 20 | Pentecost 13 |
| Aug. 21-27 — Proper 16, Ordinary Time 21 | Pentecost 14 |
| Aug. 28-Sept. 3 — Proper 17, Ordinary Time 22 | Pentecost 15 |
| Sept. 4-10 — Proper 18, Ordinary Time 23 | Pentecost 16 |
| Sept. 11-17 — Proper 19, Ordinary Time 24 | Pentecost 17 |
| Sept. 18-24 — Proper 20, Ordinary Time 25 | Pentecost 18 |

| | |
|---|---|
| Sept. 25-Oct. 1 — Proper 21, Ordinary Time 26 | Pentecost 19 |
| Oct. 2-8 — Proper 22, Ordinary Time 27 | Pentecost 20 |
| Oct. 9-15 — Proper 23, Ordinary Time 28 | Pentecost 21 |
| Oct. 16-22 — Proper 24, Ordinary Time 29 | Pentecost 22 |
| Oct. 23-29 — Proper 25, Ordinary Time 30 | Pentecost 23 |
| Oct. 30-Nov. 5 — Proper 26, Ordinary Time 31 | Pentecost 24 |
| Nov. 6-12 — Proper 27, Ordinary Time 32 | Pentecost 25 |
| Nov. 13-19 — Proper 28, Ordinary Time 33 | Pentecost 26 |
| | Pentecost 27 |
| Nov. 20-26 — Christ The King | Christ The King |

Reformation Day (or last Sunday in October) is October 31 (Revised Common, Lutheran)

All Saints' Day (or first Sunday in November) is November 1 (Revised Common, Lutheran, Roman Catholic)

# U.S. / Canadian Lectionary Comparison

The following index shows the correlation between the Sundays and special days of the church year as they are titled or labeled in the Revised Common Lectionary published by the Consultation On Common Texts and used in the United States (the reference used for this book) and the Sundays and special days of the church year as they are titled or labeled in the Revised Common Lectionary used in Canada.

| Revised Common Lectionary | Canadian Revised Common Lectionary |
|---|---|
| Advent 1 | Advent 1 |
| Advent 2 | Advent 2 |
| Advent 3 | Advent 3 |
| Advent 4 | Advent 4 |
| Christmas Eve | Christmas Eve |
| Nativity Of The Lord / Christmas Day | The Nativity Of Our Lord |
| Christmas 1 | Christmas 1 |
| January 1 / Holy Name of Jesus | January 1 / The Name Of Jesus |
| Christmas 2 | Christmas 2 |
| Epiphany Of The Lord | The Epiphany Of Our Lord |
| Baptism Of The Lord / Epiphany 1 | The Baptism Of Our Lord / Proper 1 |
| Epiphany 2 / Ordinary Time 2 | Epiphany 2 / Proper 2 |
| Epiphany 3 / Ordinary Time 3 | Epiphany 3 / Proper 3 |
| Epiphany 4 / Ordinary Time 4 | Epiphany 4 / Proper 4 |
| Epiphany 5 / Ordinary Time 5 | Epiphany 5 / Proper 5 |
| Epiphany 6 / Ordinary Time 6 | Epiphany 6 / Proper 6 |
| Epiphany 7 / Ordinary Time 7 | Epiphany 7 / Proper 7 |
| Epiphany 8 / Ordinary Time 8 | Epiphany 8 / Proper 8 |
| Transfiguration Of The Lord / Last Sunday After Epiphany | The Transfiguration Of Our Lord / Last Sunday After Epiphany |
| Ash Wednesday | Ash Wednesday |
| Lent 1 | Lent 1 |
| Lent 2 | Lent 2 |
| Lent 3 | Lent 3 |
| Lent 4 | Lent 4 |
| Lent 5 | Lent 5 |
| Passion / Palm Sunday (Lent 6) | Passion / Palm Sunday |
| Holy / Maundy Thursday | Holy / Maundy Thursday |
| Good Friday | Good Friday |
| Resurrection Of The Lord / Easter | The Resurrection Of Our Lord |

| | |
|---|---|
| Easter 2 | Easter 2 |
| Easter 3 | Easter 3 |
| Easter 4 | Easter 4 |
| Easter 5 | Easter 5 |
| Easter 6 | Easter 6 |
| Ascension Of The Lord | The Ascension Of Our Lord |
| Easter 7 | Easter 7 |
| Day Of Pentecost | The Day Of Pentecost |
| Trinity Sunday | The Holy Trinity |
| Proper 4 / Pentecost 2 / O T 9* | Proper 9 |
| Proper 5 / Pent 3 / O T 10 | Proper 10 |
| Proper 6 / Pent 4 / O T 11 | Proper 11 |
| Proper 7 / Pent 5 / O T 12 | Proper 12 |
| Proper 8 / Pent 6 / O T 13 | Proper 13 |
| Proper 9 / Pent 7 / O T 14 | Proper 14 |
| Proper 10 / Pent 8 / O T 15 | Proper 15 |
| Proper 11 / Pent 9 / O T 16 | Proper 16 |
| Proper 12 / Pent 10 / O T 17 | Proper 17 |
| Proper 13 / Pent 11 / O T 18 | Proper 18 |
| Proper 14 / Pent 12 / O T 19 | Proper 19 |
| Proper 15 / Pent 13 / O T 20 | Proper 20 |
| Proper 16 / Pent 14 / O T 21 | Proper 21 |
| Proper 17 / Pent 15 / O T 22 | Proper 22 |
| Proper 18 / Pent 16 / O T 23 | Proper 23 |
| Proper 19 / Pent 17 / O T 24 | Proper 24 |
| Proper 20 / Pent 18 / O T 25 | Proper 25 |
| Proper 21 / Pent 19 / O T 26 | Proper 26 |
| Proper 22 / Pent 20 / O T 27 | Proper 27 |
| Proper 23 / Pent 21 / O T 28 | Proper 28 |
| Proper 24 / Pent 22 / O T 29 | Proper 29 |
| Proper 25 / Pent 23 / O T 30 | Proper 30 |
| Proper 26 / Pent 24 / O T 31 | Proper 31 |
| Proper 27 / Pent 25 / O T 32 | Proper 32 |
| Proper 28 / Pent 26 / O T 33 | Proper 33 |
| Christ The King (Proper 29 / O T 34) | Proper 34 / Christ The King / Reign Of Christ |
| | |
| Reformation Day (October 31) | Reformation Day (October 31) |
| All Saints' Day (November 1 or 1st Sunday in November) | All Saints' Day (November 1) |
| Thanksgiving Day (4th Thursday of November) | Thanksgiving Day (2nd Monday of October) |

*O T = Ordinary Time

414

# About The Authors

**J. Ellsworth Kalas**, a renowned author and preacher, now serves as a professor of homiletics at Asbury Theological Seminary. Before joining the Asbury faculty, he spent 38 years as a pastor in four churches in Wisconsin and Ohio, and five years as an associate in evangelism with the World Methodist Council. Kalas is the author of approximately twenty books and ten adult study quarterlies for the United Methodist Publishing House, and is particularly well known for his popular *Back Side* series.

**David J. Kalas** is the pastor of Emmanuel United Methodist Church in Appleton, Wisconsin. Prior to moving to Wisconsin in 1996, he served for fifteen years in youth and pastoral ministries in Virginia and Ohio. Kalas is a graduate of the University of Virginia (B.A.) and Union Theological Seminary of Virginia (M.Div.).

**Frank G. Honeycutt** is the senior pastor of Ebenezer Lutheran Church in Columbia, South Carolina. He is the author of *Percolated Faith* (CSS) and *Preaching to Skeptics and Seekers* (Abingdon), as well as numerous journal articles on preaching and ministry. Honeycutt is a graduate of Clemson University (B.A.), Lutheran Theological Southern Seminary (M.Div.), and Lutheran School of Theology at Chicago (D.Min. in Preaching).

**Stephen M. Crotts** is the director of the Carolina Study Center, a campus ministry based in Chapel Hill, North Carolina. A member of the Fellowship of Christian Athletes, Crotts is a popular speaker and a frequent contributor to Christian magazines. Among his CSS publications are *Long Time Coming!* and *The Beautiful Attitudes.* Crotts received his education at Furman University (B.A.) and Emory University (M.Div.).


**R. Robert Cueni** is the president of Lexington Theological Seminary in Lexington, Kentucky. He previously served as senior pastor of Country Club Christian Church (Disciples of Christ), a 3,000-member congregation in Kansas City, Missouri. A graduate of Kent State University (B.S.), Christian Theological Seminary (M.Div.), and San Francisco Theological Seminary (D.Min.), Cueni is the author of eight books, including *Questions Of Faith For Inquiring Believers* (CSS) and *Dinosaur Heart Transplants: Keys To Renewing A Mainline Church.*